D1521749

THE SCENES OF INQUIRY

THE SCENES OF INQUIRY

On the Reality of Questions in the Sciences

NICHOLAS JARDINE

CLARENDON PRESS · OXFORD
1991

Oxford University Press, Walton Street, Oxford OX2 6DP
Oxford New York Toronto
Delhi Bombay Calcutta Madras Karachi
Petaling Jaya Singapore Hong Kong Tokyo
Nairobi Dar es Salaam Cape Town
Melbourne Auckland
and associated companies in
Berlin Ibadan

Oxford is a trade mark of Oxford University Press

Published in the United States
by Oxford University Press, New York

British Library Cataloguing in Publication Data
Jardine, N. (Nicholas)
The scenes of inquiry.
1. Philosophy of Science
I. Title
501
ISBN 0–19–823935–1

Library of Congress Cataloging in Publication Data
Jardine, Nicholas.
The scenes of inquiry: on the reality of questions in the sciences/
Nicholas Jardine.
p. cm.
Includes index.
1. Science—Philosophy. 2. Science—History. 3. Reality.
I. Title.
Q175.J3463 1991 501—dc20—90–49045
ISBN 0–19–823935–1

Typeset by Cambrian Typesetters, Frimley, Surrey
Printed and bound in Great Britain by
Biddles Ltd, Guildford & King's Lynn

Printed and bound in
Great Britain by Biddles Ltd.
Guildford & King's Lynn

331593

For Rachel

Acknowledgements

In the course of the past four years Simon Schaffer has discussed with me at length the main topics of this work, and has shared with me his awe-inspiring knowledge of the historical and sociological literature on the formation of scientific disciplines. On historiographical issues I have greatly profited from discussions with Peter Burke, John Forrester, Bruno Latour, Antonio Pérez-Ramos, and Quentin Skinner, and from altercations with Michael Ben Chaim and Andrew Cunningham. On the history of natural history I have been much helped by Michael Bravo, Mike Dettelbach, Shelley Innes, Myles Jackson, Emma Spary, Jennifer Tucker and other members of the Cabinet of Natural History (Cambridge Group for the History of Natural History and the Environmental Sciences). My interpretations of philosophical writings beyond the confines of the analytic tradition have been guided by students and colleagues: Andrew Bowie, Gerd Buchdahl, Janine Crawley, Anna-Katherina Mayer, and Sue Morgan. Mary Hesse offered constructive comments on drafts of this work, and a shrewd anonymous referee for Oxford University Press stung me into rethinking and rewriting the entire book. Angela Blackburn has given much-needed encouragement and advice. Irene McLoughlin, June Mitchell, Pat Pawley, and Maureen Sauzier gave efficient help with the word-processing, and Laurien Berkeley offered many useful and perceptive copy-editorial suggestions.

My heartiest thanks to all the above.

Contents

1. INTRODUCTION: FOCUSING ON QUESTIONS 1

The Origin of the Present Work 1
The Aims of the Work 2
Metaphysical Assumptions 4
Plan of the Work 5

PART I. LOCAL REALITY

2. SCENES OF NATURAL HISTORY 11

Introduction 11
An Agenda of Natural History 12
Foci of Controversy 17
Blumenbach and the Formative Drive 25
Kant: Teleology and Mechanism 28
Forays Beyond the Bounds of Sense: Herder, Kielmeyer
and Goethe 33
Schelling and Oken: Kingdoms Beyond the Bounds of Sense 43
Shifting Scenes 50

3. LOCAL REALITY AND INTERPRETATION 56

Local Reality 56
Some Difficulties 58
Local Reality and Intelligibility 62
Strengths of our Account of Local Reality 65
Gadamer: Interpretation of Classic Works 68

4. EXPLAINING SCENES 77

Introduction 77
Presuppositions 79
Methodical Commitments 83
Access to Methods and Practices 90

5. THE ORIGINS OF METHODS 94
Introduction 94
Common Sense 96

Pontifical Disciplines   99
Exemplary Disciplines   103
Genuine Innovation   107
Remote Factors: Sites of Origin and Modes of Diffusion   109
Remote Factors: Stimuli to Change   114
Conclusion   119

6. LEGITIMATION AND HISTORY   121
Types and Contexts of Legitimation   121
History in the Sciences   124
Strategies of Historical Legitimation   130
Disciplinary Histories: Four Examples   132

7. A NEW HISTORIOGRAPHY   146

PART II. ABSOLUTE REALITY

8. ABSOLUTE REALITY AND DISSOCIATION   155
Absolute Reality   155
Hacking's Challenge   155
Implications of Dissociation   160
Meeting Hacking's Challenge   161

9. THE SOCIOLOGICAL CHALLENGE   168
Introduction   168
Collins: Calibrations Fair and Foul   170
Interest Theory   177
Networks and Multiple Constraints   185

10. RHETORIC, AESTHETICS AND RELIABILITY   193
Introduction   193
Placing Experiments in Natural Philosophy   196
Discourses of Chemistry   200
The Challenge of Literary and Aesthetic Strategies   204
Meeting the Literary and Aesthetic Challenge   205
The Very Possibility of a Reliable Aesthetics   208

11. CONCLUSION: BEWARE OF SCIENCE   225

INDEX OF NAMES   241

1
Introduction: Focusing on Questions

THE ORIGIN OF THE PRESENT WORK

In his autobiography R. G. Collingwood tells of his obsession with the Albert Memorial: 'Everything about it was visibly mis-shapen, corrupt, crawling, verminous; for a time I could not bear to look at it, and passed with averted eyes; recovering from this weakness, I forced myself to look and to face day by day the question: a thing so obviously, so incontrovertibly, so indefensibly bad, why had Scott done it?' He goes on to relate how his daily communings with the Memorial led him to a series of reflections on questions, and in particular on the historian's need to excavate and grasp the questions whose resolution was attempted in past works. My own Albert Memorial was a book, Lorenz Oken's *Lehrbuch der Naturphilosophie*, which I first read in the English translation of 1847 entitled *Elements of Physiophilosophy*. This extraordinary document offers a derivation of the entire universe from God, 'the primordial zero', through the three 'kingdoms of nature', that is, minerals, plants and animals, to the noblest product of nature, man. It is set out in 3,652 numbered sections, of which the first reads: 'Philosophy, as the science which embraces the principles of the universe or world, is only a logical, which may perhaps conduct us to the real, conception.' The last declares: 'The fourth science is the *Art of War*, the art of motion, histrionism, music, poetic art of science, the light. As in the art of poetry all arts have been blended, so in the art of war have all sciences and all arts. The art of War is the highest most exalted art; the art of freedom and of right, of the blessed condition of Man and humanity—the Principle of Peace.' In the body of the work are to be found such wondrous pronouncements as: 'The nose is the thorax repeated in the head;' 'The animal is a detached blossom moving freely in the air;' 'The fish is a mussel from between whose shells a monstrous abdomen has grown.'

Like Collingwood I was led by communings with a seemingly grotesque work to a series of questions about questions. How could the apparently deranged questions addressed by Oken have appeared real or well-posed to him and his readers? How can we come to understand such questions, despite their unreality for us? Though Oken was a controversial figure, he had a solid international reputation as an anatomist and natural historian, and was a founder both of the popular scientific journal *Isis* and of the Gesellschaft deutscher Naturforscher und Aerzte, said to have provided the model for the British Association for the Advancement of Science. What are the historical and epistemological implications of so recent an involvement of the sciences with such questions? When and how did the questions addressed by Oken become real for communities of scientists? When and how did they cease to be regarded as real questions? How are we to explain such emergence and dissolution of questions? How can we justify our conviction that many of Oken's questions are not merely unreal for us, but absolutely unreal, or at least, absolutely less real than the questions addressed in present-day sciences?

THE AIMS OF THE WORK

This work is primarily addressed to students of the sciences—philosophers, historians and sociologists. To them it advocates a radical shift of concern from the answers and doctrines that have been propounded by the sciences to the questions and problems that they have posed. I argue that such a shift of focus not only makes it possible to overcome long-standing obstacles to the understanding of the sciences but also opens up exciting new fields of inquiry. The work carries also a message for practitioners of the sciences. To them it advocates an interest in their own methods and practices, especially the social, institutional, literary and aesthetic practices that they rarely articulate and expose to criticism. I suggest that without such critical reflections on the part of scientists, the sciences will remain prisoners of myths which limit and distort their inquiries.

How have beliefs changed in the various scientific disciplines? What factors have been operative in the formation of scientific beliefs? How do doctrinal conflicts arise in the sciences and how are they resolved? How are factual and theoretical claims communicated and promoted? How are they interpreted and appropriated? How do they achieve general acceptance or rejection? The researches of present-day historians and sociologists of science are for the most part directed to such issues. And these are the issues that have occasioned the major methodological debates of the past two decades: between exponents of 'internal' rational explanations of doctrinal change and exponents of 'external' explanations in terms of social and political factors; between 'intellectualist' approaches which concentrate on doctrines and 'praxis-oriented' approaches which concentrate on activities and techniques; between protagonists of a historiography centred on individual biographies and protagonists of historiographies centred on institutions, research programmes, traditions of inquiry, etc.; between those who regard scientific facts as discoveries about nature and those who regard them as social constructs.

The shift of historical and sociological concern which I advocate is from scientific doctrines to the questions posed in the sciences—from the ways in which answers gain credence in the sciences to the ways in which new questions are brought into being and old ones dissolved. Such a shift brings into view, I shall suggest, a series of new and fascinating issues concerning the formation, maintenance and deconstruction of scientific disciplines. Further, it integrates the study of the social and institutional practices of the sciences with the narration and explication of their subject matters and doctrines. In so doing it holds promise of a historiography and sociology of the sciences that will overcome the long-standing and ill-natured oppositions between internal and external, intellectualist and praxis-oriented, individualist and collectivist, realist and social constructivist, attitudes to the sciences.

The philosophy of science, too, is at present almost exclusively focused on scientific doctrines. How do observations and experimental findings gain general acceptance? What are the virtues of hypotheses and theories—truth, utility, beauty—that scientists do, or should, cultivate and pursue? To what extent are theoretical conflicts in the sciences resoluble in the light of observational and experimental evidence? Is it generally possible to understand a scientific theory from the standpoint of a radically different theory? What is it for some scientific claims to explain others, to support others, to reduce others? Such issues are of central concern to all the various brands of philosophers of science—

realists, anti-realists, quasi-realists, constructive empiricists, fictionalists, pragmatists.

Here too, my suggestion is that the time is ripe for a shift of concern from answers to questions. Here again I suggest that such a shift opens up fresh and fertile fields for investigation. It focuses attention on issues concerning the claims of the sciences to have accumulated real questions; on the dissociation whereby questions real from one scientific standpoint may be unreal from others; on the crucial roles in the realization of questions of calibration of the local methods and practices of the sciences against precedents and standards; on the challenges to the reality of scientific questions posed by the prevalence in the sciences of appeals to authority, to vested interests and to literary and aesthetic sensibilities. In so doing it relocates the issue of the objectivity of the sciences. Moreover, it promises new and fruitful links between philosophy of science and the sociology and social history of the sciences.

METAPHYSICAL ASSUMPTIONS

In the first, historically directed, part of the work metaphysical assumptions are kept to a bare minimum. The central notion here is that of a scene of inquiry, the range of questions that are locally real, that is, real in a community of practitioners of a given discipline at a given time. The questions real in a community are identified as those which they can see how, in principle, to 'get to grips with'—a little more explicitly, they are the questions for which there exist considerations that would be acknowledged in the community as providing grounds for preferring one full and direct answer over all the others. It is further claimed that there is an intimate connection between the local reality of questions and the understanding of questions. Understanding of questions real in one's own community involves appreciation of the considerations that would be taken in that community to be relevant to those questions. Understanding of questions unreal in one's own community but real in another community involves appreciation of the considerations that would be taken in that other community to be relevant to those questions.

The first part of the work is deliberately non-committal on metaphysical issues concerning the goals of inquiry in the sciences. In particular, in the account of local reality of questions no constraints are imposed on the kinds of consideration that may be held to provide grounds for favouring one answer to a question over others. The motive for this neutrality is straightforward. Study of changes in the scenes of inquiry of disciplines is proposed as a type of historical inquiry applicable across the entire range of the sciences; but there can be no doubt that truth has by no means always been the primary goal in the sciences.

In the philosophically directed second part of the work I take a stand on the issue of the proper goal of the sciences. Truth ought to be the primary goal of the sciences. This assumption motivates the account of absolute reality of questions with which this part of the work opens. Whereas the local reality of a question in a community is defined in terms of the considerations they would take to favour one full and direct answer over the others, absolute reality is defined in terms of considerations reliably indicative of the truth of a full and direct answer.

PLAN OF THE WORK

The next chapter opens with a general account of the concerns of natural historians in the latter part of the eighteenth century. There follows a study of certain remarkable developments in the field of natural history in the German lands around 1800, developments which culminated in the apparently bizarre enterprises of Lorenz Oken, mentioned above. The study is designed to exemplify a drastic shift of scene within a discipline, a major change in the range of questions real for certain communities of its practitioners. It offers an illustration of the way in which study of the methods and presuppositions of past practitioners of a discipline enables us to understand questions that have become entirely alien to us. Further it provides some of the historical raw materials for the deliberations of the subsequent chapters.

Chapter 3 starts with an account of the reality of questions in a community of inquirers. I go on to discuss the relations between local reality and the understanding of questions. The chapter concludes with some general reflections upon historical interpretation, in which I explore certain parallels between my views and Hans-Georg Gadamer's account of the interpretative understanding of past works.

The remaining chapters of the first part of the work are

concerned with the explanation of changes in scenes of inquiry. In Chapter 4 I discuss some of the ways in which shift of scene may be brought about by changes in presuppositions and changes in methodological commitments. I argue for the fundamental role of local and often tacit methods, practices and techniques as determinants of scenes of inquiry, and I discuss the problems of access that these pose for the historian.

Chapter 5 is concerned with methodological innovation. I offer a critical examination of certain large claims about the role of common sense as matrix for the methods of the sciences. There follows a discussion of transference of methods between disciplines and of the ways in which some disciplines may serve others as models or arbiters of method. The chapter concludes with a brief discussion of the social, institutional and technological factors that may stimulate methodological innovation: changes in teaching curricula; changes in the social roles of practitioners of the sciences; changes in instrumentation and the practices and routines of technicians; changes in the organization, architecture and resources of scientific institutions; changes in technologies of representation and communication.

In Chapter 6 I consider the strategies and standards of legitimation that may stimulate methodological change and secure acquiescence and compliance in methods and practices. I emphasize the diversity of the types of legitimation operative in the sciences: appeal to the norms of logic and epistemology; appeal to interests; appeal to authority; appeal to literary and aesthetic sensibilities; appeal to exemplary successes. I go on to argue for the importance of writing about the history of disciplines as a primary context for the various types of legitimation.

In Chapter 7 I first recapitulate my main hypotheses about the factors responsible for setting and shifting scenes of inquiry. I then outline my programme for a new historiography of the sciences centred on the formation, transformation and dissolution of scenes of inquiry, arguing that such a historiography overcomes the oppositions between internalist and externalist, intellectualist and praxis-oriented, individualist and collectivist approaches.

The second part of the work is primarily concerned with challenges to the objectivity of the sciences on the score of the reality of the questions they address.

Chapter 8 opens with an account of absolute reality of questions in terms of amenability in principle to evidential considerations reliably indicative of their resolutions. The historical diversity of styles of inquiry in the sciences is shown to constitute a cogent challenge to the absolute reality of the questions currently posed in the sciences. Various strategies for resisting this challenge are explored. In particular, I argue that the challenge can be met if calibration against precedents and standards can be shown to have been a predominant factor in bringing about methodological changes in the sciences.

It is openly boasted by many sociologists of science, and secretly feared by not a few philosophers solicitous of the welfare of the sciences, that recent studies in the sociology and social history of the sciences threaten to discredit, nay, may even have discredited, the objectivity of the sciences. In particular, it is widely claimed by sociologists that their scrutiny of the 'soft underbelly' of science— the manœuvres, transactions and negotiations that lead up to consensus on matters of scientific fact—show scientsts' declarations about the roles of reliable procedures, rational discussions, fair calibrations of instruments, replications of experiments, etc., to be *ex post facto* legitimations which conceal the very different practices actually operative in the production of consensus. According to exponents of one major recent approach to the sociology of science, the so-called 'interest theory', close study of the processes that eventuate in consensus shows that its primary determinants are the social, political and factional interests of practitioners of the sciences and of those to whom they address their claims. According to exponents of a yet more recently developed approach, the so-called 'network theory', the processes of production of consensus on knowledge claims and of trans- formation of social structures and roles are inextricable, the mechanism underlying both cognitive and social change being one of formation of networks of alliance, control and delegation involving heterogeneous 'actants': scientists and non-scientists, inanimate objects and instruments, men and machines, texts and readers, etc. Both interest theoretic and network theoretic studies have yielded findings which suggest that many of the methods and practices effective in securing consensus in the sciences are neither calibrated nor amenable to calibration. The absolute reality of the questions addressed by the sciences is thus called in question. In Chapter 9 I discuss and seek to mitigate these threats to the view that reliable methods and practices play dominant roles in the generation of consensuses in the sciences.

Both sociological interest theory and network theory entail major roles in the formation of consensus in the sciences for strategies of appeal to literary and aesthetic sensibilities. Moreover, a series of important recent studies has documented in convincing detail the substantial parts played by such strategies in the formation and transformation of scientific disciplines. In Chapter 10 I review some of these studies and discuss the reliability and amenability to calibration of literary and aesthetic strategies. In particular, I seek to rebut certain doctrines prevalent in philosophical aesthetics which imply that such strategies could not possibly be reliable.

This work and its companion *The Fortunes of Inquiry* are concerned with the claims of the sciences to have accumulated real questions and true answers. The final chapter opens with a defence of the basic assumptions and strategies used in evaluating those claims. The enterprise of the two works is then subjected to a reflexive assessment, in which my accounts of reality and truth are exposed to self-appraisal. I go on first to defend the right of the philosopher to offer advice to scientists and then to offer such advice. I urge scientists to beware of the complacency induced by the myths of the unity, rationality and 'world-guidedness' of science. The scenes of inquiry of the sciences will, I suggest, remain limited and distorted unless scientists become more reflective, taking serious account of the findings of sociologists and social historians about the diversity of the social practices of the sciences and the prevalence and effectiveness in the sciences of strategies of appeal to authority, to history, to vested interests and to literary and aesthetic sensibilities.

I
LOCAL REALITY

2
Scenes of Natural History

My aim in this chapter is to give substance to the notion of transformation of a scientific discipline through shifts of scene— changes in the ranges of questions real for communities of its practitioners. The material is largely drawn from German writings on natural history in the closing decades of the eighteenth century and the opening decades of the nineteenth.

The opening sections—an account of the agenda of natural history in the mid-eighteenth century and some indications of the natural historical controversies of the latter half of the century—set the stage both for the specific episodes in German natural history which follow and for many of the examples drawn from natural history in later chapters. I then describe a specific framework for the pursuit of natural history set out by J. F. Blumenbach and Immanuel Kant—a framework that was widely adopted in the German lands round the turn of the eighteenth century. This framework set definite limits on the legitimate concerns of natural historians. In the following sections I consider first some relatively modest ventures beyond the limits set by Blumenbach and Kant, then the far from modest schemes of Goethe, Schelling and Lorenz Oken. In the final section of the chapter I sketch an interpretation of these changes in terms of shifts of scene of inquiry.

A pre-emptive remark is in order. I do not claim that the often peculiar story of German natural history around the turn of the eighteenth century is a typical instance of the transformation of a scientific discipline. On the contrary, it is chosen precisely because it is atypical in a particular respect. These developments involved unusually drastic and explicitly articulated changes in the ranges of questions real for inquirers. It is, indeed, my claim that shifts of scene of inquiry constitute a fundamental aspect of historical development in all scientific disciplines. But shifts of scene have usually been less visible than those that I shall describe.

AN AGENDA OF NATURAL HISTORY

The entry 'histoire naturelle' in the eighth volume (1768) of the
Encyclopédie of Denis Diderot and Jean d'Alembert gives a lucid
account of the subject matter, relations to other disciplines,
methods and practical applications of natural history in the mid-
eighteenth century.

The scope of natural history is announced at the outset:

It includes all the beings which live on the earth, which rise into the air or
which dwell in the bosom of the waters, all the beings which cover the
surface of the earth and all those which are hidden in its bowels. Animals,
vegetables and minerals constitute the three principal parts of *Natural
History*.

The primary task of the natural historian is to provide complete
descriptions of animals, vegetables and minerals. Such descriptions

include the interior parts of each object as well as the exterior parts: they
convey as far as possible the proportions of shape and weight, measures of
the extent and of all the qualities that can give a proper idea of the
structure of the principal parts of each thing. By such descriptions one can
compare one object with another and judge the resemblance and
difference which are found in their structure; one can recognize the
different ways which nature employs to produce the same effect; and thus
one arrives at general results which are the most precious achievements
for *Natural History*.

The account goes on to consider the branches of natural history
and their uses, starting with anatomy.

Up to the present anatomy has hardly had any other object but man; this
is doubtless the principal object; but the human body does not include all
the models of the mechanism of the 'animal economy'. There are in
animals structures very different from those of man . . . In comparing
some with others and relating them all to man one may know better man
in particular and the mechanism of nature in general.

The importance of comparative anatomy for medicine and
surgery, both human and veterinary, is emphasized.

The article then turns to botany, 'one of the principal and most
extended branches of *Natural History*'. The treatment is polemical.
Botanists are accused of excessive concern with questions of
nomenclature and of 'the chimerical pretension of following in
their systems the unintelligible order of nature, which cannot be

conceived except by the Creator'. Instead, they should content themselves with establishing a clear vocabulary for the description of plants. Then they would be able to concentrate on the most important and difficult tasks of botany:

not to name plants, but to know their properties, to know how to cultivate useful plants and destroy those which are harmful, and to observe the structure and all the parts which co-operate in the 'vegetable economy'.

These tasks are then discussed in considerable detail. The study of the virtues of plants is of special importance for medicine.

Thus botany contains a great part of *materia medica*, which is entirely included in *General Natural History* because this science covers not only plants, but also all the animals and all the minerals which have medicinal virtues. Their properties are so precious that to discover them naturalists ought to join all their knowledge with that of medical men.

There follows an equally enthusiastic account of the role of botanists in agriculture, horticulture and arboriculture. Improvement of plants and protection of them from disease and degeneration require a knowledge of the 'vegetable economy' (that is, plant physiology).

Knowledge of this economy is the most elevated goal of botany; to attain it one must start with a detailed examination of all the parts of plants; it is a simpler kind of anatomy than that of animals, but one which requires equally expert researches and equally delicate operations. The great observers have made rapid progress in it; the invention of the microscope has given them the means of revealing the least parts of vegetables. Through the anatomical exposition of all plants . . . one may cast new light on the mechanism of vegetation. Great discoveries have already been made concerning the development of germs, the growth of plants, the suction of roots and leaves, the flow and evaporation of sap, the reproduction of vegetables, etc.

The article goes on to point to the close relations between the 'economies' of plants and animals.

One can compare the sap of plants with the blood of animals . . . plants take their nourishment by the suction of roots and leaves as animals do by their mouths or the suckers which serve them as a mouth; digestions, secretions and evacuations happen in plants; they have sexes which are very distinct by virtue of the organs suited to form, support and nourish the embryos which are the germs of plants; finally, the polyp has as much analogy with plants as with animals.

There follows a brief mention of the third kingdom of nature, minerals, whose study is linked to chemistry, needed for the exact definition of minerals, and to the 'theory of the earth' (that is, consideration of the processes through which the earth has come to be in its present state).

After this survey of the branches of natural history comes an excursion on its current fashionability.

The great number of these cabinets of natural history manifestly proves the taste of the public for this science; one can form these only through arduous researches and a considerable expenditure, for the price of natural curiosities has currently risen to a very high level . . . But everything has its vicissitudes, and the empire of fashion extends to the threshold of the sciences. The taste for abstract science succeeded the taste for the science of antiquities; then experimental physics was cultivated more than the abstract sciences; at present *Natural History* occupies the public more than experimental physics or all other sciences. But will the reign of *Natural History* also have its term?

The question is a rhetorical one. Natural history is not really threatened; for it is the foundation of the physical sciences as well as providing delightful exercise for body and mind.

The final section of the article is concerned with the means for the teaching, learning and advancement of natural history. The key to success is diligent observation and collaborative enterprise. Books and natural history cabinets, which provide 'an epitome of the whole of nature', are important aids. Yet more important is the study of plants, animals and minerals in their natural habitats. On the basis of the most extensive possible comparison of the properties and structures of the earth's inhabitants the natural historian may arrive at an arrangement which determines 'the method he prescribes for himself in the composition of his books and the order that one follows for the arrangement of a cabinet of natural history'. However, the article concludes, serious errors result if it is forgotten that such arrangements are human conventions, not natural systems in accord with the laws of nature.

This article is by no means impartial. The general policy of the *encyclopédistes* underlies its Baconian emphasis on description and comparison, its dismissive attitude to the quest for a natural system, its didactic tone and its constant concern with utility and practical applications.[1] And that policy underlies an omission remarkable for the period: God. Even in enlightened France it was customary to present knowledge of God through his works, and in particular of his benevolence as evidenced in the providential design of living beings, as a primary goal and justification for natural history. However, the majority of the views expressed are commonplaces of prefaces, reviews and introductions to textbooks in the period. (It is, for example, possible to piece together similar views on the scope, aims and value of natural history from the extensive reflections of Albrecht von Haller (1708–77) acknowledged as a reformer of the subject by the main agents in the developments in German natural history which we shall retail.)[2] We have here an index both of the agenda of natural history and of its place in the European commonwealth of learning at the beginning of the period with which we are concerned.

The account of the central concerns of natural historians is an accurate one. The central task of natural history was, indeed, generally taken to be complete and precise description of the earth's inhabitants, these being partitioned into the three 'kingdoms of nature': minerals, plants and animals. Though a special affinity between the study of plants and the study of animals was generally acknowledged, the study of living beings was never treated as a distinct form of inquiry: there was no such discipline as biology in the period. There was, as the article indicates, much concern in the period with questions of nomenclature and ordering. The controversy was especially fierce in botany, the realm most affected by Linnaeus's new binomial nomenclature and his new sexual scheme for the definition and arrangement of genera.[3] The heat of debate about the merits of rival schemes for the naming and ordering of plants, animals and minerals is by no means entirely attributable to doctrinal differences concerning the

[1] For an excellent brief account of the goals of the *encyclopédistes* see R. Darnton, 'Philosophers trim the tree of knowledge: the epistemological strategy of the *Encyclopédie*', in *The Great Cat Massacre and Other Episodes in French Cultural History*, London, 1984, ch. 5.
[2] On von Haller's reflections on natural history see O. Sonntag, 'The self-image of Albrecht von Haller', *Isis*, 65 (1974), 336–51.
[3] See F. A. Stafleu, *Linnaeus and the Linnaeans: The Spreading of their Ideas in Systematic Botany, 1735–89*, Utrecht, 1971.

natural system, its form and its attainability. It reflects a crisis of comprehension of the natural world brought about by the flood of information about new and exotic forms that resulted from the ever more extensive commercial and colonial ventures of the European nations. It reflects also the crucial importance of naming and ordering for the practical activities of natural historians—the planting out of botanical gardens, the labelling and storage of plant specimens in herbaria, the arrangement of natural curiosities in cabinets, the exchange and sale of seeds, specimens and stock.

The article accurately portrays the nature of natural historians' interest in the internal structure and function of plants and animals. Animal anatomy was, indeed, as the account implies, centred on the study of human structure; and the study of the functions of parts of plants and animals, that is, 'animal economy' and 'vegetable economy', was viewed as an extension of anatomy—as 'anatomy in motion'.

Particularly striking is the testimony to the extent of popular interest in natural history. Throughout the century, not only Paris, but the whole of Europe, was swept by a series of collectors' crazes—for 'formed stones', for pickled monstrosities, for stuffed birds, for pinned insects, for shells, for aquatint miniatures and spectacular folios illustrating natural curiosities.[4] There was an extensive market in exotic specimens, complete with regular auctions, professional collectors, dealers and speculators and spectacular booms and slumps. In its emphasis on study in the wild and on the benefits to body and mind of natural history, the article reflects also the new responsiveness of the period to the sights, sounds and odours of untrained nature. This new sensibility, pioneered in such works as Rousseau's *Le Botaniste sans maître* and von Haller's *Die Alpen*, ties in with other potent themes well represented in the *Encyclopédie*: revulsion from the luxury, artificiality and foul air of city life; sentimental nostalgia for the healthy simplicities and vivifying air of the countryside; fascination

---

[4] On 18th-cent. natural history crazes see K. Pomian, *Collectionneurs, amateurs et curieux: Paris-Vénise, XVIᵉ–XVIIIᵉ siècle*, Paris, 1987; D. E. Allen, *The Naturalist in Britain: A Social History*, London, 1976, ch. 2; Y. Laissus, 'Les Cabinets d'histoire naturelle', in R. Taton, ed., *Enseignement et diffusion des sciences en France au dix-huitième siècle*, 2nd edn., Paris, 1987; S. P. Dance, *A History of Shell Collecting*, rev. edn., Leiden, 1986.

with the tales of exotic lands and peoples unleashed in the flood of popular travel literature.[5]

Turning to the uses and applications of natural history, the article gives clear indications of its links with medicine and agriculture. Given the declaredly utilitarian bias, the concentration on botanical matters is unsurprising. For in this period the botanic and physic gardens become of major economic importance as the main source of materia medica; as providers of seed and stock for gardens and estates; as sites of experiments in breeding, propagation and grafting; as places of acclimatization and cultivation of new and exotic plants from foreign lands.[6]

Lastly, it may be noted that the activities and applications of natural history detailed in the article are indicative of the offices and roles open to the natural historian: physician; teacher in the medical faculty of a university or at a medical or veterinary school; curator of the cabinets of natural history that proliferated in universities, academies, courts and the homes of the wealthy; intendant of a botanic or physic garden; teacher of agriculture or rural economy; stipendiary of an academy in some branch of natural history; author of natural history textbooks or of popular works in natural history; herbalist, collector or physician–naturalist to an expedition.[7]

FOCI OF CONTROVERSY

The following sketches deal with the controversial issues in eighteenth-century natural history that provide the immediate

[5] See e.g. D. G. Charlton, *New Images of the Natural in France: A Study in European Cultural History*, Cambridge, 1984; P. Van Tieghem, *Le Sentiment de la nature dans le préromantisme européen*, Paris, 1960; A. Corbin, *Le Miasme et la jonquille*, Paris, 1982.

[6] On the activities and institutions of natural history in France in this period see Y. Laissus, 'Le Jardin du Roi', in Taton, ed., *Enseignement et diffusion des sciences en France*. See also C. C. Gillispie, *Science and Polity in France at the End of the Ancien Regime*, Princeton, NJ, 1980, chs. 2, 3 and 5; C. Salomon-Bayet, *L'Institution de la science et l'expérience du vivant: Méthode et expérience à l'Académie Royale des Sciences 1666–1793*, Paris, 1978; J. Roger, *Buffon*, Paris, 1990.

[7] All these roles were played in the course of a long career by L. J.-M. Daubenton (1716–1800), who provided much of the material for the entry 'histoire naturelle' (by Diderot): see the article 'Daubenton' by Camille Limoges, in C. C. Gillispie, ed., *Dictionary of Scientific Biography*, New York, 1970–80, vol. xv, Suppl. 1.

context for the developments in German natural history with which we shall be concerned.

The quest for a natural system

The great disputes of the first half of the eighteenth century over systems of ordering of minerals, plants and animals concerned artificial systems, systems which promised reliable and rapid allocation of specimens to genera and species rather than representation of their natural affinities.[8] However, almost all the major proponents of artificial systems—Linnaeus, Tournefort at Paris, Boissier de Sauvages at Montpellier, C. G. Ludwig at Leipzig—had acknowledged the natural system as an ideal for natural history, though perhaps an unattainable one. Such a system would respect the natural affinities of minerals, plants and animals and would thus be faithful to God's plan as revealed in nature. Linnaeus, in particular, had explicitly presented the natural system as a goal for natural history. He had himself published and presented in lectures fragmentary natural systems of plants and animals. Moreover, he had lent urgency to the quest by suggesting that a grasp of natural affinities would yield insights both into the medicinal virtues of plants and into the proper conditions for their cultivation. In the latter part of the eighteenth century the form of the natural system, and the prospects and means for attaining it, became major concerns in natural history.

The eighteenth-century debate about the natural system is often presented as a conflict between protagonists of, on the one hand, a 'great chain of being' in which all species of creatures from the rudest minerals up to man form a linear progression and, on the other hand, the view that the natural affinities of species reveal a hierarchy of discrete groups. This is grossly misleading: despite the astonishing variety of their views on the form of the natural system, it is hard to find authors who consistently maintained either of these extreme views. Undoubtedly the commonest image of the natural system was that of a map, species corresponding to points on the map and relative proximities on the map corresponding to their relative affinities: notable users of this image were Linnaeus himself and Antoine-Laurent de Jussieu, botanist at the

---

[8] The following account is largely based on H. Daudin, *De Linné à Lamarck: Méthodes de la classification et idée de série en botanique et en zoologie (1740–1790)*, Paris, 1926, repr. 1983.

Jardin du Roi. (It is an image with an obvious appeal to botanists, for it may be read as a planting scheme for a garden.) But other images abounded. Simon Pallas (1741–1811), explorer and botanist at the St Petersburg Academy of Sciences, suggested on occasion that the natural affinities of living beings could be represented by a tree, on occasion that they were best represented by a network on the faces of a polygon. Johann Hermann, curator of the zoology cabinets at Strasbourg, suggested in 1783 that the natural affinities of animals form a network in three dimensions. P. D. Giseke writing in 1792 represented the natural orders of plants that his teacher Linnaeus had set out in his lectures at Uppsala as a two-dimensional disposition of circles of different sizes. Michel Adanson, traveller and botanist at the Académie des Sciences, presented a natural system of plants in the form of families arranged in natural series.

Views on the way in which to attain the natural system were no less varied than views on the form of the system itself. In mineralogy there was dispute between those who recommended the use of physical characters alone and those who held that a natural system should be based on a mixture of physical and chemical characters or on chemical characters alone. In botany Linnaeus appears to have held that natural groups of all ranks in the hierarchy of living beings could, in principle, be defined by essential characters relating to the generative organs—but he conceded the importance in practice of consideration of habitus, that is, overall appearance. At the other extreme, in his *Familles des plantes* of 1763–4 Adanson proposed formation of natural groups based on estimates of overall similarity in which equal weight was attached to all characters. Between these extremes we have a variety of proposals for differential weighting of characters in the formation of natural groups. For example, in his *Genera plantarum* of 1789 A.-L. de Jussieu proposed a weighting of characters according to their importance for the 'plant economy'; though in practice he made extensive use of a posteriori weighting of characters according to their constancy in groups of plants whose naturalness was obvious at a glance. In zoology there was comparable dispute about the weighting of characters and, in particular, about the relative importance for a natural system of external habitus and internal anatomy.

Opposition to the quest for a natural system sprang from a

variety of sources. There was the straightforward empiricist
distrust of speculative systems, in evidence, for example, in the
Encyclopédie article discussed above. There was the view, also in
evidence in the article, and powerfully presented in Buffon's
monumental *Histoire naturelle*, the first volume of which appeared
in 1749, that the futile quest for a natural system distracts attention
from the true task of a natural historian, a description of the
earth's inhabitants in their natural surroundings. (In Buffon's case
the opposition was reinforced by his view that all systems are mere
fictions: only individuals and their lineages exist in reality.)
Finally, it was widely argued in the closing decades of the century
that the key to an understanding of the earth's inhabitants lies not
in the ordering and grouping of individuals, but in a synthetic
approach, one which considers minerals, plants and animals in
relation to each other and to the history of the earth as a whole. In
mineralogy this was reflected in a shift from concern with mineral
types to concern with entire rock formations and the processes
whereby they have been formed.[9] In botany it was reflected in the
move from bare recording of plant distributions to systematic
study of the relations of assemblages of plants to climate and soil.[10]
In zoology too there was a shift of concern from issues of
classification and ordering to concern with diversity of form and
behaviour in relation to the various 'conditions of existence'.
Moreover, there developed a substantial body of speculation
about the ways in which the present distributions of plants and
animals relate to the history of the earth, including the changes in
the environment wrought by man.

Anatomy and physiology

Where debates about natural and artificial systems of classification
concentrated mainly on plants, animals provided the primary locus
of debate about anatomy and physiology. We have already noted
one major development in late eighteenth-century anatomy, the
move from an approach exclusively centred on the human body to
one which considered the internal structure of other animals as of

[9] See e.g. R. Laudan, *From Mineralogy to Geology: The Foundations of a Science*, Chicago, Ill., 1987.

[10] See e.g. J. Browne, *The Secular Ark: Studies in the History of Biogeography*, New Haven, Conn., 1983, chs. 1 and 2; M. Nicolson, 'Alexander von Humboldt, Humboldtian science and the origins of the study of vegetation', *History of Science*, 25 (1987), 167–94.

interest in its own right and which recognized the diversity of kinds of anatomical structure in the animal kingdom. Correlated with the rise of this comparative approach was the development of typology, the presentation of the anatomical structures of a variety of forms as modifications, degenerations, elaborations, etc., of common plans or types.[11] Thus Daubenton wrote of 'a general prototype in each kind on which each individual is modelled, but which seems to be altered or perfected by circumstances' and also of 'a primitive and general design, which one can follow a very long way, and in accordance with which everything seems to have been conceived'.[12] A related major shift in the late eighteenth-century anatomy concerned the units of description. Instead of concentrating on individual organs—the heart, the kidney, the lungs—anatomical studies increasingly focused on entire systems of organs—the vascular system, the excretory system, the respiratory system. To see the significance of this shift we need to consider certain developments in the allied field of physiology or 'the animal economy'.

In the mid-eighteenth century physiology was, as noted above, generally regarded as an extension of anatomy. In the latter part of the century this way of regarding physiology was widely called in question. In place of a concentration on the functions of particular organs we find a new focus on the co-ordination of functions in the preservation of life.[13] And in place of a treatment of particular functions as consequences of the activities of particular organs—as 'anatomy in motion', in von Haller's famous phrase—functions were considered as in some measure independent of particular anatomical structures. Thus in the anatomical writings of Daubenton's student, Félix Vicq d'Azyr (1748–94), anatomist at the Académie des Sciences, veterinarian, hygienist and personal physician to Marie Antoinette, organ systems are classified

[11] On typology in anatomy in the late 18th cent. see e.g. T. Lenoir, 'Generational factors in the origin of *romantische Naturphilosophie*', *Journal of the History of Biology*, 11 (1978), 57–100; B. Balan, *L'Ordre et le temps: L'Anatomie comparée et l'histoire des vivants au XIXe siècle*, Paris 1979, 161 ff.; H. B. Nisbet, 'Herder, Goethe and the natural type', *Publications of the English Goethe Society*, 27 (1967), 83–119.

[12] Daubenton, in Buffon, *Histoire naturelle*, iv (Paris, 1753), 215, 379.

[13] On the so-called 'vitalist' physiology of the late 18th cent. see e.g. T. M. Brown, 'From mechanism to vitalism in 18th-century English physiology', *Journal of the History of Medicine*, 7 (1974), 179–216; F. Duchesneau, *La Physiologie des lumières: Empirisme, modèles et thèories*, The Hague, 1982, chs. 8 and 9.

according to the functions they realize, and there is emphasis on the diversity of the organ systems which carry out a given function in different types of animals.[14] In the physiological system proposed by Paul-Joseph Barthez (1734–1806), Professor of Medicine at Montpellier, a central role is played by a 'vital principle'.[15] This principle manifests itself in the 'sympathy' which integrates the responses of organs to stimuli and in the 'synergy' which integrates the operations of organs involved in the behaviour of the animal. In the writings of John Hunter (1728–93) 'the principle of life', which is expressed in the various vital powers of living matter, is presented as prior to the organization of the body: 'organization may arise out of living matter, and produce action; but . . . life never can arise out of, or depend on, organization'. And Hunter, like Vicq d'Azyr, emphasized (and displayed in the famous museum at his London residence) the diversity of the anatomical structures which carry out the various functions co-ordinated by the living principle.[16] In the writings of Johann Friedrich Blumenbach, Professor of Medicine at Göttingen from 1778 to his death in 1840, we find postulated a similar priority of vital forces and functions over the particular anatomical structures which enact them. Blumenbach's scheme is crucial for the developments in German natural history with which we shall be concerned; but to grasp its significance we must first consider one particular branch of eighteenth-century physiology, the 'theory of generation'.

Generation

The 'theory of generation' dealt with the processes involved in the formation of adult individuals.[17] The following passage from Blumenbach neatly summarizes the doctrinal conflict that provides the context for his famous treatise *Ueber den Bildungstrieb* (On the Formative Drive):

It is either supposed that the prepared, but at the same time unorganized rudiments of the foetus, first begins to be gradually organized when it

[14] See especially his *Traité d'anatomie et de physiologie*, i Paris, 1786.

[15] On Barthez see Duchesneau, *La Physiologie des lumières*, ch. 9.

[16] On John Hunter see S. J. Cross, 'John Hunter, and animal œconomy, and late eighteenth-century physiological discourse', *Studies in the History of Biology*, 5 (1981), 1–110.

[17] A good introduction to 18th-cent. theories of generation is E. Gasking, *Investigations into Generation, 1651–1828*, London, 1967.

arrives at its place of destination at a due time, and under the necessary circumstances. This is the doctrine of Epigenesis; Or, we deny every sort of generation, and believe that the germ of every animal, and every plant that ever has lived and ever will live, were all created at one and the same time, namely, at the beginning of the world; and that all that is necessary is, that one generation should be developed after the other. Such is the celebrated theory of evolution.[18]

Of particular importance for an understanding of Blumenbach's position is the celebrated controversy on generation between his teacher and predecessor as Professor of Medicine at Göttingen, von Haller, and Kaspar Friedrich Wolff (1734–94), from 1776 Professor of Anatomy at the St Petersburg Academy of Sciences.[19] Their dispute centred on the interpretation of the development of the chick. Von Haller believed that he had observed continuity between the membranes of the egg yolk and the intestine of the chick. From this he inferred that the foetus must have existed, preformed though invisible, in the egg even before fertilization. The apparent spreading of a network of blood vessels over the surface of the yolk he interpreted as a filling of pre-existing vessels as the heart pumps blood into them. This blood, he supposed, brings back the food that thickens the preformed organs and renders them opaque and hence visible. Wolff interpreted the same phenomena quite differently. In his view adult structures resulted from processes of differential solidification of an originally homogeneous fluid. Distribution of fluid to the growing parts took place through the action of a *vis essentialis*. He questioned the inferences that von Haller had drawn from the alleged continuity between the yolk membrane and the intestine of the foetus. And he argued that the streaming of material from the yolk to the developing foetus took place under the influence of the *vis essentialis* before the formation of the blood vessels.

In considering this clash it is important to note how far from inescapable were the empirical objections raised in the period against the doctrine of preformation (or 'evolution'). Thus the inheritance of both maternal and paternal characteristics, the formation of hybrids and the occurrence of monstrous births could

---

[18] J. F. Blumenbach, *An Essay on Generation*, London, 1792, trans. by A. Crichton from *Ueber den Bildungstrieb und das Zeugungsgeschäfte*, 3rd edn., 5.

[19] The following account is largely based on S. A. Roe, *Matter, Life and Generation: Eighteenth-Century Embryology and the Haller–Wolff Debate*, Cambridge, 1981.

all be explained away by allowing for an influence of external factors on the growth of the parts performed in the egg. And the phenomena of regeneration could be accounted for by postulating a distribution of complete and partial germs throughout the body. Finally, the objection that visible structure is absent in the earliest phases of development of the egg was readily met by postulating transparent or invisibly small structures, a line of defence that appeared to be confirmed by microscopic examination and by the appearance of structure in homogeneous living matter when it was treated with alcohol or vinegar. Von Haller and Wolff both held strongly empiricist views, but given the inconclusiveness of the data it is hardly surprising that much of their debate was fought out at the metaphysical level.

For von Haller, as noted above, anatomical organization is prior to the performance of vital functions. So it was natural for him to assume that the living egg had organs from the outset; and in particular that it had from the outset a heart which manifested in its contractions the most fundamental of vital forces, namely, irritability. For Wolff, however, organs and organization were the product, not the source, of the most fundamental vital force, the *vis essentialis*. For von Haller both gravitational force and the vital force of irritability were implanted in matter by God at the Creation. The successive production of the preformed beings under the guidance of irritability, like the regular revolutions of the heavenly bodies under the rule of gravity, were to be seen as the lawlike working out of God's original plan. To invoke forces which bring about organization, as did Wolff's *vis essentialis*, was to usurp the prerogative of the Creator. (Von Haller had the same objection to Buffon's *moule intérieur*, which was supposed to organize the 'organic molecules' contributed by the male and female generative material.) Wolff, however, argued that postulation of a *vis essentialis*, which selectively distributes nourishment, is required if we are to have a *theoria* of generation, that is, a derivation of the phenomena of generation from a principle which gives their sufficient reason. He objected to the preformationists' appeal to God on the grounds that it was tantamount to a refusal to treat generation as a natural phenomenon for which sufficient reason can be given. And he answered the charge that his *vis essentialis* usurped the Creator's role by insisting that 'nothing is demonstrated against the existence of Divine Power, even if bodies are produced by natural forces and natural causes; for these very forces and causes and nature itself claim an author for themselves, just as much as organic bodies do'. Unlike Haller's transcendent God, Wolff's was immanent in Nature.

BLUMENBACH AND THE FORMATIVE DRIVE

Blumenbach's *Ueber den Bildungstrieb* (On the Formative Drive), a version of which first appeared in 1780,[20] explicitly sets out to refute preformationist accounts of generation, and in particular the 'ovist' theory of his teacher, von Haller, a theory which Blumenbach himself had accepted in his youth.

Like Wolff, Blumenbach criticizes von Haller's belief that the observed continuity of the foetal intestine of the chick with the yolk membranes implies their coexistence from the beginning. He points out that when certain insects have laid their eggs in plants, there are formed galls whose tissues are continuous with those of the egg.[21] Here the inference from continuity to original coexistence is obviously fallacious. Moreover, he claims, strong evidence against preformation is provided by J. G. Koelreuter's hybridization experiments on tobacco plants, *Nicotiana*.[22] (Koelreuter had shown that it is possible to obtain a complete reversion of hybrid progeny to the type of the male parent by a sequence of back-pollinations.) However, it is the phenomena of regeneration, especially the astonishing regenerative powers shown by the green polyp, that Blumenbach presents as the conclusive refutation of preformation.[23] Preformationists try to account for regeneration by postulating invisible 'germs' distributed throughout the adult body. Blumenbach directs a battery of heavy-handed mockery at the evidence alleged in support of the existence of such germs— virgin births, tumours filled with hair and teeth, etc.[24] He regards it as highly significant that when regeneration occurs the new parts are always much smaller than those they replace.[25] This is indicative of a reorganization of living matter at the site of damage rather than accretion of material to a 'germ' as postulated by preformationists.

[20] 'Ueber den Bildungstrieb (Nisus formativus) und seinen Einfluss auf die Generation und Reproduktion', *Göttingisches Magazin der Wissenschaften und Literatur*, 1 (1780), 247–66.   [21] *Essay on Generation*, 35–6.
[22] Ibid. 56.   [23] Ibid. 17–18.   [24] Ibid. 43–51.
[25] Ibid. 18–19.

Blumenbach's central contention is as follows:

That there is no such thing in nature, as pre-existing germs: but that the unorganized matter of generation, after being duly prepared, and having arrived at its place of destination takes on a particular action, or nisus, which nisus continues to act through the whole life of the animal, and that by it the first form of the animal, or plant is not only determined, but afterwards preserved, and when deranged, is again restored. A nisus, which seems therefore to depend on the powers of life, but which is distinct from the other qualities of living bodies (sensibility, irritability, and contractility), as from the common properties of dead matter: that it is the chief principle of generation, growth, nutrition, and reproduction, and that to distinguish it from all others, it may be denominated the Formative Nisus (*Bildungstrieb*, or *Nisus formativus*).[26]

The existence of this formative drive is confirmed not only by the phenomena of generation, but also by direct observation of processes of development: Blumenbach cites in particular the formation of the transparent filamentous *conferva fontinalis*, which can be completely observed using a microscope.[27] Further confirmation is obtained by analogy with the evident operation of formative processes in the inorganic world—for example, in the formation of snowflakes and of dendritic silver.[28]

Blumenbach distinguishes sharply between his *Bildungstrieb* and Wolff's *vis essentialis*.[29] The latter is concerned only with the distribution of nutriment, and this does not correlate closely with the formation of organs, the province of the *Bildungstrieb*. However, he offers no positive account of the nature of the formative drive. Rather it is proposed as a heuristic in the search for empirical laws, analogous in status to Newtonian gravitational attraction.

Obviously for most readers it is a quite superfluous reminder that the word '*Bildungstrieb*', like the words 'attraction' and 'gravity', should serve no more and no less than to designate a force whose constant operation may be recognised from experience, but whose cause . . . is for us a *qualitas occulta*. Ovid's saying, *causa latet, vis est notissima*, holds for all these forces. The only profit from the study of these forces is to

---

[26] *Essay on Generation*, 20.
[27] Ibid. 62–3.
[28] Ibid. 61–2.
[29] Ibid. 26–8.

characterise their operations more nearly and to reduce them to general terms:[30]

In the sequel Blumenbach illustrates the heuristic powers of his postulate by deriving from observation a number of laws governing the operation of the *Bildungstrieb*: 'The activity of the nisus is an inverse ratio to the age of the organized body;' 'The Formative Nisus is much more active in the embryo of mammalia than in those of oviparous animals;' etc.[31] He goes on to indicate how alteration of the direction (*Richtung*) of the *Bildungstrieb* may be used to explain departures from the normal course of development. Such alteration of direction may give rise to monstrous births.[32] Moreover, changes in mode of life may bring about change in the direction of the *Bildungstrieb* resulting in 'degeneration' of the original type and the production of races. This, Blumenbach suggests, is how the races of domestic animals have derived from their original wild stocks.[33]

To grasp the full range of the roles attributed to the *Bildungstrieb*, however, it is necessary to read *Ueber den Bildungstrieb* in conjunction with Blumenbach's textbooks of physiology and natural history.[34] From these it becomes clear that for Blumenbach the *Bildungstrieb* has priority amongst the basic vital powers: it is the first of them to manifest itself, being followed, in turn, by irritability and sensitivity; and it regulates and integrates the activities of the other 'vegetative' functions responsible for the preservation of life—nutrition, secretion and digestion. The various directions of the *Bildungstrieb* are responsible for the

---

[30] Ibid. 21–2. There are many precedents for appeal to the example of Newton's gravitational attraction to justify postulation of forces active in living matter but of unknown inner nature; for example, Albrecht von Haller had used the analogy with Newtonian gravitation to justify his postulation of irritability as a force inherent in muscle (see Roe, *Matter, Life and Generation*, 33, 96–9).

[31] *Essay on Generation*, 75, 78.

[32] On 18th-cent. obsession with this topic see P. Tort, *L'Ordre et les monstres: Le Débat sur l'origine des déviations anatomiques au XVIIIᵉ siècle*, Paris, 1980.

[33] *Essay on Generation*, 83–4.

[34] *Handbuch der Naturgeschichte*, Göttingen, 1779, and many subsequent editions; *Institutiones physiologicae*, Göttingen, 1787. On Blumenbach's natural history and physiology see T. Lenoir, 'Kant, Blumenbach, and vital materialism in German biology', *Isis*, 71 (1980), 77–107; *The Strategy of Life*, Dordrecht, 1982, ch. 1; P. McLaughlin, 'Blumenbach und der Bildungstrieb: Zum Verhältnis von epigenetischer Embryologie und typologischem Artbegriff', *Medizinhistorisches Journal*, 17 (1982), 357–72; Duchesneau, *La Physiologie des lumières*, ch. 8.

diversity of internal structure and external appearance of living beings. Moreover, Blumenbach suggests in his later writings, substantial changes in the direction of the *Bildungstrieb* may have been responsible for the replacements of types that have accompanied revolutions in the history of the earth.[35]

KANT: TELEOLOGY AND MECHANISM

For forty years (1756–96) Kant gave regular lectures at the University of Königsberg on 'physical geography'. His course covered not only geography in the narrow sense—topography and climate—but also such topics as the past migrations of living beings, their present distributions in relation to climate and the diversity of human races, communities, customs and moral and political beliefs.[36]

In an introduction to this course, Kant distinguished between two types of division of natural objects. On the one hand, there are 'logical divisions according to concepts' such as those employed by Linnaeus. On the other hand, there are 'physical divisions according to time and space' which relate to the history and present distributions of beings on earth.[37] By way of an example of such a history of the earth's inhabitants Kant ventures some remarks on the derivation of the various breeds of dog.[38] In 1775 he introduced into the course a substantial discussion of the formation of human races: *Von den verschiedenen Racen der Menschen* (On the Different Races of Mankind).[39] This treatise is a contribution to the extensive eighteenth-century literature on the unity of mankind, and in particular to the heated debate that followed the publication of Henry Home's (Lord Kames) defence of a polygenetic theory in his *Six Sketches on the History of Man* of 1774. Kant opens his defence of a single origin of mankind with a distinction between a physical genus (*physische Gattung*) and a logical genus (*Schulgattung*). Physical genera are defined, following Buffon, by the ability of their members to produce fertile offspring; logical genera are defined in terms of similarity of

---

[35] On replacement of species see especially Blumenbach, *Beyträge zur Naturgeschichte*, p. 1, Göttingen, 1790, 20–3.

[36] See J. A. May, *Kant's Concept of Geography and its Relation to Recent Geographical Thought*, Toronto, 1971.   [37] Ibid. 259.

[38] Ibid. 261.

[39] Kant, *Vorkritische Schriften*, ed. A. Buchenau, ii, Berlin, 1912, 443–60.

form.[40] Study of logical genera Kant assigns to the description of nature (*Naturbeschreibung*); study of physical genera he assigns to history of nature (*Naturgeschichte*).

The history of nature, which we still almost entirely lack, would teach us the alteration of the form of the earth; and likewise the alteration which the earth's creatures (plants and animals) have undergone through natural migrations; and the deviations from the original form of the stem-kind (*Urbild der Stammgattung*) that have thence arisen. It would presumably reduce a great array of apparently distinct species to races of the same kind and would convert the logical system of description of nature into a physical system for the understanding.[41]

Kant proceeds to define races as derivations (*Abartungen*) of a common stem which are constantly handed on from generation to generation, and which produce intermediates when miscegenation occurs.[42] The original stem of mankind was, Kant maintains, equipped with hereditary 'germs' (*Keime*), responsible for the development of particular parts, and 'predispositions' (*Anlagen*), responsible for the relations between the parts.[43] The manifestation of these 'germs' and 'predispositions' has been variously developed and suppressed in response to environmental conditions, in particular the amount of sunlight and the quality of the air. In this 'pre-critical' treatise on human races Kant presents the purposive organization of the stem of the human races as a providential arrangement which cannot be explained by mechanical laws.[44] Moreover, Kant shows no hesitation in attempting to reconstruct the form of the original men.[45]

Kant's two 'critical' treatises on human races, *Bestimmung des Begriffs einer Menschenrasse* (Definition of the Conception of a Human Race) of 1785 and *Über den Gebrauch teleologischer Prinzipien in der Philosophie* (On the Use of Teleological Principles in Philosophy) of 1788, are less dogmatic and far subtler.[46] In place of a simple story of adaptation of the races to climatic zones, Kant speculates in his 1785 paper on a sequence of migrations and cross-breedings, a history of such complexity as to render it impossible to determine the form of the original human race. Moreover, he dispenses with the simple appeal to a

---

[40] Ibid, 445.   [41] Ibid. 451 n.   [42] Ibid. 446.
[43] Ibid. 450.   [44] Ibid. 451.   [45] Ibid. 458.
[46] Kant, *Schriften von 1783–1788*, ed. A. Buchenau and E. Cassirer, Berlin, 1913, 223–240, 287–516.

providential plan inexplicable by mechanical laws. Instead, in the 1788 paper (written in response to Georg Forster's hostile review of the 1785 paper), he claims that appeal to final causes is indispensable for us in the explanation of living beings, and that the question of the reality and source of purposive organization in nature is a metaphysical one, beyond the bounds of *Naturwissenschaft*. These doctrines are developed more fully in Kant's *Critique of Judgement* of 1790.

In this magisterial and forbidding work Kant characterizes final causation as a mode of causation in which something is both cause and effect of itself—as, for example, trees both give rise to and originate from trees, and the tree as a whole both sustains and is sustained by its parts. Beings that exhibit such final causality Kant calls 'natural ends' (*Naturzwecke*).[47]

Natural ends face the naturalist with a dilemma. On the one hand, 'All production of material things must be estimated as possible on mere mechanical laws'. On the other hand, it follows from the occurrence of natural ends that 'some products of material nature cannot be estimated as possible on mere mechanical laws, that is, for estimating them a quite different law of causality is required, namely that of final causation'.[48] No conflict of assertions about nature herself arises, since these are maxims of reflection, concerning only the ways in which we are bound by our cognitive constitution to interpret nature.[49] To us natural ends cannot but appear 'accidental' (*zufällig*) if considered as having arisen through the operation of mechanical laws. It is, nevertheless, on the cards that teleology and mechanism are reconciled in the 'inner ground of nature', although that inner ground is inaccessible in principle to discursive intelligences such as ourselves.[50]

Although the maxims of mechanism and teleology are not, on Kant's reckoning, in substantive conflict, they do create an evident practical dilemma. For the investigator of living beings has to recognize, on the one hand, that he must seek as far as possible to explain their development and behaviour in mechanical terms and, on the other hand, that in virtue of the limitations of his finite discursive intelligence he cannot hope to succeed in this task. In an appendix on 'The Theory of the Method of Applying the

---

[47] Kant, *Critique of Judgement*, §64; trans. J. H. Bernard, New York, 1951, 217 ff.   [48] Ibid. 70. 234.
[49] Ibid. 70. 234–5.   [50] Ibid. 71. 235–6.

Teleological Judgement' Kant addresses the issue. His general scheme for a solution is as follows:

Hence, if the naturalist would not waste his labour, he must, in judging of things the concept of any of which is indubitably established as a natural purpose (organised beings), always lay down as basis an original organisation [*ursprüngliche Organisation*] which uses that very mechanism in order to produce fresh organised forms or to develop the existing ones into new shapes (which, however, always result from that purpose and conformably to it.)[51]

We have already mentioned Kant's application of such a scheme in his account of the differentiation of human races from an original stem-race. Here Kant speculates on a bolder application in which common stems for whole groups of species would be inferred from agreements in anatomical structure.

The agreement of so many genera of animals in a certain common schema, which appears to be fundamental not only in the structure of their bones but also in the disposition of their remaining parts—so that with an admirable simplicity of original outline, a great variety of species has been produced by the shortening of one member and the lengthening of another, the involution of this part and the evolution of that—allows a ray of hope, however faint, to penetrate into our minds that here something may be accomplished by the aid of the principle of the mechanism of nature (without which there can be no natural science in general). This analogy of forms, which with all their differences seem to have been produced according to a common original, strengthens our suspicions of an actual relationship between them in their production from a common parent . . .[52]

In a famous footnote Kant goes on to propose as an 'adventure of reason' an extreme application of his scheme, speculating on the genesis of all types of living beings from a single original organization, 'the womb of mother earth'.[53]

Kant then returns to the crucial question of the way in which we may envisage the realization of natural ends through the operation of mechanical laws. He briskly dismisses preformationist accounts of the generation of living beings: they appeal uneconomically to 'supernatural contrivances'; they are forced to treat monstrous births as components of the original design; and they are unable to

[51] Ibid. 80. 267.   [52] Ibid. 80. 267–8.   [53] Ibid. 80. 268–9.

account for the production of hybrids.[54] He then warmly endorses Blumenbach's theory of epigenetic development through the operation of mechanical laws under the guidance of a *Bildungstrieb*.

As regards this theory of Epigenesis, no one has contributed more either to its proof or to the establishment of the legitimate principles of its application—partly by the limitation of a too presumptuous employment of it—than Herr Hofrat Blumenbach. In all physical explanations of these formations he starts from organised matter. That crude matter should have originally formed itself according to mechanical laws, that life should have sprung from the nature of what is lifeless, that matter should have been able to dispose itself into the form of self-maintaining purposiveness—this he rightly declares to be contradictory to reason. But at the same time he leaves to natural mechanism, under this to us indispensable *principle* of an original *organisation*, an undeterminable but yet unmistakable element, in reference to which the faculty of matter in an organised body is called by him a *formative impulse* . . .[55]

In the later editions of his natural history and physiology textbooks Blumenbach returned the compliment, citing the *Critique of Judgement* with approval and writing in an unmistakably Kantian vein about the way in which the formative drive connects 'merely mechanical' with purposive modifications in living beings.[56]

The natural historical scheme established in practice by Blumenbach and in theory by Kant was of remarkable effectiveness. It largely resolved the long-standing controversy over the process of generation. It offered a new integration of anatomy and physiology, and it did so in such a way as to open up a programme of empirical research. It has been shown that this scheme for the pursuit of mechanical (and chemical) explanations within a teleological framework was widely followed by natural historians, anatomists and physiologists in the German lands; and it has been suggested, rightly I believe, that there are close affinities between it and Georges Cuvier's widely followed functional approach to comparative anatomy.[57]

---

[54] Kant, *Critique of Judgement*, 81. 271–3.   [55] Ibid. 81. 274.

[56] On Blumenbach's response to Kant see P. R. Sloan, 'Buffon, German biology, and the historical interpretation of biological species', *The British Journal for the History of Science*, 12 (1979), 109–53; Lenoir, 'Kant, Blumenbach and vital materialism in German biology'.

[57] T. Lenoir, 'The Göttingen School and the development of transcendental Naturphilosophie in the Romantic era', *Studies in the History of Biology*, 5 (1981), 111–205; 'Teleology without regrets: the transformation of physiology in Germany: 1790–1847', *Studies in History and Philosophy of Science*, 12 (1981), 293–354. See

There can be little doubt that the appeal of the Blumenbach–Kant scheme lay not only in the questions it opened up, but also in its exclusion of divisive and sensitive questions about God's role as creator and sustainer of the natural world.[58] However, the way in which the scheme excluded God from natural history entailed a remarkable list of further exclusions. In particular, it outlawed all questions about the natural system, conceived as God's plan in nature. Further, it ruled out all questions about the inner nature of the formative drive and other vital forces, along with all questions about the way in which the original organizations themselves arose. In the next two sections we shall consider certain attempts to get to grips with these and other questions beyond the bounds of Kantian sense.

FORAYS BEYOND THE BOUNDS OF SENSE: HERDER, KIELMEYER AND GOETHE

J. G. Herder was one whom Kant himself castigated for venturing beyond the bounds of sense in the field of natural history. There was, in fact, much common ground between Kant and his former student on the aims and methods of natural history. Both rejected a natural history limited to mere description and ordering in favour of one that would take into account the adaptations of living beings to past and present conditions of existence. Both held such an extended natural history to be of outstanding pedagogic importance. And both were committed to a rigorous exclusion from natural history of metaphysical questions unamenable to empirical investigation. In particular, both rejected 'physico-theological' speculations about providential design in nature.

The opening books of the first volume of Herder's massive *Ideen zur Philosophie der Geschichte der Menschheit* (Ideas for a Philosophy of the History of Mankind) of 1784 survey the universe, starting with accounts of the development of the solar system and of the history of the earth and proceeding to an outline

---

also J. L. Larson, 'Vital forces: regulative principles or constitutive agents? A strategy in German physiology, 1786–1802', *Isis*, 70 (1979), 235–49. D. Outram, 'Uncertain legislator: Georges Cuvier, laws of nature in their intellectual context', *Journal of the History of Biology*, 19 (1986), 323–68.

[58] This exclusion is announced by Kant with memorable force and clarity in the *Critique of Judgement*, 68. 230.

of the progressive development of minerals, plants and animals.[59] Mankind Herder presents as the end-product and culmination of this scale of beings.

From stones to crystals, from crystals to metals, from these to plants, from plants to brutes, and from brutes to man, we here see the *form of organisation* ascend; and with this the powers and propensities of the creature have become more various, till at length they have all united in the human frame, at least as far as they were susceptible of being comprised in it. Here the series stops; we know no creature above man organised with more diversity and art: he seems the highest point obtainable by terrestrial organisation.[60]

Herder relates all that sets man above the beasts—language, humanity, reason and religion—to the superlative physiological and anatomical organization of the human body, and in particular to man's bipedal gait.[61] The entire series of created beings, from crystals to man, manifests a single underlying plan or type, of which man is the most perfect manifestation.

Thus it is anatomically and physiologically true, that the analogy of *one organisation* prevails through the whole animated creation of our Globe: only the farther from man, the more the vital element of the creature differs from his, and Nature, ever true to herself, must proportionately deviate from his standard of organisation: the nearer him, the closer has she drawn together the classes and radii, to combine what she could in him, the divine centre of the terrestrial creation.[62]

All created beings—minerals, plants and animals—are, Herder claims, manifestations and embodiments of hidden active powers. (It is no wonder that he is often said to have been the prototype for Goethe's Faust.) From the successive increments in anatomical perfection at successive rungs on the ladder of living beings we may infer the existence of a progression in the underlying combinations of the active organic powers. Thus in plants the reproductive power predominates, in insects the power of irritability, and in mammals the power of perception.[63] These powers,

[59] Herder, *Outlines of a Philosophy of the History of Man*, trans. T. Churchill, London, 1800, 107.
[60] Ibid. 41. On the context and interpretation of Herder's ambiguous pronouncements on the unity of type see Nisbet, 'Herder, Goethe and the natural type'.
[61] *Outlines of a Philosophy of the History of Man*, 108.
[62] Ibid. 51.   [63] Ibid. 111–12.

as well as the inorganic powers of electricity and magnetism are, Herder suggests, probably manifestations of a single fundamental power, the *Grundkraft*. Moreover, they are immortal. Hence, if we have cultivated our powers well, we may hope for new and better bodies in the afterlife.[64]

In his review of the first two volumes of the *Ideen*, Kant does, indeed, concede some areas of agreement between himself and Herder in the realm of natural history: a common commitment to epigenesist as opposed to preformationist accounts of the development of living beings; and a common acknowledgement of the role of migration and climate in the differentiation of the human races.[65] However, the review as a whole has been aptly characterized as 'a brief but brutal bombardment'. Kant attacks Herder's extravagant uses of analogical reasoning, pouncing with especial relish on his extrapolation from the scale of living beings to human reincarnation in the afterlife. He denounces Herder's metaphorical language with its poetic appeals to imagination and feeling; and he memorably contrasts Herder's conception of philosophy with his own view of it as a discipline 'whose cultivation consists more in the pruning than in the sprouting of luxuriant shoots'.[66] Kant insists that, for all his declarations to the contrary, Herder does in fact venture far into the forbidden territory of metaphysics. He is especially critical of Herder's speculations about goal-directed organic powers and of his attempts at a naturalistic derivation of man's higher faculties. Herder's hypotheses concerning the production of the series of visible organizations by invisible organic powers he dismisses as an attempt to 'explain what one does not understand by means of that which one understands still less'. Such hypotheses he declares to be 'wholly outside the field of *Naturlehre* and to belong to merely speculative philosophy'.[67]

---

[64] Ibid. 123–6.

[65] Kant, *Gesammelte Schriften*, Akademie edn., viii, Berlin, 1923, 43–66. On Kant's attack on Herder see R. T. Clark, *Herder: His Life and Thought*, Berkeley, Calif., 1955, ch. 10; M. Reidel, 'Historizismus und Kritizismus: Kants Streit mit G. Forster und J. G. Herder', *Kant-Studien*, 72 (1981) 41–57; F. Beiser, *The Fate of Reason: German Philosophy from Kant to Fichte*, Cambridge, Mass., 1987, ch. 5.

[66] *Gesammelte Schriften*, 55. In *Vom Erkennen und Empfinden der menschlichen Seele* of 1778 Herder had defended 'poetic' use of signs and analogies as a source of knowledge, invoking both a principle of continuity in the scale of living beings and a correspondence between the powers of the human mind and the hidden powers at work in nature. Kant gives no indication of cognizance of Herder's spirited defence of such analogical inferences.   [67] Ibid. 53–4.

A more precisely articulated version of the doctrine of the succession of organic powers is to be found in Karl Friedrich Kielmeyer's *Rede ueber die Verhältnisse der organischen Kräfte* (Address on the Relations between Organic Forces).[68] This he delivered in 1793, three years after his return to Stuttgart from Göttingen where he had studied under Blumenbach.[69] The occasion of the address was the sixty-fifth birthday of Karl Eugen, Duke of Württemberg, founder and patron of the ferociously disciplinarian Hohen Karlsschule, at which Kielmeyer taught zoology and chemistry and curated the natural history cabinets.

The opening remarks of the address clearly echo the central tenets of the Blumenbach–Kant programme for seeking within a teleological framework empirical laws governing the development of living beings.[70] On the basis of his extensive comparative anatomical and physiological observations Kielmeyer recognizes five vital forces. He then proposes a series of specific laws concerning the relations and interactions of the vital forces. The most general of these laws applies both to stages in the development of each individual living being and to stages in the entire sequence (*Stufenfolge*) of kinds of living beings. This is the law of succession of organic forces, according to which (setting aside some complications) the reproductive (i.e. formative) force at first predominates, then the force of irritability, and finally the force of sensibility.[71] All this is very much in the Blumenbachian manner. In notable respects, however, Kielmeyer's address transgresses the boundaries set by the Blumenbach–Kant scheme for research. Explicit transgressions include a passing remark about the way in which one might seek to understand the emergence of the first organizations on earth, and a tentative speculation about a *Grundkraft* of which all forces in nature, organic and inorganic, are manifestations.[72] Implicit violations

---

[68] Kielmeyer, *Rede ueber die Verhältnisse der organischen Kräfte unter einander in der Reihe der verschiedenen Organisationen, die Geseze und Folgen dieser Verhältnisse*, Stuttgart, 1793; ed. H. Balss, *Sudhoffs Archiv*, 23 (1930), 247–65, 248–50.

[69] On Kielmeyer see W. Coleman, 'Kielmeyer, Carl Friedrich', in Gillispie, ed., *Dictionary of Scientific Biography*, vii. 366–9; D. Kuhn, 'Uhrwerk oder Organismus: Karl Friedrich Kielmeyers System der organischen Kräfte', *Nova Acta Leopoldina*, NS 36 (1970), 157–67; Lenoir, 'The Göttingen School'.

[70] *Rede ueber die Verhältnisse der organischen Kräfte*, 261.

[71] Ibid. 262.

[72] Ibid. 264.

include the recurrent reference to organs as 'expressions' (*Aeusserungen*) of organic forces and the claim that the entire course and condition of living nature must 'arise from' (*hervorgehen*) this balance of forces.[73] Taken literally such language is entirely at variance with the Blumenbach–Kant scheme, according to which the vital forces regulate the organization of living matter and the functions of living organs, but certainly do not constitute living matter or living organs.

Much bolder ventures beyond the bounds of Kantian sense are to be found in Goethe's writings. Goethe saw himself as the instigator of a new science of morphology whose subject matter was 'the form, formation and transformation of organic natures'.[74] His major contributions to this new science were in the fields of plant anatomy and the comparative anatomy of the vertebrate skeleton.[75] In 1786 he circulated the claim that he had discovered the intermaxillary bone in man, a discovery to which he later claimed he had been guided by the idea of an ideal type of the vertebrates.[76] In 1790, two years after his first Italian journey, he published his *Versuch, die Metamorphose der Pflanzen zu erklären* (An Attempt to Explain the Metamorphoses of Plants).[77] In this work he sought to show that all the organs of the plant can be considered as progressive modifications of a single fundamental organ, the primordial leaf (*Urblatt*). In his post-1790 writings on the vertebrate skeleton, Goethe makes use of the same notion of serial modification of a basic organ, treating the various sorts of vertebra as well as the components of the skull as modifications of the primordial typical vertebra. In these writings Goethe presents the variety of vertebrate skeletons as derivations from a basic plan

[73] Ibid. 265.

[74] Goethe, *Gedenkausgabe der Werke, Briefe und Gespräche*, ed. E. Beutler, Zurich, 1948–66, xvii. 115; on Goethe's introduction of the term *Morphologie* see the entry in the index to vol. xvii, p. 995.

[75] The following account is indebted to Nisbet, 'Herder, Goethe and the natural type'; H. Bräuning-Oktavio, 'Vom Zwischenkieferknochen zur Idee des Typus: Goethe als Naturforscher in den Jahren 1780–1786', *Nova Acta Leopoldina*, NS 18 (126) (1956); T. Lenoir, 'The eternal laws of form: morphotypes and the conditions of existence in Goethe's biological thought', in F. Amrine, F. J. Zucker and H. Wheeler, eds., *Goethe and the Sciences: A Reappraisal*, Dordrecht, 1987, 17–28.

[76] Bräuning-Oktavio, 'Vom Zwischenkieferknochen zur Idee des Typus', offers convincing evidence that Goethe's claim about the role of the ideal type is a retrospective fabrication.

[77] *Goethe's Botanical Writings*, trans. B. Mueller, Honolulu, 1952.

or type (*Bauplan, Urtyp*); and he offers a detailed reconstruction of the basic skeletal plan of the vertebrates.[78]

Derivation of the various particular anatomical structures of living beings from their types can be seen, Goethe claims, to take place in accordance with lawlike processes. There are many disparities between Goethe's various accounts of these processes. However, certain claims recur. There is, for example, repeated appeal to a principle of compensation according to which development of some parts occurs at the expense of others.[79] Goethe frequently describes series of anatomical structures as manifesting an enhancement (*Steigerung*) or perfection (*Vervollkommnung*) of a typical or ideal structure.[80] The progression from seed leaves, via ordinary leaves, sepals and petals to the generative organs of plants is one of enhancement. The development of larval or foetal into adult forms manifests the process of perfection; so too does the succession of animal organizations that culminates in the human form.[81] On occasion Goethe characterizes enhancement and perfection as processes of differentiation of originally similar parts—thus, for example, the chain of identical vertebrae in the type of the vetebrate skeleton is variously perfected through differentiation into specialized vertebrae and the segments of the skull.[82] Further, Goethe often invokes a law of polarity by which he explains perfection and enhancement as the resultant of the opposition between processes of specification, separation and disintegration, on the one hand, and condensation, concentration and integration, on the other.[83]

Goethe's attitude to purpose in nature shows important affinities

[78] Goethe's clearest and most extended account of the laws of derivation from a type is in the opening sections of his 'Erster Entwurf einer allgemeinen Einleitung in die vergleichende Anatomie, ausgehend von der Osteologie', written in 1795 and published in *Zur Naturwissenschaft überhaupt, besonders zur Morphologie*, Stuttgart, 1817–24: *Die Schriften zur Naturwissenschaft*, ed. Akademie der Naturforscher (Leopoldina) Zu Halle, Weimar, 1947– , ix. 119–51.

[79] See Goethe, *Die Schriften zur Naturwissenschaft*, ix. 125.

[80] See G. Uschmann, *Der morphobiologische Vervollkommungsbegriff bei Goethe und seine problemgeschichtlichen Zusammenhänge*, Jena, 1939.

[81] *Die Schriften zur Naturwissenschaft*, ix. 202–9.

[82] Ibid. 124–8.

[83] See the list of passages cited under *Polarität* in the index of Goethe, *Gedenkausgabe der Werke, Briefe und Gespräche*, ed. Beutler, xviii. 1002. On Goethe's conception of polarity see R. C. Zimmermann, 'Goethes Polaritätsdenken im geistigen Kontext des 18. Jahrhunderts', *Jahrbuch der deutschen Schiller-Gesellschaft*, 18 (1974), 303–47.

to Kant's.[84] Like Kant he rejects 'physico-theological' accounts of living beings which appeal to providential design; and, like Kant, Goethe considers living beings as natural ends, 'at once cause and effect of themselves'. Moreover, there are points of resemblance between, on the one hand, Goethe's morphological types and the lawlike processes by which particular structures are derived from them and, on the other hand, Kant's stem-kinds and the processes by which the present variety of creatures has been derived from them. For Goethe recognition of types is a precondition for seeing the true relationships of living beings, just as for Kant postulation of stem-kinds is a precondition for an understanding of the present variety of living beings. Comparative anatomy is crucial for the recognition of Kantian stem-kinds just as it is for Goethean types. Moreover, Goethe's concept of type is as strictly teleological as Kant's concept of stem-kind. Just as for Kant derivation from stem-kinds fits the various living beings to their surroundings, so according to Goethe transformation of a type yields forms which harmonize with the diverse 'conditions of existence'.[85]

In other respects, however, Goethe's types are strikingly different from Kant's stem-kinds. Stem-kinds cannot be observed since they existed only in the remote past. At best their form can be reconstructed from the present-day distributions of living beings together with inference about their past migrations and the past climates and conditions to which they were exposed; but Kant is pessimistic about the feasibility of this. Goethe's types, on the other hand, do not exist as individuals: 'no individual can serve as a model for the whole'.[86] They are however, visible: Goethe is insistent that the type can be literally seen in arrays or series of individual living beings. So, paradoxically, Kant's stem-kinds are real objects that cannot be seen, whereas Goethe's types are ideal objects that can be seen.

[84] Goethe himself gave an account of the impact on him of Kantian philosophy, and in particular of the *Critique of Judgement*: 'Einwirkung der neueren Philosophie', *Werke*, ed. E. Trunz, xiii, Hamburg, 1955; *Goethe's Botanical Writings*, 228–32. The basic work on Goethe's relations with Kantian philosophy is K. Vorländer, 'Goethes Verhältnis zu Kant in seiner historischen Entwicklung', *Kant-Studien*, 1 (1897), 60–99, 315–51; 2 (1898), 161–236. A sensible general discussion of the issue is J. Gauss, 'Goethe und die Prinzipien der Naturforschung bei Kant', *Studia Philosophica*, 29 (1970), 53–8.

[85] See e.g. Goethe, *Die Schriften zur Naturwissenschaft*, ix. 125–8. This aspect of Goethe's morphology is discussed by Lenoir, 'The eternal laws of form'.

[86] *Die Schriften zur Naturwissenschaft*, 121.

In claiming to be able to 'grasp the whole in intuition'—to literally see the ideal types from which the various structures of plants and animals are derived, Goethe laid claim to precisely the kind of holistic and synthetic understanding that Kant had denied to merely human intelligences. The question arises: How did Goethe suppose it possible to achieve such synthetic understanding just by looking?

Goethe wrote extensively about the processes whereby we may arrive at insight into types and the laws by which the varied structures of living beings are derived from them. However, his pronouncements are often cryptic and not always consistent; the following remarks are, therefore, tentative. Morphological types are, in Goethe's terminology, pure or original phenomena (*reine Phänomene, Urphänomene*). The quest for pure phenomena Goethe describes as follows:

The object of our work would then be to demonstrate; (1) an *empirical phenomenon*, of which every individual is conscious in Nature and which later is elevated to (2) a *scientific phenomenon* by experimentation, by representing it under circumstances and conditions differing from those in which we first encountered it and in a more or less effective sequence; and (3) the *pure phenomenon* now standing for it as the result of all experiences and experiments. It can never be isolated, appearing as it does in a constant succession of forms. In order to describe it, the human intellect determines the empirically variable, excludes the accidental, separates the impure, unravels the tangled, and even discovers the unknown.[87]

Types, like other *Urphänomene*, are perceived only when individual phenomena are ordered in the light of systematic observation and experiment. In the case of recognition of morphological types the relevant preliminary ordering is the arrangement of specimens in series which exhibit their structural relations to best advantage. Only then is it possible to 'see' the type in the series of specimens or, equivalently, to see the series as derived by law-governed transformation of the type.

What kind of seeing is this which enables Goethe to intuit a series of anatomical structures as derivations from an ideal type?

There is ample evidence to suggest that the seeing which transports Goethe beyond the bounds of Kantian sense is intimately connected with aesthetic appraisal. At least from the

[87] *Werke*, ed. Trunz, xiii. 25; *Goethe's Botanical Writings*, 228.

time of his first Italian journey, 1786–8, Goethe treats original types as ideals of beauty for all kinds of phenomena.[88] The original landscape (*Urlandschaft*), which he saw in the Neapolitan and Sicilian countryside, is the ideal that inspired the unsurpassable descriptions of nature of Homer, Hesiod and Pindar. The original woman (*Urweib*), whom Goethe sought in a succession of lovers, is an ideal of beauty both physical and spiritual. The original form of man that Goethe sought to ascertain from study of statues of Greek gods is likewise an ideal of beauty. And in this case the connection between aesthetic appraisal and his new science of morphology is explicit. For on his return from Italy Goethe attended lectures on anatomy and made measurements on human bodies in the attempt to establish the human physical ideal.

Further evidence that for Goethe recognition of morphological types is guided by aesthetic insight emerges when we consider the terms he uses to describe the lawlike processes by which particular animal and plant structures are derived from original types. Enhancement (*Steigerung*), perfection (*Vervollkommnung*), and polarity (*Polarität*), are all for Goethe terms of aesthetic appraisal.[89] On the one hand, they are used as terms of critical and art-historical appraisal to describe the relations between art works and their prototypes—Goethe's *Torquato Tasso* is an enhancement of his *The Sorrows of Young Werther*; the civilized Ionic style is a perfection of the austere and lofty Doric style, and so on. On the other hand, these terms are used to describe the processes whereby the artist derives the particular work of art from the source of his inspiration. The two uses are intimately connected: for it is a commonplace of the aesthetic theory of the period that aesthetic appraisal involves an imaginative re-enactment of the process of creation of the work of art.

In the 'Critique of Aesthetic Judgement', the first part of the *Critique of Judgement*, Kant talks of the way in which aesthetic appraisal of sublime objects occasions imaginative representations which 'strive after something which lies beyond the bounds of experience'.[90] And, as we have already noted, in the second part of the work he is inspired by consideration of purposive

[88] The following remarks are indebted to H. Trevelyan, *Goethe and the Greeks*, Cambridge, 1942, ch. 2.
[89] See C. M. Wilkinson and L. A. Willoughby, *Goethe as Poet and Thinker*, London, 1962, chs. 6, 10 and 11.   [90] Kant, *Critique of Judgement*, 49. 157.

organization in nature to voice certain 'presentiments' about the unknowable 'inner ground of nature' and the powers of an 'archetypal' productive intellect, matters which clearly lie beyond the bounds of Kantian sense. One who supposed that aesthetic appraisal involves a re-enactment of the processes of creation might well find in Kant support for the view that through aesthetic intuition one may grasp the 'inner ground of nature'.

That this was the message Goethe had read into Kant is, I think, implied by his comments on *The Critique of Judgement* in his 'Intuitive Judgement' (*Anschauende Urteilskraft*).[91] 'In my efforts to utilise if not actually master the Kantian theory, it sometimes seemed to me as if the worthy man were proceeding roguishly and ironically, at one point appearing to set narrow limits to our perceptive capacity and at another beckoning furtively beyond them.' As an instance of such beckoning beyond the bounds of sense Goethe cites Kant's invocations of the concept of an archetypal intelligence. He concludes as follows:

To be sure, the author seems to be referring here to a godlike understanding; yet since it is possible in the moral realm to ascend to a higher plane, drawing close to the Supreme Being through faith in God, virtue and immortality, the same well might hold true in the intellectual realm. Through contemplation of ever-created Nature we might make ourselves worthy of participating intellectually in her productions. Had not I myself ceaselessly pressed forward to the archetype, though at first unconsciously, from an inner urge; had I not even succeeded in evolving a method in harmony with Nature? What then was to prevent me from courageously embarking upon the adventure of reason as the old gentleman of Königsberg himself calls it?

That Goethe here has in mind morphological investigations becomes clear when we remember that Kant's 'daring adventure of reason' was inspired by comparative anatomical phenomena and concerned the derivation of all living beings from a single original organization.[92]

---

[91] *Die Schriften zur Naturwissenschaft*, ix. 95–6; *Goethe's Botanical Writings*, 232–3.

[92] It should be noted that Kant's *Critique of Judgement* is but one of several contexts for Goethe's aesthetic morphology. Other significant contexts are provided by Petrus Camper's lectures on art and anatomy and by the treatises on physiognomy of Lavater, with whom Goethe was in active correspondence and collaboratrion in the decade before his Italian journey: see N. Jardine, 'What did Goethe see in women and other productions of nature and art?', forthcoming.

In the *Critique of Judgement* Kant had intimated the possibility of a reconciliation of teleology and mechanism in 'the supersensible principle of nature, external to us, as well as in us'. Goethe's aesthetic scrutiny of nature is directed outwards, towards the external manifestations of Kant's 'supersensible principle'. For Schelling and his followers, however, the quest for knowledge of nature beyond the bounds of Kantian sense leads inwards.

SCHELLING AND OKEN: KINGDOMS BEYOND THE
BOUNDS OF SENSE

In Schelling's *On the World-Soul* of 1798 both Goethe's speculations on the metamorphoses of plants and Kielmeyer's law of succession of organic forces are cited with approval.[93] Future ages, Schelling claims, will recognize Kielmeyer's *Rede ueber die Verhältnisse der organischen Kräfte* as marking 'the epoch of a wholly new natural history'. In the course of the next three years Schelling developed these themes in the context of an elaborate programme for the a priori construction of a philosophy of nature (*Naturphilosophie*).[94] This construction re-enacts the entire process whereby both the outer world of nature and the inner world of consciousness were engendered by an archetypal productive intuition. The starting-point for the construction of the outer world is an original polarity of forces, the product of the original act by which the self (*das Ich*) sets itself up in opposition to nature.

The construction itself proceeds dialectically through successive manifestations and partial resolutions of the original conflict. In the first phase the inorganic *Kräfte* are constructed, magnetism and electricity appearing as manifestations of the primordial conflict, and chemical process as its partial resolution. In the second phase the vital *Kräfte*, sensibility, irritability and the galvanic or life process, are in turn constructed as the higher analogues of the inorganic *Kräfte*; and Kielmeyer's law of succession of the vital forces is derived a priori. The priority of vital forces over vital organs, adumbrated in Kielmeyer, becomes

[93] F. W. J. Schelling, *Sämmtliche Werke*, ed. K. F. A. von Schelling, Stuttgart, 1856–61, ii. 565.
[94] The best general account of Schelling's *Naturphilosophie* remains K. Fischer, *Schellings Leben, Werke und Lehre*, 2nd edn., Heidelberg, 1899. An important recent study is R. Marks, *Konzeption einer dynamischen Naturphilosophie bei Schelling und Eschenmeyer*, Munich, 1985.

explicit: 'Sensibility is there before its organs have been formed; brain and nerves rather than being causes of sensibility are themselves already its product'.[95]

It is in this context that Schelling set out his programme for a 'wholly new natural history' in his *First Sketch of a System of Naturphilosophie* of 1799. He first notes that some have interpreted the succession of organizations (*Stufenfolge der Organisationen*) as evidence of a genealogy of types, even supposing that all types of living beings may be the progeny of a single ancestral type. This is impossible, Schelling claims.

The distinctness of the stages at which we now see the organizations fixed evidently presupposes a ratio of the original forces peculiar to each one; whence it follows that nature must have initiated anew each product that appears fixed to us . . .[96]

When properly understood comparative anatomy and physiology testify not to a genealogy of species but to development directed towards an original ideal. Given that the various types of organization are determined by and expressive of ratios of organic forces, it should be possible in principle to derive a priori the entire sequence of types of organization through which nature strives to realize the original ideal.[97] Schelling goes on in a striking passage to contrast such a 'history of nature herself' both with the standard descriptive natural history and with the genealogical natural history that Kant had proposed.

Natural history has up to now been only the description of nature, as Kant has very rightly remarked. He himself suggests the name 'natural history' for a special branch of the science of nature, namely knowledge of the gradual alterations that the various organizations of the earth have undergone through the influence of external nature, migrations from one climate to another, etc. If only the idea just set out were practicable, the name 'natural history' would assume a much higher import, for it would then actually convey a history of nature herself, namely of how through continual deviations from a common ideal she gradually brings forth the whole multiplicity of her products and thus realises that ideal, not indeed in the individual products, but in the whole.[98]

Here we have a proposal for an a priori derivation of the entire natural system, a system that is conceived not as the plan of a

[95] Schelling, *Sämmtliche Werke*, iii. 155.   [96] Ibid. 63.
[97] Ibid. 64–5.   [98] Ibid. 68.

transcendent creator, but as the realization of an ideal immanent in nature. Schelling himself produced no such system. However, natural history was one of the disciplines in which *Naturphilosophie* achieved a substantial following, and the opening decades of the nineteenth century see a considerable number of classificatory enterprises that can be read as attempts to implement Schelling's programme. The most remarkable of these is due to Lorenz Oken, declared follower of Schelling and at the time of publication of his system Professor of Natural History and Medicine at the University of Jena, and a close acquaintance of Goethe.[99]

In an address in 1809, *On the Value of Natural History, especially for the Education of the Germans*, Oken protests that the cultivation of natural history only for its practical and commercial fruits in medicine and agriculture leads to a 'senseless enumeration, description and naming of animals'.[100] In place of such an ignoble, 'profiteering' natural history he pleads for a natural history that will be an integral part of the new *Naturphilosophie*.[101] This noble natural history will unify the German people with themselves and the world; it will give them an understanding of their own nature and their relations to plants and animals; and it will imbue them with manly resignation when their power falls short of their understanding.[102] Such is the natural history elaborated by Oken in his *Lehrbuch der Naturphilosophie*, 1809–11.[103]

Oken's *Lehrbuch* is ambitious. In it he offers nothing less than a derivation, from the original zero (God) and its polarization into the positive and negative series of numbers, of the whole system of

[99] On Oken's career see A. Ecker, *Lorenz Oken*, Stuttgart, 1880; M. Pfannenstiel, 'Lorenz Oken', *Berichte der naturforschenden Gesellschaft zu Freiburg i. Br.*, 41 (1951), 7–20. The only detailed study of Oken's *Naturphilosophie* known to me is G. Busse, 'Philosophische und geistesgeschichtliche Grundzüge der Lehre Lorenz Okens', D. Phil. thesis, Freiburg im Breisgau, 1950, to which the present account is much indebted. On Oken's systematics of the plant and animal kingdoms see also J. B. Stallo, *General Principles of the Philosophy of Nature*, Boston, Mass., 1848, 230–330; S. J. Gould, *Ontogeny and Phylogeny*, Cambridge, Mass., 1977, 40–5; H. Querner, 'Ordnungsprinzipien und Ordnungsmethoden in der Naturgeschichte der Romantik', in R. Brinkmann (ed.), *Romantik in Deutschland*, Stuttgart, 1978, 214–25.

[100] Oken, *Gesammelte Schriften*, ed. J. Schuster, Berlin, 1939, 258–9.
[101] Ibid. 260–3.   [102] Ibid. 264 ff.
[103] 3rd edn., Zurich, 1843, trans. into English by A. Tulk as *Elements of Physiophilosophy*, London, 1847. Oken's other major natural historical work, *Lehrbuch der Naturgeschichte*, Leipzig, 1813, Jena 1826, is 'merely narrated, without grounds', that is, it provides only classification and description without deriving the classification from the principles of *Naturphilosophie*.

'products of nature', organic and inorganic, together with their principal activities and functions.

The third volume of the *Lehrbuch* deals with the development of the animal kingdom. In its preface Oken boasts that he has 'established for natural history grounds of classification that are entirely new, covering the whole body and applying to all animals' and that he has 'on that basis arranged all the animals according to their faculties'.[104] He goes on to insist that his work is considered and methodical: he does not dash off just anything that comes into his head. One of the methods he has followed he calls 'the factual [*sächliche*] method'. It is a constructive method which 'always links the object which follows with the most important of the preceding ones'. His other method, the *naturphilosophische*, exploits correspondences between part and whole in the cosmos.[105] To exemplify the two methods Oken instances his two derivations of the thesis that the primordial organism from which all others are composed is a vesicle (*Bläschen*). According to the *sächliche* method 'the organic must become a vesicle, since it is a galvanic process which can take place only between the elements. The action of air is necessarily an external one, so it divides the slime inwards into the earthy and the watery, cell wall and cell content.' According to the *naturphilosophische* method 'the organic must be a vesicle because it is the image of the planet'.[106]

The core of Schelling's technique of *Konstruktion* is the dialectical procedure whereby successively 'higher' and more specialized natural processes and products are derived as the successive manifestations and partial resolutions or syntheses of the primordial strife between expansive and contractive forces. There are evident affinities with Oken's *sächliche* method. In carrying out his constructions of natural processes and bodies Schelling has frequent recourse to analogies between natural products that are generated at corresponding moments of the successive epochs of construction. Such are the analogies between, on the one hand, the inorganic forces of magnetism, electricity and chemical process and, on the other hand, the 'higher' organic forces of sensibility, irritability and galvanism. Similarly, a substantial role is played in Schelling's cosmogony by the view that analogous patterns of differentiation arise in the successive epochs

---

[104] *Lehrbuch*, vol. iii, pp. iv–v.   [105] Ibid. p. vi.
[106] Ibid. p. vii.

of construction of the cosmos. Oken's *naturphilosophische* method has much in common with Schelling's constructive use of analogy.[107]

The first stage in Oken's developmental history of living beings is the construction of the vesicles of slime mentioned above. In isolation these occur in water as Infusoria; variously combined they constitute other types of organism. The second stage is the construction of the plant kingdom. The third stage, which synthesizes the other two, is the construction of the animal kingdom, culminating in man, the complete and perfect realization of God. The original ideal, for Schelling unrealizable in any particular finite product of nature, is for Oken fully realized in man.[108] (In later writings Oken treats the ideal warrior-hero as an as yet unrealized perfection of mankind.) The basis of the construction is provided by a ranking of the organic processes associated with each of the four elements. From this is derived a partition of 'the animal body' into tissues, organs and organ-systems, themselves ranked according to the rank of the process or processes that they enact. The system of types of animal is constructed by addition and reduplication of successively higher-ranking organs culminating in man, who possesses all organs in their highest forms: hence Oken's pronouncement, 'The animal kingdom is but a dismemberment of the highest animal, man.' In the demarcation and ranking of types it is sense organs, the noblest organs, that provide the primary criteria.

The principal ranking of types, the 'axis' of Oken's system, is the sequence of seventeen classes, from infusorians to mammals, shown in Table 2.1.[109] In the course of its development from fertilized egg to adult an animal of a given type passes in turn through stages representative of each of the classes that rank below the class to which it belongs.

The foetus is a representation of all animal classes in time. At first it is a simple vesicle, stomach, or vitellus, as in the Infusoria. Then the vesicle is doubled through the albumen and shell, and obtains an intestine, as in the

---

[107] Ibid. vii. 106. There is, however, little parallel in Schelling for the numerological correspondences invoked by Oken, for example, in his 'derivation' of his theory of elements from the Trinity in the 'mathesis' of the first book of the *Lehrbuch*.

[108] Herder's *Ideen*, i. is one obvious source for such views.

[109] Based on 3rd edn., 484–5. In earlier edns. only four circles are recognized.

TABLE 2.1 *Oken's construction of the series of classes of animals*

Dominant element	Dominant sense	Dominant organ-system	Circles	Classes
Earth		Alimentary Gastric Intestinal Absorbent	Protozoa	Infusorians Polyps Jellyfish
Water	Tactile	Vascular Venous Arterial Cardiac	Conchozoa	Shellfish Snails, slugs Squids
Air		Respiratory Cutaneous Branchial Tracheal	Ancyliozoa	Worms Crustaceans Insects
Fire	Taste Smell Hearing Sight	Osseous Muscular Nervous Sensory	Sarcozoa

Aesthesiozoa | Fish Reptiles Birds Mammals |

Corals . . . With the appearance of the osseous system, into the class of Fishes. With the evolution of muscles, into the class of Reptiles. With the ingress of respiration through the lungs, into the class of Birds. The foetus, when born, is actually like them, edentulous.[110]

The criteria used to demarcate and rank the classes of animals are iteratively applied within each class to provide a demarcation and ranking of orders, families, genera and species. The resultant scheme is of great complexity. In it there are correspondences between types of different categories in the hierarchy: such are the parallels between classes of animals and families of birds and fishes shown in Table 2.2.[111] There are also correspondences between 'lower' and 'higher' types of the same category: such are the parallels between orders of fish and orders of birds and between families of fish and families of birds, likewise shown in Table 2.2.

[110] Oken, *Elements of Physiophilosophy*, 45. On this aspect of Oken's system see Gould, *Ontogeny and Phylogeny*, ch. 3.
[111] Based on 2nd edn., 40. In the 1st edn. only the parallelisms of classes and orders are worked out.

TABLE 2.2 *Parallelisms in Oken's system*

Animals		Fish		Birds	
Circles	Classes	Orders	Families	Orders	Families
Protozoa	Infusorians	I	Lampreys	I	Tree-creepers
	Polyps		Pipe-fish		Woodpeckers
	Jellyfish		Shad		Cuckoos
Conchozoa	Shellfish	II	Eels	II	Sparrows
	Snails, slugs		Haddock		Crows
	Squids		Gobies		Parrots
Ancyliozoa	Worms	III	Tunnies	III	Songbirds
	Crustaceans		Bream		Flycatchers
	Insects		Perch		Hawks
Sarcozoa	Fish	IV	Herrings	IV	Geese
	Reptiles		Salmon		Herons
	Birds		Pike		Fowl
Aesthesiozoa	Mammals	V	Sharks	V	Bustards

All these correspondences are reflected in 'analogies' of anatomical structure. Some of these analogies involve transformations of a structural type similar to those postulated by Goethe. Indeed, Oken and Goethe became involved in a bitter priority dispute over the 'discovery' that the skull is derived from a transformation and fusion of a series of primordial vertebrae.[112] Others of Oken's analogies, however, involve transformations stranger and more extreme than anything countenanced by Goethe: 'the nose is the thorax repeated in the head'; 'the limbs of insects are the ribs of mammals'; 'the fish is a mussel from between whose shells a monstrous abdomen has grown'.

Oken's system is an extraordinary feat of synthesis. It takes a decisive stand on every one of the major controversial issues in the natural history of the period—the basis of the process of generation, the form of the natural system, the relation between

[112] See R. Zaunick, 'Oken, Carus, Goethe: Zur Geschichte des Gedankens der Wirbel-Metamorphose', in *Historische Studien und Skizzen zur Natur- und Heilwissenschaft, Festgabe Georg Sticker zum 70. Geburtstage dargeboten*, Berlin, 1930; H. Bräuning-Oktavio, *Oken und Goethe im Lichte neuer Quellen*, Weimar, 1959.

form and function, the role of God in the natural world. Moreover, it is a system which tightly integrates the description, classification, anatomy, physiology and chemistry of living beings.

In the period 1820–50 we find a substantial body of natural historical writing which shows marked affinities with the work of Goethe and Oken.[113] Notable exponents of this 'transcendental' approach include J. F. Meckel and K. G. Carus in Germany, Étienne Geoffroy Saint-Hilaire and Étienne Serres in France, and Robert Knox, John Goodsir and Richard Owen in the British Isles. At the level of specific doctrines there are great disparities between these transcendental natural historians. However, they are united by a well-marked cluster of general commitments: to the interpretation of the diversity of living beings as an unfolding or enactment of original ideas and forces; to the specification of morphological types and morphological laws; to the tracing of parallels between individual development (both normal and abnormal) and the ideal succession of living beings.

SHIFTING SCENES

What kind of story has just been told? What is the significance of this chronicle of changes in the scope, contents and methods of natural history? In particular, how are we to interpret the formation of the Blumenbach–Kant scheme for the pursuit of natural history and the transition from that scheme to transcendental natural history in the style of Goethe, Oken and their followers and emulators?

One type of answer can be ruled out with confidence. This can hardly be read as a story of scientific progress. From the standpoint of our biology the natural historical concerns of Blumenbach, Kant, Herder, Kielmeyer, Goethe, Schelling and

[113] See e.g. E. S. Russell, *Form and Function: A Contribution to the History of Animal Morphology*, London, 1916, chs. 4–8; Querner, 'Ordnungsprinzipien und Ordnungsmethoden'; D. Knight, *Ordering the World: A History of Classifying Man*, London, 1981, ch. 1; P. F. Rehbock, *The Philosophical Naturalists: Theories in Early Nineteenth-Century British Biology*, Madison, Wis. 1983; T. A. Appel, *The Cuvier–Geoffroy Debate: French Biology in the Decades before Darwin*, New York, 1987; A. Desmond, *The Politics of Evolution: Morphology, Medicine, and Reform in Radical London*, Chicago, 1989; and the articles by T. Lenoir, P. F. Rehbock and E. Richards in A. Cunningham and N. Jardine, eds., *Romanticism and the Sciences*, Cambridge, 1990.

Oken are entirely alien. This alienation does not arise from their having given what are, according to present-day biology, largely false answers to genuine questions. Nor does it arise from their having addressed what are, from our scientific viewpoint, genuine but eccentric or uninteresting questions. Rather, I suggest, the alienation is engendered by their having addressed what are for the most part, for us, unreal questions. If pressed to pass judgement on the developments retailed above, we may perhaps conclude that in the relevant period German natural history was not yet 'on the secure path of a science'. But there is little scope for further adjudication—too few of the questions they addressed are, by our lights, real questions; too few of their beliefs are for us even candidates for truth. Consider again some of Oken's wondrous pronouncements: 'The organic must be a vesicle because it is the image of the planet;' 'The animal kingdom is but a dismemberment of the highest animal, man.' I hope that the above account has made it clear that the way in which we are alienated from Oken's beliefs does not have to do primarily with understanding. We are able to gain an understanding of the questions Oken posed by seeing how his methods of inquiry enabled him to get to grips with them. But such understanding does not make the questions any the more real for us. Nor is the problem one of interest, salience or centrality. The weirdness of Oken's questions for us does not result from our finding them dull, obscure or marginal. The problem is simply that from our standpoint the questions Oken addressed are not real questions.

More profitable perhaps are readings that would cast our story into one of the various genres of 'history of ideas' or 'intellectual history': for these are types of history in which we can engage without undue regard to the reality of questions or the truth of answers from the standpoint of present-day scientific beliefs. In accordance with the traditional type of history of ideas one may read the story in terms of motifs, themes and topoi, their sources and their fortunes. To thicken our story into an interesting specimen of this genre we would have to undertake some prosopography: Who taught whom? Who read whom? etc. We would have to embark on some philology, investigating in detail the roles and connotations of key terms: *Organisation*, *Stufenfolge*, *Differenzierung*, etc. Above all, we would have greatly to refine, and doubtless correct and qualify, our account of the various authors' natural historical beliefs in relation to their beliefs in other domains.[114]

In accordance with currently more fashionable modes of intellectual history our story would be read as a sketch of the careers of certain research programmes or research traditions in natural history. To thicken the narrative into such an account the primary task would be to show that the beliefs and methods retailed are suitably representative of those which prevailed in whole communities of inquirers.[115]

My contention is that by concentrating on doctrines rather than questions these approaches fail to engage with the most fundamental feature of the episodes in natural history that we have retailed.

One more existing mode of interpretation deserves mention before I venture my own. Michel Foucault presented the shift from eighteenth-century natural history to nineteenth-century biology as one manifestation of the shift from a classical 'episteme', concerned with the ordering of things on the basis of their external and visible characteristics, to a modern episteme, concerned with origins, historical formations, hidden structures and inner processes.[116] In particular, he argued that inquiries into the historical development of living beings presuppose a comparative anatomy in which the forms and dispositions of organs and organ-systems are seen as the consequences of physiological and functional requirements. Thus he came to the paradoxical conclusion that it was Cuvier, opponent of the transmutation of species, who 'made Darwin possible'.

There has been widespread acceptance of the core of Foucault's thesis, namely, that natural history was transformed around 1800 by a new concern with internal process and structure in living beings. The validity of this central claim is clearly illustrated by the changes in German natural history that we have retailed. Other

[114] Parts of the story have been ably elaborated along these lines: see e.g. R. Löw, *Philosophie des Lebendigen: Der Begriff des Organischen bei Kant, sein Grund und seine Aktualität*, Frankfurt, 1980; Busse, 'Philosophische und geistesgeschichtliche Grundzüge der Lehre Lorenz Okens'.

[115] As noted above, Lenoir has made a strong case for the existence of a 'Göttingen School', whose natural historical and physiological inquiries were prosecuted in accordance with the Blumenbach–Kant scheme: Lenoir, 'The Göttingen School'.

[116] M. Foucault, *Les Mots et les choses*, Paris, 1966; trans. as *The Order of Things*, London, 1970, chs. 7 and 8.

aspects of the thesis are, however, controversial. There has been much debate about the nature of epistemes and the way in which they supposedly exercise control over the disciplines. Moreover, certain specific aspects of Foucault's thesis have been called in question.[117] It seems, for example, that he dated the emergence of biology as a discipline too early in the nineteenth century; that he generalized too readily from developments in French natural history to developments in natural history as a whole; and, above all, that he took Cuvier's own inflated estimate of the novelty of his approach in natural history too much at face value. For our purposes, however, the interest of Foucault's position lies neither in his specific claims about the career of natural history nor in his general notion of episteme, but in the way in which he describes the consequences of change of episteme. According to Foucault, when a new episteme takes over, new topics and types of inquiry 'become possible'. In its concern with the coming into being of problems Foucault's interpretation of the tranformation of natural history around 1800 is close to mine.

The interpretation that I advocate construes the development of natural history in the German lands in terms of changes in the range of questions that were real or valid for natural historians—as a story of shifts in the scene of natural history. What does our story look like when spelled out in these terms?

First let us consider the Blumenbach–Kant scheme for seeking empirical laws within a teleological framework. This scheme can be seen as having made real a substantial range of new questions. Types of natural historical and physiological questions opened up include: questions concerning the geographical distribution and anatomical structures of the original organizations from which existing living forms have derived; questions concerning alterations in the direction of the formative drive in response to 'revolutions' of climate and habitat in the history of the earth; questions concerning the mechanical and chemical processes which affect the vital forces and which mediate their operations; questions concerning the ways in which anatomical structures relate to the external appearances of living beings and adapt them to their conditions of existence. On the other hand, a considerable body of

---

[117] See the papers in the special issue of *Revue d'histoire des sciences et leurs applications*, 23 (1970), devoted to Foucault's views on the epochal significance of Cuvier.

fundamental questions is explicitly invalidated, being declared to be in principle beyond the range of evidential considerations. Thus excluded are all questions concerning the relations between God and the natural world, along with all questions about the underlying reasons for the apparent harmony between mechanism and purposive formation in living beings, all questions about the inner nature and origin of the vital forces and their immanence in living matter and all questions about the way in which the original organizations themselves came into being.

Herder's treatment of living beings in his *Ideas for a Philosophy of the History of Mankind* clearly addresses questions about the nature of vital forces and the origins of purposive organization that are unreal from the standpoint of the Blumenbach–Kant scheme. (There is, however, little question of deliberate breaching of the Kantian bounds by Herder. Indeed, it is arguable that the way in which Kant sets those bounds in the *Critique of Judgement* is, in part, a response to Herder's enterprise.) Kielmeyer's *Rede* is, on my reading, an equivocal document, operating within a well-defined scene of inquiry at the level of explicit declaration but raising questions outside that scene at the levels of intimation and metaphor. In Goethe the breaching of the Kantian bounds is more decisive. With his aesthetic intuitions, whereby series of anatomical structures are seen as derivations from original plans, Goethe claims direct access to questions about the 'inner ground' of purposive organization in nature that are unreal from the Blumenbach–Kant standpoint. There is, however, ample room for disagreement about the extent of deliberation in Goethe's ventures beyond the bounds of Kantian sense. (My own view is that Goethe's apparent naïvety on such issues is a contrived and ironic stance; that he not only deliberately ventures into the forbidden territory, but quietly mocks Kant for setting such bounds on inquiry.)

Schelling's position is far more clear-cut. In his early works there is elaborated a rich and powerful methodology designed to engage with an entire range of natural historical questions that are illegitimate under the Blumenbach–Kant scheme. Here we find fully articulated and made real questions about the underlying ground of purposive development and differentiation in nature; questions about the origin and inner nature of the life-forces; questions about the ways in which the life-forces are materialized as functioning organs; questions about the genesis of the entire sequence of living beings; questions about the form and significance of the natural system. Moreover, Schelling leaves us in no doubt that his breaching of the barriers erected by the Blumenbach–Kant scheme is a deliberate one: for example, he remarks bluntly that those who assert that it is impossible to 'go beyond' the *Bildungstrieb* are best answered by doing so.[118]

In the writings of Oken and other exponents of transcendental natural history in the first half of the nineteenth century we see a series of attempts to answer the new questions that had been opened up by Goethe and Schelling—questions about the relations between form and function, about the structure of the natural system, about the origin of living beings, about the laws of their development and differentiation.

How are such changes in scenes of inquiry to be explained? The developments in natural history that we have retailed are strongly indicative of a central explanatory role for methodological change. However, before we can make headway on the topic of explanation we need to consider more carefully what it is for a question to be real for a community of inquirers. That is the subject of the next chapter.

[118] Schelling, *Sämmtliche Werke*, ii. 529.

3

Local Reality and Interpretation

What is it for a question to be locally real, that is, real or well posed for a community of inquirers? And how does the local reality of questions relate to their intelligibility? So far we have contented ourselves with vague and programmatic pronouncements on these issues. Thus, we have claimed that a question is real in a community of inquirers when they can see how, in principle, to 'get to grips' with it. Moreover, we have suggested that understanding of questions real in a community involves appreciation of the considerations that would be taken in that community to be relevant to their resolution. The time has come to be a little more precise.

To start with we may note that there are two salient ways in which a question may be unreal or invalid for us. First, a question may be unreal for us because there is no consideration that we would take to have the faintest bearing on it. Questions unreal for us on this score include: Why is there something rather than nothing? Does the absolute exist? Is the organic the image of the planet? (a question to which, as we have seen, Lorenz Oken addressed himself). Such questions may be said to be unreal for us by virtue of utter inscrutability. Secondly, a question may be unreal or invalid for us because it rests on a presupposition that we reject. Questions unreal for us on this score include: How does the Prime Mover move the heavenly spheres? Why is there nothing rather than something? Who discovered that the Thames is the longest river in Europe? Such questions may be said to be unreal for us by virtue of presupposition failure. Clearly our account of the reality of questions in a community of inquirers should exclude questions that are unreal for them on grounds of utter inscrutability or of presupposition failure.

The connection between the local reality of questions and their presuppositions is worrying, because the notion of presupposition is controversial on many scores. Much of this controversy concerns matters that need not detain us. However, there is one central issue that we are bound to confront. Consider the question 'Is the King of France bald?' The view standard among linguists is that if in fact there is no King of France the question has no direct answer. However, some semantic theorists deny this, claiming that if there is in fact no King of France the direct answer to our question is that the King of France is not bald—'Of course he isn't bald. He doesn't exist!' More generally, on the orthodox view, failure of presupposition deprives questions of direct answers. On the heterodox view, in most of the alleged examples of pre-supposition failure the questions do have direct answers, answers whose truth is, as William Lycan tastefully puts it, of 'forehead-smacking obviousness'.[1] The issue between the orthodox and heterodox views is an intractable one. The intuitions about particular cases that play so large a role in the dispute seem highly suspect: here, as on so many other issues in semantic theory, there is ample room for the thought that there may be no fact of the matter. It is, therefore, most desirable to have an account of local reality that is neutral on this issue.

We say that an answer to a question is *straight* when it is both direct and adequate, in the sense that it conveys all the information that is called for. Further, let us say that evidential consideration E is *relevant* to question $Q?$ in community C just in case E is taken in C to favour one over (the disjunction of) all the other assertions taken in C to be straight answers to $Q?$ Our more precise account of the local reality of questions—their validity in communities of inquirers—is as follows:

Question $Q?$ is real in community C just in case there is an evidential consideration E that is relevant to $Q?$ in C.

The account of local reality is readily extended from questions to assertions. Writing $A?$ for the question whether or not A, we have:

A is real in community C just in case $A?$ is real in C.

Our account of local reality appears to meet all the requirements set out above. It clearly precludes the reality in a community of

---

[1] The heterodox view is aggressively and wittily championed in S. Boer and W. G. Lycan, *The Myth of Semantic Presupposition*, Bloomington, Ind., 1973, and W. G. Lycan, *Logical Form in Natural Language*, Cambridge, Mass., 1986, ch. 4.

questions that are inscrutable for them or whose presuppositions
are rejected by them. Moreover, it achieves these effects whilst
remaining neutral on the issue of the proper semantic treatment of
presupposition failure. To see this let us consider first the case in
which members of *C* react to presupposition failure in the way
predicted by the orthodox treatment of presupposition, then the
case in which they react in the way predicted by the heterodox
treatment. In accordance with the orthodox treatment they would
deny that a question whose presupposition fails has a direct
answer: 'Is the King of France bald?—'That's unanswerable,
because there isn't one.' So *a fortiori* the question lacks a straight
answer for them. Hence, on our account, the question is unreal for
them. In accordance with the heterodox treatment, on the other
hand, they would opt for a negative direct answer: 'Is the King of
France bald?'—'Of course not, there isn't one.' However, that
does not imply that 'The King of France is not bald' constitutes for
them a straight answer; for straightness requires adequacy, that is,
provision of all that the question calls for. An adequate answer in
this case requires further information, namely, that there is no
such person as the King of France. So, again, the question lacks a
straight answer for them and is, in consequence, unreal for them.
Of course, in practice people react variously to presupposition
failure, sometimes as predicted by the orthodox treatment,
sometimes as predicted by the heterodox treatment. That is why
the issue appears so intractable. But our account is immune to
such variability. It requires only that questions whose presuppositions are denied be not credited with straight answers; and
this requirement is, it seems, universally satisfied.

SOME DIFFICULTIES

There is a series of issues on which our account stands in need of
further clarification and defence. The issues are finicky and the
following remarks are tentative.

Presupposition

It may be objected that to the extent that the notion of local reality
of questions is linked with the notion of presupposition it is
rendered incurably vague. What one person takes to be a
presupposition of a question, whose failure deprives the question

of a straight answer, may be taken by another to be a conversational or contextual implication, whose failure makes the question merely odd or potentially misleading. Thus one person innocent of having beaten his grandmother may well deny the possibility of giving a straight answer to the famous question 'Have you stopped beating your grandmother yet?' But another innocent on this score may hold that the straight answer to the question is 'No', and that the question merely insinuates but does not presuppose past grandmother-abuse.

It should, I think, be conceded that the notion of local reality of questions inherits from the notion of presupposition a host of borderline cases. It may, however, be noted that there are few borderline cases of the types of presupposition that will be of central concern to us, namely, existential presupposition (typified by the relation between assertions of the form 'X exists' and questions of the form 'Is X . . . ?') and explanatory presupposition (typified by the relation between assertions of the form 'X has an explanation' and questions of the form 'What is the explanation of X?').

In our account of the reality of a question in a community we have so far considered only the case in which a presupposition of the question is rejected in the community. What of the cases in which the presupposition is either unreal or of indeterminate status in the community? In typical instances it seems that the question inherits unreality from unreality in a presupposition and indeterminacy of status from indeterminacy in the status of a presupposition. But multiplicity of presuppositions and layering of presuppositions place many difficulties in the way of a general account.[2]

Relevance

In one respect the notion of relevance proposed is a stringent one. To be relevant to a question in a community a consideration must be taken by them to favour just one over the disjunction of all the other assertions that they take to be straight answers to the question. The need for such stringency is obvious. To admit as relevant any consideration that members of C would take to favour some straight answers to a question over others would

---

[2] The complexity of these issues is evident from the papers in C.-K. Oh and D. A. Dineen, eds., *Presupposition*, New York, 1979.

trivialize the account of local reality when applied to what, how and why questions. For the reality of such questions in a community would then be demonstrable simply by citing arbitrary assertions that they would rule out on grounds of absurdity, whilst conceding their status as straight answers. However, it might be objected that our account is too stringent on this score. Suppose that there are evidential considerations that members of a community C would acknowledge as good grounds for eliminating certain 'serious candidate' straight answers to a question $Q?$, but that there are no evidential considerations that they would acknowledge as giving some single direct answer the edge over all the others. Our account does not admit the reality of such a question in community C even though for them the question, being in principle partially determinable by them, is one that has for them 'something in it'. It may seem that we should allow that R is relevant to $Q?$ in C when R would be acknowledged by members of C as favouring some over others of the straight answers that they would take to be serious contenders. Quite apart from the difficulty of explication of the notion of a serious contender, this line of thought is resistible. Let us say that $Q?$ contains $Q'?$ when all straight answers to $Q'?$ are straight answers to $Q?$ We may then note that whilst on our account a question that is in principle only partially determinable in a community is not real in that community, the question nevertheless contains a question real in that community—on our account there is, for them, quite literally 'something in' such a question.

In other respects, however, our notion of relevance is far from stringent. For an evidential consideration to be relevant to a question for a community it is not required that it would be recognized by them as *directly* relevant to the question it validates: relevance may be mediated by extended inference, and may rest on many premisses. Nor is it required that the evidential consideration be one that they would at once recognize as relevant: allowance is made for reflection and consultation.

Communal acknowledgement

What connection is there between what is, or would be, communally acknowledged and what is, or would be, acknowledged by individual members of a community C? Two sorts of difficulty stand in the way of a 'democratic' account which identifies acknowledgement in *C* with acknowledgement by a sufficient majority of members of *C*. Difficulties are posed by deference to experts and other forms of division and delegation of cognitive labour. More intractable difficulties are posed by the gulfs that may arise between what most members of a community privately believe and what claims they would in practice be prepared to honour and defend. Consider, to take an extreme instance, a research institute populated by physicists each privately convinced of the fictionalist construal of the fundamental laws of physics. Each member of the community believes '$e = mc^2$' to be a whopping fib. But they are prepared, as a community, to stand by Einstein's famous formula. Moreover, in such an instance, it would typically be common knowledge in the community that this was their policy. It is my hunch that an account of communal acknowledgement should be in terms of agreement (often tacit) in the community about whose claims on what issues they would be prepared to honour and defend rather than in terms of majority belief within the community.[3]

Evidential considerations

For *E* to count as an evidential consideration for *C* we require that *E* be potentially evident under appropriate circumstances to members of *C* (or, at least, to those members of *C* regarded in *C* as competent to appreciate, register, witness or assimilate evidence of the relevant kind). We propose no further constraints on what may constitute evidential considerations for a community. They do not have to be considerations that we regard as reliably indicative of the truth. Nor do they have to be considerations that are taken in the relevant community to be reliably indicative of the truth— for that community may be one in which in certain domains of inquiry truth is not the primary aim. They do not have to be considerations that we regard as potentially evident. They do not have to be empirical considerations: they may, for example, be theological or aesthetic considerations. They may be self-evident

---

[3] Cf. Erving Goffman's suggestion concerning the way in which a 'veneer of consensus' is maintained in a group: 'Together the participants contribute to a single over-all definition of the situation which involves not so much a real agreement as to what exists but rather a real agreement as to whose claims concerning what issues will be temporarily honored': *The Presentation of Self in Everyday Life* [1959] London, 1967, 21. See also the account of collective belief in M. Gilbert, 'Modelling collective belief', *Synthese*, 73 (1987), 185–204.

considerations. (Note that if *A* is self-evident for *C*, it itself renders *A?* valid in *C*.) Crucially, it is not required of evidential considerations in *C* that they either be, or be held in *C* to be, actually accessible to members of *C*. Suppose that time travel is impossible and that there is not now extant information relevant to the resolution of questions about the precise coloration of the various types of dinosaur. Even on these suppositions such questions remain real for us, because we hold that relevant evidence would be available to normally sighted, zoologically competent, binocular-wielding members of our community, were they *per impossibile* suitably placed in the Mesozoic jungles.

LOCAL REALITY AND INTELLIGIBILITY

How does the reality of questions and assertions from a particular cognitive standpoint relate to their intelligibility from that standpoint and from other standpoints?

Reality and intelligibility are distinct notions. This is perhaps most evident in the case of questions and assertions that are unreal for us because we hold their presuppositions to be false. The question 'Who discovered that the Thames is the longest river in Europe?' is unreal for us who hold (or at least would defer to acknowledged experts who hold) that the Thames is not the longest river in Europe. But this does not render the question in any way unintelligible to us. Though reality and intelligibility are distinct, our account of local reality fits in naturally with an account of local intelligibility which relates them intimately.

Let us call the totality of the beliefs and commitments of a community their 'cognitive frame'. The cognitive frame of a community will in general include beliefs to the effect that certain evidential considerations are relevant to certain questions. It will include also the beliefs and methodological commitments that are held in the community to explain or justify those relevances.

Let us consider first questions that are real for us. (Since, on our account of local reality, the local reality of an assertion is determined by the local reality of the corresponding question, we may without loss of generality confine our attention to questions.) Here my suggestion is that an adequate understanding of such questions consists in an understanding of the ways in which they are made real or valid in our cognitive frame. Such understanding involves both appreciation of the considerations taken in our community to be relevant to their resolution and a grasp of the ways in which our communal beliefs and methods render those considerations relevant for us.

When we turn to questions that are unreal for us, a wide range of types of understanding has to be considered. First there will be cases in which understanding is achieved by seeing how the question would be validated by evidential considerations in a cognitive frame derived from our own by extension and modification. Thus, to take the simplest of instances, we understand the question 'Who discovered that the Thames is the longest river in Europe?' by seeing how it would be validated in a cognitive frame that differed from our own in including the belief that the Thames is the longest river in Europe. Then there will be cases in which to achieve understanding the interpreter must try to see how a question is validated in a cognitive frame that is substantially distinct from his own. Such understanding will be readily achieved when the alternative cognitive frame is one with which he is already familiar. Thus it is, for example, that the agnostics and atheists among us Europeans generally have at least a measure of understanding of Christian dogma; and thus it is that a competent historian of medieval astronomy can understand questions about, say, the mode of obedience to the Prime Mover of the motors of celestial orbs. Even when the relevant alternative cognitive frame is initially unfamiliar to the interpreter, there will be instances in which understanding is readily obtained. For example, the relevant cognitive frame may be a contrived one into which the reader is initiated by a fictional narrative. The relevant cognitive frame may be one with which the interpreter has a measure of tacit familiarity because it is the cognitive frame of classic works constitutive of his own cultural tradition or because it is ancestral to the cognitive frame of some present-day discipline. Or the relevant cognitive frame may be one to which the interpreter can gain access via interpretations already essayed by anthropologists or historians. Finally, there are questions whose understanding requires the interpreter to master cognitive frames to which there is no such introduction or ready initiation: the cognitive frames of distant cultures untrodden by anthropologists, of past disciplines untouched by historians, of esoteric or avant-garde writing unspoiled by critics.

By way of illustration let us reflect again on some of Lorenz Oken's more extraordinary pronouncements.

The nose is the thorax repeated in the head.

The animal is a detached blossom moving freely in the air.

The fish is a mussel from between whose shells a monstrous abdomen has grown.

The reader of the last chapter will, I hope, have gained a measure of insight into such mysterious identifications. A partial understanding is consequent on a grasp of the way in which Oken constructs the elaborate system of classification and ranking of plants and animals of which these particular correspondences form a fragment; for thus we get a hold on some of the evidential considerations deemed relevant by Oken to these assertions. To obtain such partial understanding it suffices to read Oken's textbook. However, much of the rationale for Oken's system of classification is not made fully explicit in his book. Further insight is gained when we consider Oken's work in the context of the views of Schelling and his circle on the ways in which the natural philosopher may 're-create' nature by retracing the steps by which minerals, plants and animals have been produced through a dialectical play of forces. In this way we obtain a fuller understanding as we come to see how and why Oken brings certain kinds of evidence to bear on questions about correspondence of anatomical structure. That is, we come to see how the questions Oken raises and the answers he offers are realized within the cognitive frame of *Naturphilosophie*.

In achieving such understanding we do not render these remarkable assertions any the more real or well posed for us. On the contrary, to the extent that we may at the outset have mistakenly attempted to grasp them in terms of anatomical correspondences of kinds recognized by present-day anatomists—functional analogy, homologies of structure, etc.—we may well find that our understanding renders these assertions less real or well posed for us than at first sight they appeared. We understand these assertions not by making them real from our standpoint, but by coming to see how and why they were real from Oken's standpoint.

STRENGTHS OF OUR ACCOUNT OF LOCAL REALITY

The four following chapters are devoted to explorations of the historiographical implications of our account of the local reality of questions and assertions. It is hoped that the reader will find in these implications considerable support for the account itself. However, much of the support for our account arises not from these remote implications but rather from its intrinsic plausibility and from the plausibility of the claims about the understanding of questions and assertions to which it is tied. Let us consider these more immediate attractions.

1. The notions of local reality and intelligibility to which we have appealed are well grounded in ordinary usage. Thus, on the one hand, we habitually make a distinction between questions and assertions that are unreal, invalid or ill posed and those that are merely silly, dull, ill mannered, recondite or irrelevant to our purposes. On the other hand, we distinguish between questions and assertions that are merely ill posed, invalid or unreal and expressions that are genuinely nonsensical.

2. Our account ties the reality of questions and assertions for us to our belief in their amenability in principle to evidential considerations. It ties the intelligibility of questions and assertions for us to our capacity to gain access to cognitive standpoints from which they are valid. The way in which we have built on these assumptions is perhaps contentious. But the assumptions themselves have, I believe, great intrinsic plausibility. They may well be regarded as the grains of truth in verificationism.

3. It has become a truism amongst anthropologists and historians that a 'judgemental' approach, one excessively concerned to ascribe truth and falsity to alien beliefs, is rarely conducive to understanding. However, failure to distinguish reality and intelligibility may make ability to adjudicate alien beliefs appear to be a condition for understanding them. For it may be imagined that understanding requires attribution to them of determinate contents susceptible of truth or falsity. In cases where it is implausible to suppose that the alien belief system embodies knowledge denied to us, inability to adjudicate will then be seen as indicative of a lack of understanding. Of course, this is not how matters stand in the business of interpretation. When belief systems radically divergent from our own are at issue, a

readiness to adjudicate the alien beliefs is very often symptomatic not of adequate understanding but rather of cultural insensitivity and misunderstanding. It is a major virtue of our account that it so explicates reality and intelligibility as to show how understanding of alien beliefs may be accompanied by, and in part constituted by, the realization that many of those beliefs are from our standpoint invalid or unreal.

4. Our account has distinguished precedents. Kant's notion of the objective validity (*objective Gültigkeit*) of a judgement shows affinities with our notion of the reality of an assertion. In particular, his famous insistence that relation to possible empirical intuitions is a condition of objective validity parallels our requirement of answerability in principle to evidential considerations; and his 'antinomies of reason' can be read as attempts to demonstrate the unreality of certain questions that we cannot avoid but which involve the extension of concepts beyond the bounds of empirical intuition—questions concerning the extent and duration of the world and the compatibility of moral freedom with mechanical causation, for example. Moreover, in allowing that such questions are 'thinkable' despite their lack of objective validity, Kant implicitly makes a distinction analogous to our distinction between reality and intelligibility.[4]

[4] P. F. Strawson, *The Bounds of Sense*, London, 1966, 38–42, and others have charged Kant with inconsistency on this score. Kant does indeed appear inconsistent if, as does Strawson (p. 18), one reads his denial of objective validity to judgements 'beyond the bounds of sense' as a positivistic denial of intelligibility to issues irresoluble by appeal to empirical considerations (a reading which is encouraged by certain passages in which Kant speaks of judgements involving application of concepts beyond the bounds of sense as devoid of content). G. Buchdahl, *Metaphysics and the Philosophy of Science*, Oxford, 1969, 8. 5, makes a solid case for crediting Kant with two notions of intelligibility: intelligibility within the phenomenal framework (objective validity) and intelligibility within the noumenal framework that is called into play when practical and theoretical reason operate beyond the bounds of sense. However, it remains problematic how according to Kant we are supposed to grasp the content of objectively invalid judgements. In the *Critique of Judgement* Kant intimates that certain objectively invalid questions (concerning the grounds of teleology and mechanism in nature) might be determinable by an 'archetypal' non-discursive intellect capable of a synthetic apprehension of nature as a whole. It is tempting, therefore, to credit Kant with the view that we may grasp the content of certain objectively invalid questions by seeing how they might be resolved by such a godlike mind. Alas, though this would further confirm the status of Kant's views as ancestral to our account of reality and intelligibility, it runs into trouble. For whilst Kant has much to say about the differences between human intellects and a hypothetical archetypal intellect, he repeatedly denies our capacity to form any positive conception of the mode of operation of such an intellect.

Closer adumbrations may be detected with less interpretive licence in later writers in the Kantian tradition who invoke relativized notions of validity. In connection with the transformation of natural history around 1800, we have had occasion to mention Michel Foucault's postulation of disjunctions in the ranges of problems real from the standpoints of successive 'epistemes': disjunctions so great as to mark the extinction and creation of entire disciplines. Ludwik Fleck is another who invokes relativized notions of the reality of questions. His 'thought-styles' are constituted by the assumptions and norms, both tacit and implicit, that together determine the ranges of questions on the agendas of communities of inquirers.[5] Fleck's emphasis on the role of local, tacit and habitual procedures as determinants of the contents of disciplines is of outstanding interest in the context of the present work. A similar emphasis on local and habitual competences as determinants of the ranges of questions that are salient in a community is found in the writings of Alfred Schutz, Harold Garfinkel and other sociologists writing in the phenomeno-logical tradition.[6] I shall suggest in the next chapter that these kinds of sociological approach to the study of tacit and habitual competences may provide valuable resources for the investigation of scenes of inquiry in the sciences.

It is, however, in a different line of development within the tradition of phenomenology that there are to be found the most significant parallels with our account of the connections between local reality and intelligibility of questions. A central project in the writings of Husserl and Heidegger is the uncovering of the 'structures' or 'pre-understandings' which constitute the horizons within which it is possible for us to have articulate experience and to raise determinate questions about the world. In Husserl these structures are universal. They are supposed to be revealed by an intuition consequent on an elaborate process of bracketing of our beliefs about the world and its occupants and constituents. In Heidegger's *Being and Time* horizons are more local and specific, having to do with ordinary and everyday modes of involvement, concern, interaction and expectation. For him the uncovering of

---

[5] L. Fleck, *Genesis and Development of a Scientific Fact* [1935], trans. F. Bradley and T. J. Trenn, Chicago, Ill., 1979.

[6] See e.g. A. Schutz and T. Luckmann, *The Structures of the Life-World*, trans. R. M. Zaner and H. T. Engelhardt, Jr., London, 1974; H. Garfinkel, *Studies in Ethnomethodology*, Englewood Cliffs, NJ, 1967.

these horizons requires not an act of intuition, but a process of interpretation.[7] In the writings of Hans-Georg Gadamer horizons of understanding, recovery of questions and interpretation of works are connected in ways which relate yet more closely to our account of local reality and intelligibility. Gadamer's theory of interpretation is, in my view, powerful and fruitful. It is with a view to appropriating a substantial part of his theory that I venture on an exploration of the resemblances and differences between his theory of interpretation and my own account of the understanding of questions.

GADAMER: INTERPRETATION OF CLASSIC WORKS

Gadamer's *Truth and Method* offers a general theory of interpretation that is centred on the interactions between the horizon of understanding of the interpreter and that of the subject of interpretation.[8] This theory, which is brilliantly elaborated by Gadamer in the context of an account of the appreciation and appropriation of classic works of art and literature, shows marked affinities with our account of local reality and intelligibility.

Two components of Gadamer's account are, for our purposes, crucial. First, there is the slightly sinister-sounding thesis of the 'enabling power of prejudice'. This is the claim that the historically conditioned expectations, moral and aesthetic norms and interpretive competences that make up the interpreter's 'horizon of understanding' are to be considered not as obstacles to the appreciation of past works, but as conditions of the possibility of their interpretation. Secondly, there is Gadamer's famous thesis of 'fusion of horizons'. According to this doctrine understanding of past works does not involve merely a scholarly reconstruction of the horizon of understanding of their originally intended audiences, but rather a response to and appropriation of the past work in which the interpreter's own horizon of understanding may be changed.

Gadamer is insistent in his denial that understanding of past works is to be attained through methodical application of rules of interpretation. However, he has much to say about the attitudes

[7] I owe most of what little understanding I have of Heidegger's *Being and Time* to Jürgen Habermas's essay 'The undermining of Western rationalism: Heidegger', in his *The Philosophical Discourse of Modernity*, trans. F. Lawrence, Oxford, 1987.
[8] 2nd ed., trans., London, 1975.

and dispositions that are conducive to understanding through the fusion of horizons. Following Collingwood[9] he insists that we recognize that 'we can understand a text only when we have understood the question to which it is an answer' and that we beware of uncritical and doctrinaire assimilations of past works, allowing ourselves rather to listen and respond to the questions that they address to us.[10]

To relate our account of local reality and intelligibility to Gadamer's theory of interpretation it is useful to introduce some terminology. The 'scene of inquiry' of an interpreter is the range of questions real for him. In general the range of questions immediately intelligible to an interpreter will extend far outside his scene of inquiry. As noted above, there will be questions whose understanding requires of the interpreter only an appreciation of the minor modifications of his cognitive frame that are needed to validate them; and there are the further questions that are real from the standpoint of cognitive frames, whether fictional or alien, with which the interpreter is already conversant. Let us call the entire range of questions that are thus readily comprehensible to the interpreter his 'scene of interpretation'. Within the scene of interpretation we may distinguish the interpreter's 'scene of response', the range of questions that engage some aspect—cognitive, moral, aesthetic, etc.—of his attention and concern. The relation of the scene of response to the scene of inquiry may vary widely. The scene of response of a workaholic scientist might be almost entirely enclosed in his scene of inquiry. At the other extreme, the scene of response of a learned, imaginative and sensitive leisured person might lie very largely outside his scene of inquiry. And for a polymathic historian and cultural anthropologist, a Vico or a Steiner, the scene of response might almost fill the scene of interpretation. For ordinary mortals, however, the sadly confined compass of the scene of response contains a smattering of questions from inside and a smattering from outside the scene of inquiry.

(This taxonomy of scenes remains in an obvious respect oversimplified. A person's interpretive activities—listening, reading, viewing, etc.—cannot be regarded as components of a single vast interpretive project. A typical person is rather to be

---

[9] Cf. R. G. Collingwood, *An Autobiography*, Oxford, 1939, chs. 5 and 7.
[10] Ibid. 310 ff, 333 ff.

seen as the locus of many interpretive projects variously corresponding to his personal interests, his profession or discipline and
the other social roles he performs. A full theory of interpretation
would have to take cognizance of this multiplicity in the interpreting
subject. In subsequent chapters we shall evade the problem by
concentrating on the inquisitive and interpretive projects of
persons *qua* practitioners of particular disciplines. For the present,
however, it may be noted that the simplification is not inappropriate given the interpreters implicitly postulated in Gadamer's
text: leisured, self-absorbed, engaged in a single master project,
that of self-education and cultivation (*Bildung*).[11]

Our account comports well with Gadamer's general views on the
interpretive dispositions conducive to understanding. Like
Gadamer we assign priority to the apprehension of questions in
the business of interpretation. Further, we are bound to endorse
his strictures against naïve and doctrinaire assimilations and his
advocacy of a preparedness to seek out and listen to the questions
that underlie past works. For on our account attainment of
understanding of works that derive from cognitive standpoints
very different from our own requires us to see how the questions
addressed in those works are realized or validated within the alien
cognitive frame. Such grasp will obviously be frustrated by naïve
appropriations which uncritically assimilate past categories,
interests, conventions and genres to those of our own period and
disciplines. Equally, as emphasized above, our account makes it
clear why such grasp is wont to be frustrated by a judgemental
approach, over-concerned to partition alien beliefs into the true
and the false and alien norms into the right and the wrong, the
rational and the irrational.

In considering Gadamer's doctrine of the fusion of horizons it is
convenient to rank texts according to the extent of the interpretive
challenge that they pose. Type 1 documents are those that deal
with questions that are real from the interpreter's standpoint, that
is, questions that appear within his scene of inquiry. Type 2
documents are those that deal with questions that are real from the
standpoint of cognitive frames with which the interpreter is
familiar, that is, questions in his scene of interpretation. Finally

[11] On German devotion to this project see W. H. Bruford, *The German
Tradition of Self-Cultivation: 'Bildung' from Humboldt to Thomas Mann*,
Cambridge, 1975.

there will be the really challenging documents, those that raise questions that are outside the scene of interpretation. Within this class we may make a further rough-and-ready distinction. To type 3 we assign documents which derive from cognitive and normative standpoints with which the interpreter has a measure of tacit familiarity by virtue of his own historical and cultural situation. To type 4 we relegate the truly recalcitrant documents, those which derive from entirely alien cognitive and normative standpoints.

Documents of types 1 and 2 scarcely concern us. Understanding of type 1 documents may, indeed, alter the interpreter's scene of inquiry by changing his beliefs about the presuppositions of questions; and a more radical change of scene of inquiry may well, on occasion, ensue from understanding of type 2 documents, for here the possibility arises that the interpreter may be converted to an alternative system of beliefs and norms. But such changes are by-products, rather than integral components, of the process of understanding itself.

Gadamer's central concern is with the classic works that are formative of cultural traditions. The interpreter will initially encounter classics of his own cultural tradition as documents of type 3, works of which he has a historically formed tacit 'pre-understanding'.[12] In coming to understand such a work the reader articulates and elaborates this pre-understanding. This articulation and elaboration will enlarge the interpreter's scene of interpretation and generally his scene of response also. Gadamer treats such articulation as the achievement of a form of self-knowledge whereby the reader comes to understand himself as a historically and culturally conditioned being. Such attainment of self-knowledge through the reading of classic works is central to the process of *Bildung*, self-cultivation, for Gadamer the primary motive for serious reading.

Gadamer's compelling account of the educative powers of canonical works fits well with our account of local reality and intelligibility. Less satisfactory, from our point of view, is his treatment of documents of type 4—works with whose cognitive

[12] However, Gadamer may appear, at least to victims of the English educational system, to overestimate the capacity of the classic to reveal itself to us without the artificial aids of historical scholarship. For an account of the fortunes of classics that has much in common with Gadamer's but is more realistic about the educational attainments of readers, see F. Kermode, *The Classic*, London, 1975.

and normative frames we have not even a tacit familiarity, because
they belong to cultural traditions other than our own, or because
they lack a continuous history of interpretation and appreciation
within our own cultural tradition. Gadamer is often dismissive of
the 'merely historical understanding' that is the best that can be
attained in such cases.[13] There is nothing in our account to
encourage such disdain for the historian's art. On our account
even such 'merely historical' understanding involves a fusion of
horizons in which the interpretive capacity of the scholar is
expanded as he comes to grips with the cognitive frame which
realized or validated the contents of the alien works.

Now let us consider Gadamer's claims concerning the enabling
power of prejudice and the historical relativity of interpretive
understanding.

A part of what is entailed by these claims, whilst doubtless
controversial in 1960 when *Truth and Method* appeared, has lost
its polemical edge. In insisting on the role of prejudice in
interpretation Gadamer is much concerned to distance himself
from recipes for historical interpretation modelled on the
supposedly neutral and objective methods of the sciences. He is
concerned also to displace Romantic theories of interpretation
with their ideal of an empathetic re-enactment by the interpreter
of the creative processes of the author. Gadamer is surely right in
diagnosing as the fallacy common to scientistic and Romantic
models of interpretation the assumption that it is both possible and
desirable for the interpreter to dissociate himself from his own
historically conditioned standpoint. A further aspect of Gadamer's
doctrine of historicity of the understanding has already been
endorsed, namely, that which concerns the role of cultural
tradition in creating a measure of tacit familiarity with classic
works. To this we may add that since understanding of past
documents, especially those of type 4, often depends on the
preservation of collateral and circumstantial documents and
artefacts, there is a more obvious and literal sense in which
cultural tradition facilitates (and its lack may frustrate) interpretation.

It is clear from such passages as the following, however, that
Gadamer relativizes to historical standpoint not only the access-

---

[13] *Truth and Method*, 267 ff.

ibility of texts, but also the constitution of the understanding of past texts itself.

But there is no possible consciousness—we have repeatedly emphasised this, and it is the basis of the historicity of understanding—there is no possible consciousness, however infinite, in which the 'object' that is handed down would appear in the light of eternity. Every assimilation of tradition is historically different: which does not mean that every one represents only an imperfect understanding of it. Rather, every one is the experience of a 'view' of the object itself.[14]

Our account of local reality and intelligibility does indeed predict a historical and cultural relativity of the constitution of understanding of texts, though it is a relativity less radical than that generally attributed to Gadamer.

On our account understanding of a question is attained when the interpreter comes to see why it is real in the community in which it is posed. In general, therefore, there will be many different modes of adequate understanding of a given question, corresponding to the variety of evidential considerations taken as relevant to it in the community in which it is posed. A more refined account would require specification of criteria for the depth and extent of these various modes of understanding. For our purposes it suffices to note certain constraints on such an account. First, on pain of making adequate understanding generally impossible, adequate understanding of a question cannot be taken to require a grasp of the totality of evidential considerations that would be acknowledged by members of the community in which it is posed as relevant to its resolution; for the roster of such considerations will in general be open-ended. Secondly, though it is obvious that some evidential considerations weigh more heavily than others in the constitution of adequate or full understanding, we can rarely if ever hope to identify a unique set of privileged considerations whose grasp is constitutive of adequate understanding. Adequate understanding of a given question may be constituted in a variety of ways.

Given such a plurality of modes of adequate understanding, it is clear that in practice the type of understanding of questions that is achieved will depend heavily on the interpreter's cognitive frame, that is, on the entire body of his beliefs and methodological

---

[14] Ibid. 430.

commitments. For this will determine the salience and accessibility to him of the various evidential considerations that validate those questions. Here then is one sense in which interpretive understanding is conditioned by standpoint.

A further form of conditioning of understanding of questions is perhaps more in the spirit of Gadamer's dicta. Let us call an understanding of a question an 'appropriation' in case it involves recognition of evidential considerations whose relevance to that question would not be acknowledged by members of the community in which it originated. 'Weak appropriations' or 'elaborations' are those in which these further considerations are in no way at odds with the evidential considerations originally acknowledged. 'Strong appropriations' or 'misprisions', on the other hand, import criteria which conflict with some at least of the original criteria.

It is hard indeed to see how elaboration and misprision in the understanding of alien texts could be systematically avoided; for that would apparently require the interpreter to reconstruct the totality of evidential relevances constitutive of the various original modes of understanding of questions, to articulate the totality of relevances constitutive of his own initial understanding, then to check the latter against the former.

There are certain very general features of the task of interpretation that aid and abet elaboration and misprision. The quest for consistency is a basic component of almost all interpretive activities. The consistency at issue may be that of a literal history or narrative, it may be that of fictional perspectives (the narrator's, those of the protagonists, that of the implied reader) or it may be that of a theory or system.[15] A cruel testimony to our need to find consistency is retailed by Harold Garfinkel. Students seeking advice on personal problems were conned by him and his co-workers into trusting the Yes–No answers to their questions given by a 'counsellor' behind a screen—answers in fact derived from a random Yes–No answering machine. They were then asked to evaluate the advice given. Most of them had managed to extract consistent, even helpful advice.[16] A kindlier instance is retailed by Stanley Fish. On his blackboard he found written by an earlier

---

[15] On consistency building see e.g. U. Eco, *The Open Work* [1962], trans. A. Cancogni, Harvard, 1989; W. Iser, *The Act of Reading* [1976], trans., Baltimore, Md., 1978, ch. 5.   [16] *Studies in Ethnomethodology*, ch. 3.

lecturer 'Jacob-Rosenbaum Levin Thorne Hayes Ohman (?)'—a list of linguists. On being told by him that it was a religious poem his students of literature extorted from it a coherent symbolism and typology.[17]

The quest for consistency entails elaboration and misprision at many levels. Elaboration is generally indispensable if a coherent overall picture is to be built up from often ambivalent and indeterminate textual cues. Misprision is likewise virtually inevitable if the interpreter is to fend off the various anomalous and dissident features that threaten the synthesis of a coherent interpretation. The consistency at issue in interpretation is rarely a simple matter of logical consistency between explicit assertions. Rather the quest is for a reading that will produce coherence in the context set by background assumptions and presuppositions. When the background assumptions and presuppositions that informed the original modes of understanding of a work are unfamiliar and inaccessible to the interpreter, yet further misprision is likely to occur.

A second major source of misprision in the interpretive process is the quest for 'relevance'. The relevance sought may be straightforwardly a matter of contemporary interest of questions and assertions. It may also have to do with the relevance to the interpreter's own personal and cultural predicament of the moral and social norms that form the 'repertoire' of the text. As Gadamer argues cogently and at great length, these aspects of interpretation are not to be construed simply as 'applications' to intellectual, social or moral issues that follow the act of interpretation, but as integral parts of the process whereby understanding is achieved.[18]

These sources of misprision will be at a premium for certain kinds of text. Misprision through the quest for relevance is likely to be operative in all interpretation of documents that lie within the interpreter's scene of response. In particular, it is virtually inevitable in the reading of canonical works of our own cultural tradition. For the status of such works as classics creates large expectations of relevance; and their continuous histories of interpretation and assimilation give rise to tacit expectations that are in part the product of past misprisions. Misprision through the

---

[17] *Is There a Text in This Class? The Authority of Interpretive Communities*, Cambridge, Mass., 1980, ch. 14.   [18] *Truth and Method*, 277 ff.

quest for consistency is especially likely to arise in the reading of works whose genres create expectations of order, harmony and coherence. Such are 'realistic' narratives, whether fictional or scientific; and such too are works that purport to set out a method, theory or system. The lure towards misprision will be especially irresistible in the case of works that are at once classic in status and systematically presented or realistically narrated: Descartes's *Discourse on Method*; Bacon's *Novum Organum*; Newton's *Principia*; Darwin's *Origin of Species*.

We have already noted how Gadamer is at pains to emphasize the 'truth' of historically conditioned creative appropriations of classic works, as opposed to that 'merely historical' understanding which seeks to reconstruct an original meaning. Without requiring us to go along with his dismissal of historical understanding, our account fits well both with his claims for the creative and morally formative aspects of the interpretive understanding of classic works and with his claims for the historically and culturally conditioned nature of such understanding.

It is a moot point whether Gadamer's claims for the relativity of interpretation go beyond what we have endorsed. On occasion he appears to suggest that historians' attempts to reconstruct original modes of understanding of texts are doomed, so that there is no firm standpoint from which misprisions can be criticized. However, the implication elsewhere is merely that the quest for original understanding is the province of dull historical scholarship and that such understanding can have only a limited bearing on civilized interpretation, appreciation and performance of classic works.

It is, I believe, a substantial virtue in our account of local reality and understanding that it allows us to appropriate much of Gadamer's brilliant treatment of the historicity of interpretive understanding and of the culturally formative powers of classic works, and that it does so without commitment to the cultural élitism and relativism often attributed to him and without endorsement of his Olympian dismissal of 'merely historical' understanding of past works.

4

Explaining Scenes

INTRODUCTION

A shift from doctrines to questions as the primary focus of concern can, I suggest, yield a historiography capable of integrating the study of the social and institutional practices of the sciences with the description and explication of their contents. Moreover, it can do justice at once to the roles in the development of the sciences of social, moral and rhetorical conventions and to the roles of individual strategy, deliberation and criticism. In this chapter and the next two I shall be concerned with what I take to be the central task of such a historiography: the explanation of changes in scenes of inquiry, the ranges of questions real for communities of inquirers.

Reality of questions in a community has been explicated in terms of communal dispositions to acknowledge the relevance of evidential considerations to those questions. In our discussions of the sources of change in scenes of inquiry it proves convenient to make a rough-and-ready distinction between immediate and remote factors. Immediate factors are the changes in cognitive frame which directly affect communal views on the answerability of questions. Remote factors affecting scenes of inquiry are, so I shall argue, a mixed bag. They include, to mention but a handful of those that will be discussed in the following chapters: changes in educational curricula; changes in the social roles of practitioners of the sciences; changes in the organization, housing and equipment of the institutions of the sciences; changes in technologies of representation and communication of scientific data and claims; criticism and testing of their methods and practices by practitioners of the sciences in response to anomaly and challenge. Our concern in this chapter is with immediate factors.

Change in presuppositions has already been signalled in the last chapter as an immediate factor productive of changes in scenes of inquiry. When a presupposition of a question is rejected in a community, that question becomes unreal in the community, because for them it is no longer possessed of a straight answer. Conversely, when new beliefs are incorporated into the cognitive frame of a community of inquirers, new questions which pre-suppose those beliefs may become real in that community.

Further immediate factors are constituted by changes in cognitive frame that affect inquirers' perceptions of relevance of evidential considerations to questions. The ways in which change in cognitive frame may affect perceptions of relevance are many and various.

Perceptions of relevance may be conditioned by beliefs which entail general restrictions on the kinds of evidence that can be brought to bear on questions. Consider, for example, the medieval natural philosophical claim that the heavenly bodies are entirely different in kind from terrestrial bodies, being immaterial and devoid of terrestrial qualities. This doctrine precludes many applications of reasons derived from terrestrial physics to the resolution of questions about the heavens. Or consider the ways in which current general physical theory places constraints on the propagation of information in the universe and hence on the spatio-temporal provenances of the data that could possibly constitute evidence for the state of affairs at a given location. There are countless more local ways in which beliefs may mediate perceptions of relevance. They may do so explicitly by serving as premisses where the perception rests on an explicit inference. For example, they may be premisses of an analogical argument which licenses transposition of evidence from one domain to another. They may do so also in a variety of tacit ways. For example, they may condition perceptions of similarity between situations, and hence transpositions of evidence from one situation to another, even when no explicit analogical inference is involved.

The major determinant of perception of relevance is, however, communal methodology: agreed means of obtaining evidence; accepted strategies for the marshalling and deployment of evidence; conventions adhered to in the criticism of claims and the conduct of controversy; shared assumptions about the division of labour and distribution of authority in inquiry; etc. There is an obvious sense in which methodological commitment is the primary immediate factor governing scenes of inquiry. For it is the primary immediate determinant of the reality of the questions that are ultimate for a community, that is, the questions whose reality for them is not itself dependent upon the reality for them of other questions. That is why it is methodological commitments rather than presuppositions that will be our main concern in this work.

In the rest of this chapter I shall consider first presuppositions then methodological commitments as factors in the explanation of scenes of inquiry. In discussing these matters I shall pay particular attention to problems of access to local beliefs, commitments and practices faced by the historian out to explain the formation, maintenance and dissolution of scenes of inquiry.

PRESUPPOSITIONS

Existential presuppositions

These are the most obvious of all determinants of scenes of inquiry. Settlement of routine existential questions gives rise to recurrent minor shifts of scene throughout the active life of a discipline. At the other extreme changes of existential presuppositions may entail massive displacements and transformations of scene that annihilate old disciplines or initiate new ones. Consider, for example, the great range of questions closed down in the early seventeenth century by the dissolution of consensus amongst astronomers on the existence of celestial orbs and the extensive field of questions opened up in the same period by the growth of a consensus on the occurrence of mutable bodies in the superlunary realm. Or consider, to take an example from the last chapter, the range of new questions opened up in German natural history and physiology at the end of the eighteenth century by the widespread acceptance of the existence of a 'formative drive' and other autonomous vital forces.

Though changes in existential commitment rank top on the score of historical researchability, they are by no means as readily excavated from the primary sources as might be supposed from standard chronicles of scientific achievement. As much recent social history of science has been at pains to show, prolonged and often complex processes of adjustment and qualification of initial claims, debate over the authenticity of findings, negotiation over assignment of credit, etc., are generally involved in the achievement of consensus even when the issues are ones deemed by all parties to be amenable to observation and experiment. Frequently a crucial role in the formation of consensus on existential questions is played by the dissemination and contestation of claims and attributions of priority concerning the discovery of the entities or phenomena at issue.[1] (Goethe's alleged discoveries of the inter-maxillary bone and of the primordial plant, mentioned in Chapter 2, well illustrate this. Far from resting on single accounts published at the times of the alleged discoveries, his partially successful attempts to claim priority involved successive elaborations of retrospective discovery stories over a period of almost forty years.)[2] To the extent that traditional historiography of the sciences relies on the discovery stories of past practitioners it tends to conceal the protraction and complexity as well as the strategic and social aspects of the activities that lead to consensus on existential questions. Further, uncritical use of the discovery stories of victorious practitioners often leads to a glossing over of dissent on such questions within and between disciplines.

Explanatory presuppositions

Questions of the form 'What is the explanation of X?' carry the presupposition that X has an explanation. In many, if not all, cognitive frames there will be a variety of values of X for which a demand for an explanation is deemed illegitimate, inappropriate or otiose. Let us call assertions that have this privileged status 'explanatorily basic'. One major class of explanatorily basic assertions consists of those whose cognitive frame rules out their explanation. Thus, quantum mechanics explicitly rules out explanations of assertions of the form 'Radium specimen a emitted a β-ray at time t'—at least it does so for those who take the cognitive frame of physics to require a specification of causes in the explanation of singular events. Or consider cognitive frames which include a metaphysical principle to the effect that to explain the

[1] On priority disputes and the retrospective recognition and simplification of discoveries see e.g. S. Woolgar, 'Writing an intellectual history of scientific developments: the use of discovery accounts', *Social Studies of Science*, 6 (1976), 423–54; A. Brannigan, *The Social Basis of Scientific Discoveries*, Cambridge, 1981; S. Schaffer, 'Scientific discoveries and the end of natural philosophy', *Social Studies of Science*, 16 (1986), 387–420; S. Woolgar, *Science: The Very Idea*, Chichester, 1988, ch. 4; A. G. Gross, 'The rhetorical invention of scientific invention: the emergence and transformation of a social norm', in H. W. Simons, ed., *Rhetoric in the Human Sciences*, London, 1989.

[2] See H. Bräuning-Oktavio, 'Vom Zwischenkieferknochen zur Idee des Typus: Goethe als Naturforscher in den Jahren 1780–1786', *Nova Acta Leopoldina*, NS 18 (126) (1956).

generation of one material substance another must be invoked. In such frames explanation of the generation of the cosmos, taken as including the totality of material substances, is precluded.[3]

A second category of explanatorily basic assertions consists of those whose cognitive frame declares all purported explanations to be unreal because in principle entirely unsusceptible to evidential considerations. In Chapter 2 we examined in detail the way in which the framework for the pursuit of natural history established by Blumenbach and Kant ruled out the possibility of explaining the inner natures and origins of vital forces as well as the origins of the basic types from which all living beings are derived. In this framework postulates about the existence of vital forces and original types appear as explanatorily basic.

There remains a host of further types of explanatorily basic assertions whose basic status is not explicitly warranted by theoretical considerations, but rather by their appearance in the context of their cognitive frames as 'natural', 'self-evident' or 'self-explanatory'. On occasion assertions of this sort play the role of foundations or axioms in a cognitive frame. Such, for example, is the role in Aristotelian cosmology of the claim that rotation is the motion natural to a sphere; and such is the role in Newtonian natural philosophy of the principle of continued rest or uniform motion of bodies acted on by no forces.[4] (It should be noted, however, that there is no general reason to assume that assertions which are foundational or axiomatic in a cognitive frame are explanatorily basic in that frame. For by no means all cognitive frames embody a commitment to the 'Archimedean' precepts that explanation requires deductive subsumption and that axioms should not themselves require further explanation.) Other types of assertion that may enjoy immunity from explanatory demands are the definitions and conventions that comprise the classificatory apparatus of a cognitive frame: 'man is a primate' in the cognitive frame of present-day biology; 'magnetism is a natural potency' in the cognitive frame of early seventeenth-century natural philosophy. In addition, structural and metatheoretic principles of the kind called by Henri Poincaré 'natural hypotheses'—principles of symmetry, invariance, continuity, etc.—may be explanatorily

[3] Cf. N. Rescher, *The Limits of Science*, Berkeley, Calif., 1984, 118–27.
[4] On 'natural states' held not to be in need of explanation see R. Cummins, 'States, causes and the law of inertia', *Philosophical Studies*, 29 (1976), 21–36.

basic in cognitive frames that attach major importance to considerations of simplicity and harmony.[5]

Explanatory presuppositions are sometimes obvious to the historian, for example, when explicit claims are made about the self-explanatory nature of certain principles. However, discernment of the full ranges of assertions that are commonly regarded as immune from explanatory demands will generally require access to beliefs about the proper substance and form of explanations in particular disciplines, beliefs that will themselves rarely be explicitly articulated.

Categorial presuppositions

A third major class of presuppositions may be called, for want of a better term, 'categorial'. These are the various formal assumptions whose violation renders applications of predicates and relational terms invalid. The following remarks are of necessity impressionistic; a fuller treatment would take us into the difficult and specialized territory of the theory of measurement.

Predicates come in categories. Thus '*Homo erectus*', '*Homo habilis*' and '*Homo sapiens*' belong to the category '*Homo*'; 'is longer than', 'is shorter than' and 'is the same length as' belong to the category 'relative length'; and 'is 3 oz.' and 'is 3.5 oz.' belong to the category 'weight in oz.'. Standard measurement theory classifies categories of predicates into scale-types in terms of the formal constraints imposed on the application of predicates in the category.[6] The category of predicates '*Homo*' constitutes a scale of the simplest type, a 'nominal scale', in which the sole constraint is that one and only one predicate in the category should apply to an object. Thus the question 'To which species of *Homo* does specimen *a* belong?' is real for us only on the assumption that *a* belongs to one and only one species of *Homo*. The category of relative lengths constitutes a more complex scale-type, an *ordinal scale*. Here the further constraint of transitivity comes into play, that is, if *a* is longer than *b* and *b* is longer than *c*, then *a* is longer

---

[5] H. Poincaré, *The Foundations of Science*, trans. H. B. Halstead [1913], Washington, DC, 1982, 152.

[6] For simple expositions of the theory of scale-types see S. S. Stevens, 'Measurement, psychophysics and utility', in C. W. Churchman and P. Ratoosh, eds., *Measurement: Definitions and Theories*, New York, 1959; E. W. Adams, 'Measurement theory', in P. D. Asquith and H. E. Kyburg, eds., *Current Research in Philosophy of Science*, East Lansing, Mich. 1979.

than c. Thus the question 'What are the relative lengths of objects in collection C?' is real for us only on the assumption that transitivity holds for the relation 'longer than' applied to objects in C. Application of predicates in the category 'weight in oz.', which constitutes a 'ratio scale', is subject to yet further constraints; for example, if the weight of a is x oz. and the weight of b is y oz., then the weight of a and b is $x + y$ oz. A host of further scale-types, some of great complexity, figure in scientific disciplines—consider, for example, the so-called 'Linnaean hierarchy' used in the classification of living beings, which has the structure of an ordinally indexed nested sequence of partitions.

Articulation of the categorial presuppositions governing the application of predicates is a distinguishing feature of the exact sciences. In other sciences, however, categorial presuppositions are rarely articulated and may pose substantial problems of access for the historian. Consider, to take an example touched on in Chapter 2, the 'natural affinities' between types of living beings that played so important a role in eighteenth-century debates about the natural system. It is often hard to tell what categorial assumptions were in play here. Certainly natural affinities were regarded as having an ordinal structure. But it is unclear whether they were supposed to have the metric structure implied by the frequently invoked analogy with geographical proximities. A similar puzzle arises in connection with the various vital forces invoked in late eighteenth-century German natural history and physiology. Clearly these are supposed to have ordinal structure, but it is hard to tell whether the constantly invoked analogy with gravitational attraction implies the fuller structure of a ratio scale.

METHODOLOGICAL COMMITMENTS

Scenes of inquiry in a science depend on the preparedness of its practitioners to acknowledge considerations as in principle relevant to the resolution of questions. The types of methodological commitment of interest to us are, therefore, those that effect such perceptions of relevance. Which types are these?

It might be thought that since our concern is with relevances acknowledged by practitioners of a science, the methods at issue must all be both explicit and acknowledged by those practitioners. However, a little reflection shows that this need not be so. Many aspects of the competent setting up and handling of instruments are strongly resistant to articulation—as is confirmed by recent studies of the problems and set-backs that arise when attempts are made to replicate experiments on the basis of even the fullest written instructions without the benefit of direct witnessing and hands-on training.[7] Yet because such habitual skills and competences condition judgements about the ranges and reliabilities of instruments they are clearly of central importance in determining relevance judgements in all experimentally based fields of inquiry. Moreover, it is possible to envisage various ways in which communal perceptions of relevance may be conditioned by methods that would not be acknowledged in the community were they to articulate and reflect on those methods. Obvious examples arise from delegation of labour outside the circle of practitioners of the science in question. For example, a community of physicians might take the outcomes of certain tests carried out by pharmacological technicians to be relevant to questions about the incidence of certain diseases, even though, if they were fully apprised of the nature of those tests, they would deny their efficacy.

There is, as far as I can see, no reason of principle ruling out as determinants of scenes of inquiry any of the entire range of types of methodological commitment. Routine competences, articulate recipes; methods followed by all mankind, methods in force only at particular sites of inquiry; methods applying to whole ranges of sciences, methods applied only in a particular field, discipline or research programme; methods devised by philosophers, methods invented by practitioners; methods learned from textbooks, methods acquired in hands-on training—all may in principle affect the perceptions of relevance on which depend the reality of questions for practitioners of a science.

When we try to formulate specific hypotheses about the roles of methodological commitment in the determination of scenes of inquiry we run into serious difficulties. As in the case of explanatory ideals, touched on above, the historical diversity of cognitive frames makes generalization a risky business. And, as we

[7] See e.g. H. Collins, *Changing Order: Replication and Induction in Scientific Practice*, London, 1985, chs. 3 and 4; S. Shapin and S. Schaffer, *Leviathan and the Air-Pump: Hobbes, Boyle and the Experimental Life*, Princeton, NJ, 1985, ch. 6. Hilarious illustrations of the difficulties of articulation of tacit competences are to be found in Julio Cortázar's *Cronopios and Famas* [1962], trans. P. Blackburn, London, 1969, 1–26, 'The Instruction Manual'.

shall argue in subsequent chapters, the diversity of the social, institutional and technological embodiments of the sciences raises yet more serious doubts about the wisdom of generalization on this score. In this chapter we shall offer only the most general of hypotheses about the methodological determinants of scenes of inquiry in the sciences, leaving more specific and venturesome hypotheses to the next chapter.

A crucial question is that of the extent to which scenes of inquiry are determined by commitment to methods applicable across the entire range of scientific disciplines—general methodologies and epistemologies—as opposed to commitments to methods peculiar to particular disciplines, fields, schools and sites of inquiry—local methodologies. Even when there is evidence of explicit commitment to a general methodology by practitioners of a range of scientific disciplines, there are many grounds for scepticism about the role of such commitment as a prime determinant of scenes of inquiry. To start with, the generality of such methodologies is achieved at the cost of abstraction from the theoretical and practical predicaments of particular forms of inquiry. It is often far from clear how they can be brought to bear on issues about the relevance of particular reasons to particular questions. This suspicion of vacuity may be reinforced by a consideration of the diversity of types of inquiry that have been presented in good faith under the aegis of particular general methodologies. Consider, for example, Baconian methodology—its formulae have proved sufficiently open to variant interpretation to allow its honest profession by such methodologically ill-assorted couples as d'Alembert and Priestley, Liebig and Ampère, Herschel the younger and Whewell.[8] Equally striking in our chosen field of natural history is the diversity of eighteenth-century approaches to physiological issues—strict mechanism in which the body is treated as a hydraulic engine; the cautious empiricism of Boerhaave and his followers; the 'vitalism' of Barthez, John Hunter, and Blumenbach—all pursued in declared conformity with Newton's rules for philosophizing.[9]

[8] On the variety of appropriations of Baconian method see e.g. R. Yeo, 'An idol of the market place: Baconians in nineteenth-century Britain', *History of Science*, 23 (1985), 251–98.
[9] See T. M. Brown, 'From mechanism to vitalism in eighteenth-century English physiology', *Journal of the History of Biology*, 7 (1981), 389–407.

Even when general methodologies are precise and stringent enough to place substantial constraints on the prosecution of inquiry, there are often grave discrepancies between the general methodology to which practitioners of a discipline officially adhere and their real practices. Such discrepancies are detectable at many levels. They may be discerned by constrasting the procedures of investigation actually employed and the reports of those same investigations written up in accordance with a general methodology. (Goethe's writings on the anatomy of the human skull, mentioned in Chapter 2, provide a good illustration of this. Notes and letters not intended for publication, composed shortly after the date at which he later claimed to have made his discovery, show that chance observations backed up by extensive reading of the anatomical writings of others were crucial. In later published writings, however, Goethe presented the discovery as having resulted from the deliberate application of a general methodology designed to reveal 'primordial phenomena'.)[10] They may be evident in specialist publications from a comparison between prefatory general methodological remarks and the modes of argumentation and marshalling of evidence implied in the body of the text. (For example, as noted in Chapter 2, the prefatory remarks in the second volume of Lorenz Oken's *Lehrbuch der Naturphilosophie* claim adherence to methods that are in line with the general principles of Schelling's *Naturphilosophie*. The body of the text, however, makes considerable use of strategies of argument and persuasion that have no such warrant: numerological arguments, theological arguments, considerations derived from orthodox empirically based treatments of comparative anatomy, etc.) They may be detected also as incongruities between the detailed arguments of specialist and internal publications and treatments more in conformity with the general methodologies to be found in review articles and textbook presentations.

Despite these cautionary remarks, it is evident that general methodological commitments have on occasion played significant roles in the determination of scenes of inquiry. For all its openness to variant interpretations as a positive programme of inquiry, appeal to 'Baconian' experimental methods surely played a major part in seventeenth-century natural philosophy in limiting scenes of inquiry by invalidating metaphysical questions about occult

[10] Bräuning-Oktavio, 'Vom Zwischenkieferknochen zur Idee des Typus'.

forms, essences and sympathies. And I have argued at length in Chapter 2 for a major role in determination of scenes of inquiry in German natural history of the teleological methodology of Kant and Blumenbach and of the *naturphilosophische* methodology of Schelling and his disciples.

Are better candidates for the role of primary determinant of scenes of inquiry to be found amongst the methods that are at once habitual or routine and universally followed by all sorts and conditions of men? An affirmative answer is likely to come from those who join T. H. Huxley, in holding that science is 'trained and organised common sense'. It has, for example, been claimed that certain methods of classification of living beings are culturally universal, and that the history of 'Western' taxonomy represents modification and elaboration rather than displacement of those fundamental procedures. Similar, and perhaps rather more plausible, claims have been made for the 'abductive' inferences whereby absent or hidden causes may be inferred from present and visible signs. Such claims will be discussed in the next chapter; for the moment we simply register our reservations about the existence of culturally universal common-sense methods of sufficient specificity to serve as primary determinants of scenes of inquiry in the sciences.

Even a cursory reading of such major recent studies of attainment of consensus in the sciences as Martin Rudwick's *The Great Devonian Controversy*, Peter Galison's *How Experiments End* and Bruno Latour's *The Pasteurization of France* shows that many of the procedures that mediate the attainment of consensus in the sciences are strictly local to particular disciplines, particular factions and particular sites of inquiry.[11] It follows that many of the methods crucial in determining perceptions of relevance, and hence in determining scenes of inquiry, are likewise local in their domains of use and application.

A rough-and-ready categorization of methods distinguishes methods of production, methods of presentation and methods of assessment.[12] By methods of production I mean all the various procedures that lead up to the written, verbal or dramatic presentation or exhibition of scientific findings and hypotheses.

---

[11] I discuss Rudwick's, Galison's and Latour's studies in chs. 5 and 9.

[12] A similar categorization of methods and practices is to be found in Shapin and Schaffer, *Leviathan and the Air-Pump*, 25.

Here belong protocols for the use of instruments, together with the often protracted processes of control, replication, simulation and data analysis involved in the separation of 'genuine' signals and effects from background noise and interference. Here belong the heuristic methods that govern the cogitations of theoreticians. Here too belong the habits and regulations that govern the division of labour and the daily routines of work in laboratories and research institutes. Methods of presentation include conventions of genre and representation, techniques of argument and narration and strategies of rhetorical and aesthetic appeal. Here too belong the demonstrative and dramatic procedures involved in 'live' displays of experimental findings before an audience. Methods of assessment include all the various procedures and conventions of refereeing, adjudication, criticism, assignment of 'burden of proof' and conduct of controversy that mediate the careers of findings and claims from their first public appearances to their consensual acceptance or rejection.

Methods of production, presentation and assessment often interact, rarely forming a tidy sequence. Such interaction is inevitable when background and auxiliary hypotheses and preparatory results have to be confirmed in order to establish a defensible case for the target hypothesis or finding. Another recurrent pattern of interaction between 'contexts of discovery' and 'contexts of justification' arises from what may be called 'the principle of prospective significance', whereby methods directly applicable to the later phases indirectly regulate the earlier phases of activity. Thus production of scientific results is strongly conditioned by practitioners' beliefs about the methods of assessment prevalent in their disciplines: both because they may themselves be committed to those methods of assessment and because they may be sensitive to the likely critical reception of their work by their peers. Conversely, interaction arises through what may be called 'the principle of retrospective significance' whereby public presentations of scientific results selectively interpret, reconstruct and regiment the modes of production of those results so as to render them publicly 'accountable', that is, to enhance their credibility according to the accepted norms of assessment.[13] The distinction between 'contexts of discovery' and

[13] On accountability as a regulator of laboratory activities see M. Lynch, *Art and Artifact in Laboratory Science: A Study of Shop Work and Shop Talk in a Research Laboratory*, London, 1985.

'contexts of justification' is further blurred by the modifications, qualifications and adaptations frequently undergone by initial findings and claims *en route* to consensus.

Methods of production, both tacit and explicit, that relate to competent use of specific instruments and experimental techniques are generally local to particular disciplines and often to particular sites or schools of inquiry.[14] Indeed, in experimental disciplines committed to different repertoires of instruments such locality is inevitable. Such methods are clearly of paramount importance in determining the scenes of inquiry of a great range of scientific disciplines: all those whose practitioners treat appeal to empirical considerations as a primary mode of resolution of questions. When we turn from the 'context of discovery' to the 'context of justification', to methods of presentation and assessment, the case for the dominance of local methods as determinants of scenes of inquiry is hardly less clear.[15] The conventions of 'objective' and 'plain' presentation in the sciences do indeed create a measure of superfical homogeneity in present-day scientific discourse. But the standards of demonstration, the assignment of burdens of proof and the batteries of persuasive strategies in use in different scientific disciplines and in different institutions and factions of a given discipline are extraordinarily various;[16] and, as intimated above, this diversity in tactics of persuasion and debate is in evidence even amongst those who declare their commitment to the same general methodology.

In the next chapter I shall consider in more detail, and with specific examples, some of the ways in which the advent of new methods and practices may shift scenes of inquiry. By way of a conclusion to the present chapter, let us reflect briefly on certain of the problems of access faced by the historian concerned with the ways in which scenes of inquiry have shifted in response to changing methods and practices of inquiry.

---

[14] On the diversity of local instrumental practices see e.g. H. Collins, *Changing Order*; P. Galison, *How Experiments End*, Chicago, Ill., 1987.

[15] See e.g. Claire Salomon-Bayet's fascinating reflections on 'institutional epistemologies': *L'Institution de la science et l'expérience du vivant*, Paris, 1978.

[16] On the diversity of rhetorical conventions and practices in the sciences see e.g. the papers in A. E. Benjamin, G. N. Cantor and J. R. R. Christie, eds., *The Figural and the Literal: Problems of Language in the History of Science and Philosophy, 1630–1800*, Manchester, 1987; C. Bazerman, *Shaping Written Knowledge*, Madison, Wis., 1989.

ACCESS TO METHODS AND PRACTICES

On the score of researchability the major problems are posed by
the prevalence of local methods that are routine and habitual,
under normal circumstances rarely discussed or even articulated
by their exponents. These problems of access are of crucial
concern to us, since it is precisely such methods that are, on our
account, the primary determinants of scenes of inquiry in the
sciences. At the level of methods of assessment the historian (and
the sociologist who is not simultaneously a competent and
experienced practitioner of the discipline in question) will be hard
put to get to grips with, for example, the tacit criteria by which
practitioners assign burdens of proof and judge the competence
and worth of other practitioners and their findings. At the level of
presentation tacit local conventions of literary genre, of modes of
representation of data, of terms of address to the reader, etc.
may prove hard of access. At the level of methods of production
especially acute problems are posed for the historian and the
uninitiated sociologist by the role in every aspect of experimental
work of habitual competences in the use of instruments. (Indeed,
here even initiation may be of little help, since hands-on training
does not generally put the trainee in a position to articulate the
competences and skills thus acquired.) The problems of access
may be exacerbated by the reticence and jealousy which often
protect local expertise. Workshops and laboratories are domains
in which there is a peculiar appositeness in Erving Goffman's
observation 'almost all information in a social establishment has
something of this exclusive function and may be seen as none of
somebody's business'.[17]

There is now a considerable body of sociological and historical
studies that pay attention to daily work in the institutions of the
sciences.[18] And there is rapidly increasing interest in the details of

[17] *The Presentation of Self in Everyday Life* [1959], Harmondsworth, 1971, 142.

[18] There is an exponentiating sociological literature on laboratory practices,
following B. Latour and S. Woolgar's pioneering *Laboratory Life: The Construction
of Scientific Facts*, Beverly Hills, Calif., 1979. Relevant historical works include:
M. Berman, *Social Change and Scientific Organisation: The Royal Institution,
1799–1844*, Leiden, 1979; J. Morrell and A. Thackray, *Gentlemen of Science: Early
Years of the British Association for the Advancement of Science*, Oxford, 1981;
M. Hunter, *The Royal Society and its Fellows, 1660–1700: The Morphology of an
Early Scientific Institution*, Chalfont St Giles, 1982; J. E. McClellan III, *Science
Reorganised: Scientific Societies in the Eighteenth Century*, New York, 1985; and, in

the local genres and conventions that have governed the writing and illustration of treatises in the sciences.[19] Of the various approaches adopted in these studies two, one derived from Californian sociology, the other from French historiography, hold, I believe, especial promise for the uncovering of local and tacit practices in the sciences.

Recently the techniques of so-called 'ethnomethodology' pioneered by Harold Garfinkel and his co-workers have been applied to the study of laboratory work.[20] The ethnomethodologists' combination of fly-on-the-wall tactics with occasional disruptive interventions has yielded rich insights into habitual competences and into the ways in which researchers selectively interpret and rationalize their activities so as to render them presentable to their peers and sponsors. Can these techniques be transposed into the history of science? At first sight there are grave difficulties. Unlike the ethnomethodologist the historian cannot literally infiltrate his subjects' places of work. Nor can he trouble his subjects as is the ethnomethodologist's wont, seeking to unmask tacit expectations and behavioural routines by violating them. There are, however, a number of other aspects of ethnomethodological procedure and sensibility that the historian of local and tacit methods and

our chosen field of natural history, A. Stroup, *A Company of Scientists: Botany, Patronage and Community at the Seventeenth-Century Parisian Royal Academy of Sciences*, Berkeley, Calif., 1989.

[19] On rhetorical strategies in present-day scientific literature see e.g. G. N. Gilbert and M. Mulkay, *Opening Pandora's Box: A Sociological Analysis of Scientists' Discourse*, Cambridge, 1984; Bazerman, *Shaping Written Knowledge*; Simons, ed., *Rhetoric in the Human Sciences* (these works contain extensive references to further literature). Historical studies of rhetorical and dialectical strategy include: O. Hannaway, *The Chemists and the Word: The Didactic Origins of Chemistry*, Baltimore, Md., 1975; W. C. Anderson, *Between the Library and the Laboratory: The Language of Chemistry in Eighteenth-Century France*, Baltimore, Md., 1984; and Benjamin *et al.*, eds., *The Figural and the Literal*. On the uses of images in the sciences see the excellent collection of articles, B. Latour and J. de Noblet, eds., *Les "Vues" de l'esprit, Culture Technique*, 14 (1985); also M. J. Rudwick, 'The emergence of a visual language for geological science, 1760–1840', *History of Science*, 14 (1976), 149–95; M. Lynch, 'Discipline and the material form of images: an analysis of scientific visibility', *Social Studies of Science*, 15 (1985), 37–66; B. Latour, 'Visualisation and cognition: thinking with hands and eyes', *Knowledge and Society: Studies in the Sociology of Culture Past and Present*, 6 (1986), 1–40. I discuss rhetorical and aesthetic strategies in the sciences in Ch. 10.

[20] H. Garfinkel, *Studies in Ethnomethodology*, New York, 1967. An exemplary application of ethnomethodological techniques to laboratory work is Lynch, *Art and Artifact in Laboratory Science*.

practices may adopt. There is the focus on daily routines at particular sites of work. There is the concern with the interplay between deeds and accounts of deeds: with the ways in which the need for public accountability prospectively conditions deeds and retrospectively conditions agents' accounts of their deeds. Whilst the historian cannot prompt such information by disruptive intervention, he can follow the ethnomethodologist in attending minutely to naturally occurring disruptions—failures of instruments, difficulties in the replication of results, defections of colleagues and allies, controversies and polemics. For such disturbances frequently provoke practitioners, their champions and their antagonists to bring into the open details of method and practice that remain unspoken or, at least, unpublished, in more clement times.[21]

The *Histoire des mentalités* pioneered by Lucien Febvre, Marc Bloch and Philippe Ariès has as its avowed aim the uncovering of past habitual commonplace beliefs, attitudes, norms and sensibilities.[22] Can the techniques of *mentaliste* history be pressed into the service of the history of the sciences? At first sight the prospects are dim. *Mentaliste* history is largely concerned with 'low culture' and in particular with popular attitudes to the great 'realities' of life: God, the weather, food and drink, sex, birth and death. Further, it is often tied to grand theories about the nature of the transformation of folk culture into civilized culture, theories that pay scant attention to the development of scientific disciplines and which have little to offer the historian of science.[23] However, at the level of historical method *mentaliste* historiography does, I believe, have plenty to offer the historian of science who would gain access to past commonplaces of doctrine and method. The *mentaliste* approach has affinities with ethnomethodology in respects whose potential value to the historian of science has already been noted: concern with local know-how and with local daily routines; and interest in reactions to disturbance (prodigies,

[21] The powers of such an approach are well evidenced in Shapin and Schaffer, *Leviathan and the Air-Pump*.

[22] Useful overviews of *mentaliste* historiography include J. Le Goff, 'Mentalities: a history of ambiguity', in J. Le Goff and P. Nora, eds., *Constructing the Past*, Cambridge, 1985; U. P. Burke, 'Strengths and weaknesses of the history of *mentalités*', *History of European Ideas*, 7 (1986), 439–51.

[23] For critiques of this aspect of *mentaliste* history see M. A. Gismondi, ' "The gift of theory": a critique of the *histoire des mentalités*', *Social History*, 10 (1985), 211–28; Burke, 'Strengths and weaknesses of the history of *mentalités*'.

riots, novelties) as indicators of commonplace and tacit norms and assumptions. However, the really distinctive feature of *mentaliste* method is the inference of commonplace attitudes and assumptions from indirect and marginal testimony—reports of inquisitors, inspectors and visitors; of dissidents and renegades; of sidekicks and confidants—and from superficial and marginal signs—details of ceremony and observance, manners and dress, style, ornament and mode of expression. The history of scientific disciplines provides, I believe, a wonderfully fertile field for the application of such techniques. In particular, at the level of methods of production, scientific instruments, together with the architecture and accoutrements of laboratories, cabinets and museums, provide a wealth of clues to tacit and commonplace procedures and practices.[24] And, at the level of methods of presentation and assessment, comparably eloquent signs are to be found in the rhetorical and aesthetic specificities of composition, layout and illustration of scientific treatises.[25]

[24] Indications of the powers of a *mentaliste* approach to the history of the sciences are to be found in R. Darnton, *Mesmerism and the End of the Enlightenment in France*, Princeton, N.J. 1968; *The Great Cat Massacre and Other Essays in French Cultural History*, Harmondsworth, 1985. In the field of natural history the *mentaliste* approach is well illustrated by Krysztof Pomian's inference of changes in attitudes to history and nature from changes in the contents of the cabinets of Parisian collectors: 'Médailles/coquilles = érudition/philosophie', *Studies on Voltaire and the Eighteenth Century*, 151 (5) (1976), 1677–1703; see also the further essays in his *Collectionneurs, amateurs et curieux: Paris, Venise: XVIe–XVIIIe siècle*, Paris, 1987. (I am indebted to Peter Burke for drawing my attention to Pomian's works.) S. Forgan, 'The architecture of science and the idea of a university', *Studies in History and Philosophy of Science*, 20 (1989), 405–34, shows the effectiveness of close reading of architecture as a source of insights into past assumptions about the practices and goals of the sciences.

[25] See e.g. the works of Hannaway, Anderson and Rudwick cited in n. 19, above.

5
The Origins of Methods

In the last chapter we offered some general hypotheses about the immediate factors that bring about changes in scenes of inquiry in the sciences. How are we to arrive at more specific hypotheses about these immediate factors, and in particular about methodological commitments whose primacy as determinants of scenes of inquiry we have emphasized? And how are we to arrive at an understanding of remote factors that affect scenes of inquiry via their effects on methodological commitments? How, for example, are we to relate methodological commitments to the institutions, cultural environments and societies that transform and are transformed by them; and how are we to relate them to the predicaments, strategies and deliberations of individual practitioners of the sciences? The questions are not easy ones. The contingencies of the careers of individual practitioners, the peculiarities of their perceptions of their situations and of the information available to them, the idiosyncrasies of their tactics and reflections, all suggest that hypotheses holding good over all periods and across the whole range of the sciences may be hard to come by. The same conclusion is strongly suggested by the manifest methodological differences between sciences, and between schools and factions in a given science; and it is reinforced by consideration of the diversity of the social and institutional embodiments of scientific disciplines and by the great discrepancies in the resources needed for their pursuit—discrepancies with respect to cost ('Big Science, Little Science' in Derek De Solla Price's famous phrase), to types of instrumentation and housing, to availability of qualified practitioners, and so on.

Striking evidence of this diversity is provided in Peter Galison's important recent study of twentieth-century experimental physics, *How Experiments End*.[1] Galison distinguishes three 'epochs' in

[1] Chicago, Ill., 1987.

the experimental investigation of the microphysical domain: the epoch of classical apparatus designed to measure the macrophysical properties from which inferences about the microphysical may be made; the epoch of cloud chamber detection of the constituents of cosmic rays; and the epoch of bubble chambers, particle accelerations and high-energy physics. He charts the extraordinary expansion in scale and cost of instruments; the lengthening time-span of experiments; and the increasing size, administrative complexity and differentiation of roles in the teams which perform experiments. Galison relates these changes in the material and social conditions of experiment to changes at every level of method and practice. As the path from experimental hint or suspicion to hard fact, from mere curiosity to 'gold-plated' event, becomes longer and more devious the methods for discerning genuine effects from background and mimicking effects become ever more complicated and diverse; the roles of data analysis and computer simulation in the preparation of experimental results are vastly expanded; and the patterns of interaction between machines, computers, analysts, straight theoreticians, experimental physicists and technicians become ever more complex.

Turning to methods of presentation and assessment of claims, we find equally radical changes. For example, there is increasing use in publications of pre-emptive analyses, designed to eliminate possible objections on the scores of background or mimicking effects. Moreover, internal publications assume increasing import-ance as the arbitrating role of grand conferences and the community of physicists 'at large' declines in favour of more specialist peer groups internal to the research organizations themselves. On top of this diachronic diversity in the methods and practices of experimental physics, Galison exhibits further methodological divergence within each epoch between schools with differing founders and authorities, educational and disciplinary backgrounds, instrumental and analytical repertoires, research priorities and theoretical commitments.

The tentative speculations which follow concentrate on the more obvious sources of change and stability in the methodological commitments of practitioners of the sciences on which scenes of inquiry directly depend. In this chapter I discuss the introduction and articulation of methods; the next is concerned with the criticism and legitimation of methods.

COMMON SENSE

'Common sense', writes Scott Atran, 'is to be considered not as a harmful subsidiary of science, but as a largely autonomous and habitually faithful ally.'[2] Certainly there has been a considerable recent resurgence of the view that many of the methods of the scientific disciplines are but refinements and specializations of 'natural' and common-sense competences generally distributed among the sorts and conditions of men. Let us look at two alleged instances.

Atran challenges standard interpretations of the classifications of living beings that are found in oral cultures. Such 'folk-taxonomies' are, he insists, to be seen neither as symbolic or magical systems nor as largely conditioned by the requirements of daily life. Rather, there is common to them all a coherent structure, the manifestation of universal common-sense dispositions. One key element of the folk-taxonomic structure is the partitioning of the totality of living beings into life-forms (plants and animals, herbs and trees, etc.) based on gross appearance, habitat and relation to man. Another key element is the recognition within the life-forms of mutually exclusive 'folk-species' whose manifest characteristics are assumed to be expressions of invariant underlying natures. Where others have represented the 'primitive' methods of folk-taxonomy as an obstacle that 'scientific' taxonomy had to overcome, Atran suggests that much of the career of natural history has involved elaboration and refinement of these culturally universal methods in response to particular practical and theoretical exigencies. Thus he interprets the development of theories about the nature of species as elaborations in response to theoretical demands of the supposedly primordial view of folk-species as having visible forms expressive of constant hidden essences. More convincing, in my opinion, is the relation he postulates between the addition of ever more ranks to the primeval two-tier scheme and the move from a local standpoint (from which the number of folk-species visible is small and few higher groups are salient) to a global standpoint (from which is evident an immense array of types showing many levels of differentiation between those of the species and the life-

[2] *Fondements de l'histoire naturelle: Pour une anthropologie de la science*, Paris, 1986, 211.

form). Only at the end of the eighteenth century, according to Atran, do we see a major break with folk-taxonomy, when the hidden natures of living beings come to be seen not merely as substrates of the phenomena of natural history, but as the subjects of a new discipline, biology.

Our second example, from Carlo Ginzburg's remarkable article 'Clues: Morelli, Freud and Sherlock Holmes', concerns the 'divinatory sciences'.[3] These depend upon 'the deciphering of various kinds of signs, from symptoms to writing'. They are concerned with the individual and the probable, unlike the geometrized 'Galilean sciences' which aim at certainty and generality. Ginzburg suggests that the arts of conjectural inference from present and manifest signs to hidden or absent realities are rooted in the practice of hunting—such an origin is, he claims, attested by the ancient Greeks' recognition of a category of conjectural (*tekmēriodēs*) inference, the particular province of hunters and fishermen as well as physicians, historians, politicians, potters, joiners and mariners. He goes on to chart the formation of new divinatory disciplines: palaeography, connoisseurship, graphology, physiognomy, phrenology, palaeontology, etc. The story culminates in the period of Freud, Morelli and Conan Doyle, the period in which, Ginzburg maintains, interpretation of signs became the articulate and self-conscious methodology of the human, as opposed to the exact, sciences.

One aspect of these claims for common sense has, in my anthropologically untutored opinion, great plausibility. This is the denial of what Bruno Latour has called 'the Great Divide', the view that progress in the sciences has come about through the displacement of irrational primitive and 'vulgar' methods by rational and disinterested scientific procedures.[4] Atran in particular inveighs effectively against French rationalist historians who have seen common sense as an obstacle to be overcome by the autonomous mathematical–experimental method of the exact sciences; he is equally cogent in his dismissal of the attitude of British anthropologists of the colonial era who conceded a measure of rationality to primitive and common-sense procedures,

---

[3] In U. Eco and T. A. Sebeok, eds., *The Sign of Three: Dupin, Holmes, Peirce*, Bloomington, Ind., 1983, 81–118.

[4] *Science in Action: How to Follow Scientists and Engineers through Society*, Milton Keynes, 1987, 211 ff.

but saw this as a rationality distorted by 'unscientific' concerns and interests.[5]

A further attractive feature of Atran's and Ginzburg's accounts is their avoidance of any suggestion that culturally universal common-sense methods are inescapable or incorrigible. Atran's book is, indeed, a tale of correction and modification of common sense. Moreover, both authors allow that the creation of certain of the scientific disciplines—the Galilean sciences according to Ginzburg, the new biology of the nineteenth century according to Atran—involved substantial breaks with common sense.

Despite these attractions there are grounds for circumspection. First, there is the worrying sense of *déjà lu*. The view of common sense as obstacle to science is a clear legacy of the Enlightenment vision of science as the triumph of reason over vulgar error and superstition. These counter-claims for the scientifically formative powers of common sense are, in turn, oddly reminiscent of the Romantic historiography of Schelling's era, with its visions of a *prisca sapientia*, preserved in folk tales and crafts, variously articulated and specified by the sciences. One suspicion that arises in connection with such assumptions is that they trade on illusions of homogeneity born of unfamiliarity and inaccessibility of pre-historic, alien and popular cultures.

Further doubts concern the specific claims for cultural commonality and continuity on which Atran and Ginzburg rest their claims. Thus where Atran's case for the prevalence in folk-taxonomies of recognition of 'life-forms' and 'folk-species' is well documented and convincing, he is able to present little evidence for his claim that the folk are wont to regard the outer forms and behaviours of living beings as manifestations of real and constant inner natures. Similarly, whilst Ginzburg makes out an impressive case for a community of commitment to semiotic methods in the human sciences at the end of the nineteenth century, there is more of playful reflexivity than conviction in the chain of conjectures by which he links hunting, Babylonian soothsaying, Renaissance connoisseurship, Cuvierian palaeontology and the detective methods of Freud and Morelli.

A final doubt, the most serious of all, concerns the level of abstraction and generality of the common-sense procedures at issue. Ginzburg's category of semiotic or conjectural inference, in

[5] *Fondements de l'histoire naturelle*, 187 ff.

particular, is extraordinarily generous; and if one sets aside Atran's contentious inclusion of a proto-Aristotelian essentialism in the body of folk wisdom, one is left with a framework that places remarkably little constraint on the classification of living beings. The universals of common-sense procedure are, I suggest, too tolerant to get to grips with the subject matters of the sciences.

PONTIFICAL DISCIPLINES

If common sense fails us as a general source of the methods that determine scenes of inquiry, perhaps we would do better to consider disciplines that presume to pontificate explicitly on the methods appropriate to inquiry in other disciplines. The roster of disciplines that have at one time or another assumed such legislative rights is lengthy: universal grammar, logic, dialectic, rhetoric, epistemology. Many scientists today pay at least lip-service to logic and epistemology as arbiters of scientific method; and there can be no doubt that such pontifical disciplines have in the past often imposed their favoured methods of argument, presentation and persuasion on substantial ranges of the sciences. We have already touched on one example, the spread of the methodology of *Naturphilosophie* in the sciences in the opening decades of the nineteenth century. This methodology never achieved widespread acceptance outside the German lands. However, there are clear-cut instances in which methodological innovations in pontifical disciplines have achieved far more general currency. Amongst the factors that may facilitate such entrenchment of a new methodology are the establishment of the pontifical discipline in the more elementary and unspecialized reaches of educational curricula and the production of works— books, artefacts, images, performances—that both reach a wide public and palatably and persuasively illustrate and instantiate the new methods. The following example shows both these features in marked degree.

Logic was famously defined by Peter of Spain (d. 1277) as 'art of arts and science of sciences, preparing the way to the principle of all methods'.[6] In the curricula of medieval and Renaissance universities logic together with the other 'trivial' subjects, grammar and rhetoric, formed the core of the general arts course,

---

[6] *Petri Hispani Summuale logicales*, ed. I. M. Bocheński, Turin, 1947, 1.

preparatory to study in the higher faculties of law, medicine and theology. A new type of logic teaching was widely seen by the humanist reformers as crucial for their educational goal, the inculcation of eloquence and civility. In the course of the sixteenth century in the majority of the Protestant universities the subject was transformed at the hands of humanist pedagogues.[7] The emphasis was shifted from the demonstrative methods of Aristotelian syllogism that had dominated medieval logic treatises. The new focus was on dialectical techniques for commanding assent— induction, analogy, argument from telling precedent and striking example, etc.—methods that were perceived as having direct relevance to the 'real worlds' of court, bar, pulpit and bedside. The new humanist logic had as its prime exemplar the orations and dialogues of Cicero; and it was in many respects derivative from the works in which Cicero himself and his continuator, Quintilian, had sought to articulate and regiment forensic and dialectical strategy.[8] The dissemination of the new logic owed much to Cicero's pre-eminence in the humanist canon and to the resultant mass of literature composed in imitation and emulation of his works. In the various branches of mathematics and natural philosophy strict adherence to the rules of humanist logic is fairly uncommon except in introductory orations, prefaces and polemics. However, a massive impact of the humanist transformation of logic teaching is evident in the eclipse in many fields of the various Aristotelian genres of 'demonstrative' presentation, in the vogue for the various forms of methodical presentation promoted by the humanist dialecticians (of which we shall consider some examples in Chapter 10) and in the increase in use of inductive, analogical and exemplary argument patterned on legal precedents.

It is a moot point how far pontifical disciplines are to be considered as genuine originators of new methods, rather than as articulators, legitimators, generalizers and amplifiers of methods and practices already present in other disciplines. The innovations of the humanist dialecticians mentioned above are not (with the

---

[7] The standard work on humanist logic is C. Vasoli, *La Dialettica e la retorica dell'umanesimo*, Milan, 1968.

[8] On imitation and emulation of Cicero in the period see G. Williamson, *The Senecan Amble*, Chicago, Ill., 1951. On the popularity of the dialogue form see R. Hirzel, *Der Dialog: Ein literarhistorischer Versuch*, ii, Leipzig, 1895, 385–93; D. Marsh, *The Quattrocento Dialogue: Classical Tradition and Humanist Innovation*, Cambridge, Mass., 1980.

possible exception of Ramist method, briefly discussed in Chapter 10) to be regarded as ground rules for entirely new genres of discourse. Rather, there was an interplay between the development and teaching of dialectical theories largely based on the dialectic of Cicero and Quintilian and a general revival, emulation and elaboration of classical literary forms and styles and of classical dialectical and forensic strategies.

On this score our earlier account of changes in scenes of inquiry in German natural history is potentially misleading; for it may make it appear that changes of scene were largely determined by exceedingly general and abstract methodological considerations that originated in the discipline of philosophy. I am confident that this was not the true situation. I have, in fact, already intimated that Kant's 'methodology of the teleological judgement' may be considered, at least in part, as an articulation and legitimation of the approach to natural history followed by Blumenbach and his students. The methodology of *Naturphilosophie* is at first sight more resistant to such an interpretation. However, it is my impression that even here abstraction from established practices in the sciences played an important role. Thus Michael Vater has emphasized the exemplary role of gravity in Schelling's metaphyics:

In all its forms, gravity remains hidden, a force observable only in what it does. Indeed, the striking feature of all manifestations of the third power—as the union of body and soul, the force that makes natural bodies a system, the synthetic connection of awareness and presentation in intuition, and the identification of concepts and intuitions in thought—is just this *invisibility*. Time, space, the individual's self-identity and cohesion, the forces that work the plurality of things into nature, the synthetic identity of self-consciousness, reason itself—these are the real structures that make phenomena possible, but are themselves hidden, or, insofar as they do appear, empty and contentless 'things'. Within appearances, only differences stand forth, never the unifying structure of appearances. And on this fact rests the whole plausibility of Schelling's postulation of a non-phenomenal or absolute dimension where the indifference of things appears as such.[9]

On this telling interpretation the Newtonian postulation of gravity serves as a model not merely, as in Blumenbach and Kant, for the

---

[9] F. W. J. Schelling, *Bruno; or, On the Natural and the Divine Principle of Things, 1802*, ed., trans. and intro. by M. G. Vater, Albany, NY, 1984, 44–5.

postulation of vital forces, but for all the most fundamental aspects of Schelling's grand venture beyond the bounds of Kantian sense. When we consider Oken's application of *naturphilosophische* methods to the three kingdoms of nature more clear-cut precedents are evident. His methods of classification on the basis of structural correspondences can, as we have already noted, be seen as a generalization of a practice that gained ground in comparative anatomy in the latter decades of the eighteenth century—the practice of representing superficially diverse living beings as modifications of the same anatomical type or ground-plan.[10] His schemes for the naming of corresponding parts in superficially diverse living beings, like other schemes of nomenclature in the newly formed discipline of comparative anatomy, probably owe much to the precedent of new nomenclatural schemes in chemistry.[11] And his constructive method for ranking minerals, plants and animals can be seen as a generalization and abstraction of the practice, common in anatomical treatises of the period, of proceeding from the anatomically simple and homogeneous to the anatomically complex and differentiated.[12]

A further reservation about the powers of pontifical disciplines to determine scenes of inquiry in their client disciplines parallels our earlier doubt about the role of universal common sense as a determinant of scenes. General methodological precepts which claim wide jurisdiction—all demonstrative sciences, all branches of natural philosophy, all the inductive sciences, all the natural sciences—are commonly, it seems, pitched at so high a level of generality as to place little constraint on the ways in which those who acknowledge them may prosecute their investigations or present their results. We have already mentioned the extraordinary diversity of procedures pursued under the aegis of Bacon's inductive method. Another fine example of such underdetermination of disciplinary practice by professed general methodology is

[10] See Daudin, *De Linné à Lamarck: Méthodes de la classification et idée de série en botanique et en zoologie (1740–1790)* [1926], Paris, 1983, ch. 3; B. Balan, *L'Ordre et le temps: L'Anatomie comparée et l'histoire des vivants au XIXe siècle*, Paris, 1979, 53–7.

[11] On the transposition to anatomy of programmes for the reform of chemical nomenclature see P. Corsi, 'Models and analogies for the reform of natural history: features of the French debate, 1790–1800', in C. Montalenti and P. Rossi, eds., *Lazzaro Spallanzani e la biologia del Settecento: Teorie, esperimenti, istituzioni scientifiche*, Florence, 1983.

[12] See e.g. Balan, *L'Ordre et le temps*, 161–6.

provided by the fortunes of Newtonian method in eighteenth-century physiology. Theodore Brown has shown how in British medicine and physiology or 'animal œconomy' around the turn of the seventeenth century the Newtonian method was held to justify an axiomatic and geometrical approach in which the body was modelled as a hydraulic machine.[13] Later the example of Boerhaave and the teachings of his followers brought the strictly mechanistic approach into disfavour. Instead there was pursued in the name of Newton and his four rules of reasoning in philosophy a variety of experimentally oriented non-mathematical approaches which cautiously forswore the attempt to specify *verae causae* for the phenomena described. In the latter part of the century in Britain, as in France and the German lands, so-called 'vitalism' came into prominence. Newtonian method was still invoked: the vital forces were treated by analogy with gravitation as general properties of matter whose inner nature is entirely inaccessible to us, but whose *modus operandi* can be investigated through experimental study of physiological phenomena. Striking direct evidence of under-determination of practice by commitment to a general methodology is provided by Michael Mulkay and Nigel Gilbert's study of the ways in which declaredly Popperian biochemists assessed their own and others' work.[14] It turned out that there was enough flexibility in their interpretations and applications of falsificationist doctrine to allow them to impute in good faith conformity to Popperian method to work of which they approved and violation to work of which they disapproved almost regardless of the actual procedures involved.

EXEMPLARY DISCIPLINES

Both universal common sense and the pontifical disciplines— grammar, rhetoric, logic, epistemology—have, it seems, generally been overrated as sources of methodological innovations in other disciplines. More important, I suspect, for the determination of scenes of inquiry is the transposition of methods from disciplines that serve not as general arbiters of method, but rather as

[13] T. M. Brown, 'From mechanism to vitalism in eighteenth-century English physiology', *Journal of the History of Biology*, 7 (1984), 179–216.
[14] 'Putting philosophy to work: Karl Popper's influence on scientific practice', *Philosophy of the Social Sciences*, 11 (1981), 389–407.

exemplars or role models. The vitalist physiology just mentioned provides nice examples. Stephen Cross in a fascinating study of the work of its leading British exponent, John Hunter, has indicated a series of respects in which procedure in the physiology of the period was modelled on that of other disciplines.[15] One such respect concerns the treatment of the internal economy of the animal as a 'natural harmony of interests' in which powers of production, circulation and exchange are regulated and balanced for the mutual benefit of the organs. As Cross shows, we have here not just an isolated metaphor from political economy but rather the transposition of an entire mode of discourse. More specific to Hunter is the extensive use of the terminology of sensationalist psychology, 'impression', 'sensibility', 'disposition', etc. in describing the modes of interaction between organs. Here again, Cross suggests, it is not merely terminology but an entire style of reasoning and writing that is imported into physiology. Yet further aspects of the methodology of vitalist physiology, most notably those associated with the 'Newtonian' treatment of vital forces as general powers of matter, appear to derive from chemistry, in which it was common practice to treat chemical affinities in this way. Cross's study strongly suggests that, for all the official subservience to Newtonian method, the scenes of inquiry of the new 'vitalist' physiology were in large measure determined by methods derived in emulation of other, more firmly established, disciplines.

The above examples are of transposition or exchange of methods involving disciplines that are, by our lights, scientific. However, there are plenty of instances in which the donor discipline has been by our standards unscientific.

A striking example is provided by the transference of legal methods and practices into seventeenth-century English natural philosophy. Thus Julian Martin has demonstrated in detail how the methods for the reform of natural philosophy set out in Bacon's *Novum Organum* were modelled on the methods he proposed for the establishment of a 'science' of common law (proposals which formed part of a larger plan for the enhancement of the autocratic powers of the Crown); and Rosemary Sargent has explored the ways in which Robert Boyle transposed legal

[15] S. J. Cross, 'John Hunter, the animal œconomy and late eighteenth century physiological discourse', *Studies in the History of Biology*, 5 (1981), 1–110.

methods for the certification, weighting and deployment of evidence into the practice of experimental natural philosophy.[16]

In the field of natural history we find substantial methodological interactions with the nascent discipline of aesthetics in the decades around 1800. These interactions occurred at many levels. There is the impact of change in aesthetic norms on fashions and crazes in the objects of natural history. Thus the early nineteenth-century shift of connoisseur's obsessions from plants and shells to insects and birds, a shift with substantial implications for the classificatory and anatomical practices of natural history, may plausibly be taken as symptomatic of the transition from Augustan sentiment to the more dynamic and receptive Romantic sensibility.[17] Similarly, there is an obvious connection between the aesthetics of sublimity and the growing concern of natural historians with mountains, caves, fossils (especially huge ones) and the powers that have shaped the earth. The connection is evident both in the techniques of illustration of mineralogical and geological treatises and in the 'sublime' plots and narrative techniques of developmental histories of the earth and its inhabitants.[18]

In the developments in natural history discussed in Chapter 2 the links with aesthetics are especially clearly in evidence. To start with, there is an evident link between the stark, schematic, neo-classical style of anatomical illustration pioneered by Petrus Camper and the development of a typological comparative anatomy. At the level of classificatory, illustrative and descriptive practices the links are most evident in anatomy—unsurprisingly, given the role of anatomy in teaching at academies of fine arts and the connections between anatomy, figure and genre painting, and the then fashionable science of physiognomy. As we have seen, the original types which Goethe recognized in series of living

[16] J. Martin, *'Knowledge is Power': Francis Bacon, the State and the Reform of Natural Philosophy*, Cambridge, forthcoming; Sargent, 'Scientific experiment and legal expertise: the way of experience in seventeenth-century England', *Studies in History and Philosophy of Science*, 20 (1989), 19–45.

[17] D. E. Allen, *The Naturalist in Britain: A Social History*, Harmondsworth, 1976, 101.

[18] See W. Lepenies, *Das Ende der Naturgeschichte: Wandel kultureller Selbstverständlichkeiten in den Wissenschaften des 18. und 19. Jahrhunderts*, Munich, 1976; D. von Engelhardt, 'Geschichte und Gesellschaft in der Naturforschung der Romantik', in M. Hahn and H. J. Sandkühler, eds., *Gesellschaftliche Bewegung und Naturprozess*, Cologne, 1981; N. Rupke, 'The study of fossils in the Romantic philosophy of history and nature', *History of Science*, 21 (1983), 389–413.

beings are not only the exemplars from which series are 'derived' by metamorphoses in accordance with morphological laws, but also ideals of beauty. Moreover, the terms he used to describe those laws of derivation, 'enhancement' (*Steigerung*), 'perfection' (*Vervollkommnung*), etc. are also his central terms of aesthetic appraisal, the terms he uses to relate particular works of art to their exemplars and prototypes. At the level of high theory the methodological links between natural history and aesthetics are evident in the writings of Kant and Schelling. In Kant's *Critique of Judgement* both aesthetic appraisal of the sublimity of nature and teleological appraisal of living beings involve quests for order, the former in the manifold of perception, the latter in the deliverances of the understanding.[19] Both forms of appraisal demand sensitivity to harmony and adaptation—adaptation of sensory material to the constructive powers of imagination in the case of aesthetic appraisal, adaptation of parts to each other and to the whole in the case of teleological appraisal. In Schelling's methodology for the construction of a system of nature the link with aesthetics is yet more intimate. In his *System of Transcendental Idealism* he explains how the archetypal 'productive intuition' that engenders the parallel histories of nature and spirit can be re-enacted in two ways: by the artist-genius lost in the work of creation; and on a lower plane by the philosopher who re-creates epoch by epoch the productions of the spirit and of nature.[20]

We have already discussed the liability of general methodological precepts to variant interpretation and application. Such openness to variant appropriation is, however, by no means peculiar to grand methodology. Even at the level of specific experimental routines and recipes there is ample room for local adaptation, elaboration and grafting on to existing techniques. Huygens's air-pump, built and operated on the basis of reports of the ones constructed by Boyle, ended up as a quite different machine, differently used for different purposes.[21] Or consider the blowpipe: both its construction and its uses in mineralogical analysis underwent extensive development, with remarkably wide

---

[19] On the parallels between aesthetic and teleological judgement in Kant see M. Podro, *The Manifold in Perception*, Oxford, 1972, ch. 2.

[20] F. W. J. Schelling, *System of Transcendental Idealism*, trans. P. Heath, Charlottesville, Va., 1978, 217–22 and 229–32.

[21] S. Shapin and S. Schaffer, *Leviathan and the Air-Pump*, Princeton, NJ, 1985, ch. 6.

local divergences, between its introduction in Sweden in the 1740s and its general establishment as a standard and uncontroversial tool in the opening decades of the nineteenth century.[22] Examples could be multiplied. Such openness to variant interpretation, application and specification is crucial in the establishment of new procedures. For acceptance of methods proposed in one discipline, school or site of inquiry in other disciplines, schools or sites of inquiry depends on the extent to which the recipients see, or can be persuaded to see, the new methods as adaptable to their own interests and concerns and as in harmony rather than conflict with their own established practices. The roles of such appropriation and grafting in the establishment of new practices are brilliantly explored in Bruno Latour's *The Pasteurization of France.*[23] There he shows in detail how Pasteurian techniques were assimilated, and in the process of assimilation transformed, by the established practices and concerns of hygienists, farmers, agriculturalists and vets, military physicians and colonial administrators.

GENUINE INNOVATION

On pain of presenting disciplines as takers in of each others' dirty washing we must not overlook the occurrence of genuine methodological innovation within disciplines. In considering such innovations it is important to bear in mind the distinction between the practitioners of a discipline and other agents whose activities contribute to the discipline. Thus innovation may involve the recognition and elaboration by practitioners of practices tacitly adopted by other agents. Linnaeus's famous method of binomial nomenclature, for example, may well be derived from a form of abbreviation sporadically used by indexers of natural history books in the period.[24] On other occasions, however, change in the methods acknowledged by practitioners follows on systematic and articulate methodological innovation and refinement at the hands of other agents. To this class belong many of the changes

[22] See D. R. Oldroyd, 'Edward Daniel Clarke, 1769–1822, and his role in the history of the blow-pipe', *Annals of Science*, 29 (1972), 213–35.

[23] Trans. A. Sheridan, Cambridge, Mass., 1988.

[24] W. T. Stearn, 'The preparation of the *Species plantarum* and the introduction of binomial nomenclature', in *Linnaeus: Species plantarum 1753: Facsimile*, i, London, 1957, 67; see also J. L. Heller, 'The early history of binomial nomenclature', *Huntia*, 1 (1964), 33–76.

occasioned by the development of new instruments and the elaboration and refinement of existing instruments. The importance of such changes in instrumental methods can hardly be exaggerated: in a vast range of experimentally based disciplines it surely constitutes the primary mechanism productive of changes of scene of inquiry.

Turning to innovation at the hands of practitioners themselves, we may note that often the pattern is one of development at the level of tacit procedure followed by explicit recognition and articulation. For example, it has been shown by Henri Daudin that certain of the methods of classification of animals promoted in the opening decades of the eighteenth century are to be seen as articulations of already prevalent ways of arranging natural history cabinets.[25] To take another example from our chosen field of natural history, consider the *principe des connexions* propounded by Étienne Geoffroy Saint-Hilaire in his *Philosophie anatomique* of 1818. This principle states that the 'analogies' between parts of the various species of animals are to be established on grounds of correspondence in relative position, rather than on grounds of function and form: 'for an organ is rather changed, atrophied, or destroyed, than transposed'. Geoffroy's more dramatic applications of the principle, in drawing analogies between parts of vertebrates and parts of insects and molluscs, for example, were contentious and led him into a violent and celebrated controversy with Cuvier.[26] But the principle itself merely articulated and generalized what had long been a common tacit practice of anatomists (including Cuvier himself), especially in the naming and labelling of the parts of skeletons.

What of the outright and fully articulate methodological innovations with which great practitioners of the sciences are often credited? Doubtless they do occur; but at least in our chosen domain of natural history it is harder than one might expect to come up with clear-cut examples. I had at first supposed Linnaeus's announcement of binomial nomenclature in his *Philosophia botanica* of 1751 to be such a case; but as noted above this probably originated as an indexer's paper-saving device. After

[25] Daudin, *De Linné à Lamarck*, ch. 1, § 5.
[26] See T. A. Appel, *The Cuvier–Geoffroy Debate: French Biology in the Decades before Darwin*, New York, 1987.

considerable search I came up with another promising candidate, W. S. MacLeay's quinary system of classification, described by David Knight as follows:

> It was based on the idea that the various groups of animals could not be fitted into linear sequences, with the different members being placed higher and lower. Rather, the groups formed circles, in which the extremes met (as in Coleridge's philosophy). If, in MacLeay's view, the naturalist took the various characters of an organism into account, he would be able to see this circular arrangement; and he would find moreover that this circle touched other circles so as to form a bigger circle. The term 'quinary' was attached to the system because the various circles were seen as having five members . . . Each set of circles consisted of two big ones, containing the highest or 'typical' group, and the next or 'subtypical' one; while below them was another equal circle, containing three smaller circles occupied by the 'aberrant' groups.[27]

If only because of its apparent dottiness, this seemed to me likely to be an outright innovation. However, both the range of distinguished naturalists who adopted the quinary system—including T. H. Huxley at the beginning of his career—and Knight's cryptic reference to Coleridge should have put me on my guard. The hierarchy of circles of affinity is a common theme in *Naturphilosophie*, and as we saw in Chapter 2 the practice of disposing species, genera and families of living beings in circles had eighteenth-century precedents. Only in its numerological details, it seems, was MacLeay's method an example of outright innovation.

REMOTE FACTORS: SITES OF ORIGIN AND MODES OF DIFFUSION

So far we have merely categorized sources of the changes in method that shift the scenes of inquiry of disciplines. How are we to reach deeper explanations of such changes? The following remarks are, alas, both sketchy and speculative.

Crucial for the understanding and explanation of the methodological innovations that originate within disciplines is the investigation of the ways in which labour is delegated and divided amongst

---

[27] *The Age of Science*, Oxford, 1987, 95.

the agents of the discipline.[28] From such studies we may hope to find out, for example, why it is that in some cases instrumental and experimental practice shows a 'life of its own' for substantial periods, whereas in others there is close interaction between developments at the theoretical level and refinements of technique at the hands of instrument-makers, technicians and experimenters. Such studies may reveal the geography of methodology—the flow of techniques and methods between disciplinary communities: metropolitan and provincial, 'in the field' and in the museum, in the hospital and in the lab, etc.[29] And, on a larger scale, such studies may uncover the alliances and conflicts of method, interests and resources that mediate the formation, fusion, fragmentation and extinction of entire disciplines.

A related line along which one may seek a deeper understanding is investigation of the channels through which methods and techniques that originate in one discipline end up, often profoundly modified *en route*, being applied in other disciplines. In the course of his reflections on interdisciplinary exchanges. Ludwik Fleck distinguished four types of twentieth-century science, ranked from esoteric to exoteric: 'Journal science', 'Handbook or Vademecum Science', 'Textbook Science' and 'Popular Science'.[30] He offered a series of brilliant, if impressionistic, observations on the simplifications, regimentations and dramatizations undergone by scientific facts and theories as they pass from the untidy and debatable frontiers of research represented in Journal Science, through handbooks and textbooks into Popular Science. Popular Science he treated as a resource, a pool of 'facts' and 'concepts' which may be fed back into Journal Science, often in fields far removed from those in which they ultimately originated. Fleck's reflections are of obvious relevance to the kinds of transposition of methods and techniques discussed above.

---

[28] Recent studies which consider the social interactions of technicians, experimenters and theoreticians include P. Galison, 'Bubble chambers and the experimental workplace', in P. Achinstein and O. Hannaway, eds., *Observation, Experiment and Hypothesis in Modern Physical Science*, Cambridge, Mass., 1985; S. Schaffer, 'Astronomers mark time: discipline and the personal equation', *Science in Context*, 2 (1988), 115–45; S. Shapin, 'The House of Experiment in seventeenth-century England', *Isis*, 79 (1988), 373–404.

[29] Exemplary investigations of the interactions and division of labour between provincial and metropolitan, field and museum, practices are to be found in J. A. Secord, *Controversy in Victorian Geology: The Cambrian–Silurian Debate*, Princeton, NJ, 1986.

[30] *Genesis and Development of a Scientific Fact* [1935], Chicago, Ill., 1979, § 4.

Further profitable lines of inquiry are suggested by consideration of Fleck's category of Textbook Science, and, more generally, by consideration of the educational and other institutional arrangements through which practitioners enter disciplines. Despite the great diversity in means of recruitment to disciplines there are certain indisputably prevalent features of the handing on from generation to generation of disciplinary practices. To take a banal example, over a wide range of disciplines university teaching has long played a substantial role in the formation of competent practitioners. Historical study of university curricula is thus an obvious source of understanding of maintenance and change of disciplinary practices. For example, as noted above, the place of logic as a study preparatory to the 'higher' studies of medicine, law and theology in the curricula of Renaissance universities helps to explain the impact of the humanists' reforms of logic.

Curricula, especially in the idealized forms in which they figure in encyclopedias, university statutes, etc., generally embody not merely a classification of the disciplines, but also evaluative rankings. Such 'pecking orders' may play important roles in determining which disciplines serve as models of procedure and presentation for others. Consider, for example, medicine and philosophy in medieval and Renaissance Italian universities.[31] Throughout the period physicians were generally required to acquire doctorates not ony in medicine but also in philosophy, 'the queen of the sciences'; and medical writers tirelessly emphasized the special links between philosophy and medicine in order to promote the dignity of medicine and to allay the suspicion that it is a merely practical art concerned only with success in curing people. This valuation of philosophy was reflected in the obsessive care of medical writers to show that their works conformed strictly to the rules of inquiry and presentation in natural philosophy as laid down by Aristotle and interpreted by his commentators (especially the Commentator, Averroës). In the sixteenth century many Italian medical writers revolted against the tyranny of Aristotle and set up Galen as the supreme authority in his stead. However, the terms of reference remained largely philosophical; Galen figured not merely as arbiter of medical practice, but also as

---

[31] The following remarks are based on J. J. Bylebyl, 'Medicine, philosophy, and humanism in Renaissance Italy', in J. W. Shirley and F. D. Hoeniger, eds., *Science and the Arts in the Renaissance*, Washington, DC, 1985.

arbiter of method and presentation of contemplative or philosophical medicine.

One obvious instrument for the maintenance and distribution of disciplinary practices is the textbook. Take the Kant–Blumenbach programme in natural history discussed in Chapter 2. From the 1790s this programme provided a framework and inspiration for a very substantial number of natural historians, physiologists and anatomists, many of whom had never studied under Blumenbach at Göttingen and are most unlikely to have read and mastered the central theoretical articulation of the programme, Kant's difficult and abstract *Critique of Judgement*. How did this come about? Part of the answer is surely provided by Blumenbach's eminently readable *Handbuch der Naturgeschichte*, a textbook widely used in German universities in the period, in which the elements of the programme are conveyed in digestible form.[32]

Textbooks are often envisaged by historians as obstacles to progress, loci of conservatism and cultural lag. Certainly there are striking examples of this: strictly Aristotelian physics manuals still being set as university texts at the beginning of the eighteenth century; geocentric cosmology still alive and well in the nineteenth century in the context of handbooks of practical astronomy for use in military colleges, and so on. But even pedagogy has its crazes. The proliferation in Protestant universities in the latter half of the sixteenth century of textbooks laid out in accordance with the fashionable Ramist method of successive binary division of the subject matter of a discipline bears witness to one such craze.[33] Another remarkable example concerns medical teaching in the German lands in the opening decades of the nineteenth century.[34] Here we find an enormously increased role in textbooks played by the history of medicine, sometimes to the virtual exclusion of presentation of current practice and theory, an increase which reflects a comparable increase in the amount of lecturing on historical topics. This 'history craze' is closely associated with the Romantic movement in German medicine, with its emphasis on

[32] By 1810 the *Handbuch* had gone through at least ten editions.
[33] On Ramus's didactic impact see e.g. W. S. Howell, *Logic and Rhetoric in England, 1500–1700*, Princeton, NJ, 1956, ch. 4; P. Dibon, 'L'Influence de Ramus aux universités néerlandaises du XVIIᵉ siècle', *Actes du XI congrès international de philosophie*, 14 (Louvain, 1953), 307–11.
[34] H. von Seemen, *Kenntnis der Medizinhistorie in der deutschen Romantik*, Zurich, 1926.

history as a record of the manifestations of the original ideas which underlie all sound medical theory and practice. It is my suspicion that further research would show such pedagogic crazes to be more frequent and more substantial in their impact on the methods of the sciences than one might suppose.

A related way in which educators may preserve and communicate disciplinary norms is through use of a canon of exemplary or cautionary works. Didactic use of a canonical work may take many forms. The work may be variously commentated, explicated, epitomized, glossed or paraphrased. The teacher may interweave his own views with the original text as further material the authority might have composed had he addressed himself to specific topics, as replies he might have offered faced with particular objections, and so on. Passages from the work may be 'demonstrated', as when a sixteenth-century anatomical demonstrator illustrated loci in Galen's works by anatomizing a corpse. Or, in the case of works that belong to what Jonathan Rée has called 'the negative canon', the teacher may expatiate on the dire consequences of its methodological shortcomings.[35] Such is the sad status that Buffon's monumental *Histoire naturelle* acquired at the hands of Cuvier and other natural historians of the museum-based 'establishment' of natural history in the opening decades of the nineteenth century.[36] And such is the status that Goethe's and Schelling's ventures into natural history and natural philosophy acquired with the deconstruction of *Naturphilosophie* at the hands of von Helmholtz, T. H. Huxley, Émil du Bois-Reymond and other propagandists of the new natural science. These are all processes in which canonical works are made visible to students. Were we to confine our attention to use of a visible canon we might well conclude that the sciences have nowadays liberated themselves from this form of subservience to authority. However, even today a substantial didactic role is played by 'invisible' canonical works, those that are invoked or presupposed as warrants and authorities, but to whose texts students are rarely directly exposed. Such are the great 'unread masterpieces',

---

[35] On 'negative canons' see J. Rée, *Philosophical Tales*, London, 1987, 55 and *passim*.
[36] On the undermining of Buffon's reputation see Lepenies, *Das Ende der Naturgeschichte*, 139–68; also P. Corsi, *The Age of Lamarck: Evolutionary Theories in France, 1790–1830*, trans. J. Mandelbaum, Berkeley, Calif., 1988, ch. 1.

Newton's *Principia*, Keynes's *General Theory*, Dirac's *The Principles of Quantum Mechanics*.

In many present-day scientific disciplines laboratories and research institutes are the obvious sites of initiation. However, in considering the roles of practical and instrumental training in the tradition of disciplines it is important not to focus too exclusively on apprenticeship in technical competence. To start with it should be remembered how recently it was that systematic training in practical techniques became an integral part of education in the sciences. In anatomy, for example, regular training in techniques of dissection was instituted only in the course of the eighteenth century.[37] For at least two centuries before that medical students had regularly witnessed, and even on occasion taken part in, dissections. But the primary didactic function of such dissections had been the demonstration of points of doctrine in anatomy and animal economy, not the inculcation of the technical skills of dissection. In chemistry, physics and physiology the systematic teaching of experimental methods, through courses of practical work carried out by the students, was instituted only in the nineteenth century.[38] Cabinets of chemical and 'mathematical' instruments, and displays of their applications and efficacies, had indeed played major roles in the teaching of natural philosophy in the eighteenth century; and there is evidence that such teaching quite often involved student participation. But the primary purpose of such displays was again demonstration—of the marvels of God's creation, of the hidden powers of nature, of the virtuosity of the natural philosopher.[39]

REMOTE FACTORS: STIMULI TO CHANGE

The diversity of the social embodiments of scientific disciplines makes it risky to generalize about the sites of origin and modes of

[37] See T. Gelfand, 'The "Paris manner" of dissection: student anatomical dissection in early eighteenth century Paris', *Bulletin of the History of Medicine*, 46 (1972), 99–130.

[38] See e.g. J. B. Morrell, 'The chemist breeders: the research schools of Liebig and Thompson', *Ambix*, 19 (1972), 1–58; D. Cahan, 'The institutional revolution in German physics, 1865–1914', *Studies in the History of the Physical Sciences*, 15 (1985), 1–66; C. Jungnickel and R. McCormach, *Intellectual Mastery of Nature: Theoretical Physics from Ohm to Einstein*, i, Chicago, Ill., 1986, ch. 4; W. Coleman and F. L. Holmes, eds., *The Investigative Enterprise: Experimental Physiology in Nineteenth-Century Medicine*, Berkeley, Calif., 1988.

[39] See S. Schaffer, 'Natural philosophy and public spectacle in the eighteenth century', *History of Science*, 21 (1983), 1–43.

tradition and diffusion of methodological innovations. It makes it yet riskier to venture hypotheses about the exigencies, opportunities and deliberations that may stimulate such innovations.

Here we shall focus on institutional and technological factors that may provoke change in local methods and practices. (In the next chapter we shall discuss the roles of practitioners' deliberations about the legitimacy of methods and practices in bringing about methodological change in their disciplines.) An obvious starting-point is consideration of daily routines of work in past and present observations, academies, philosophical societies, mechanics institutes, museums, physic and botanic gardens, laboratories, research institutes, etc. The topic is a vast one, the subject of an exponentiating historical and sociological literature.[40] The following bare indications of major instigators of change makes no pretence at originality or completeness. Of paramount importance are changes in local repertoires of instruments, as are the interactions and exchanges of role between humans and machines: processes whereby, on the one hand, human practices are taken over and standardized as mechanical operations and, on the other hand, there are developed new technical skills in the installation, maintenance and use of instruments. Less commonly studied by historians of science is architectural innovation, in my view of the utmost importance in its conditioning of day-to-day routines, of patterns of communication among practitioners and between practitioners and their public, and of modes of exercise of authority and division of administrative, cognitive and instrumental labour.[41] It should be noted that none of these types of innovation will normally bring about immediate settlement into new methods and practices; the pattern will generally be one of more or less protracted interaction between methodological change and modi-

[40] See Ch. 4, n. 18.

[41] See O. Hannaway, 'Laboratory design and the aim of science: Andreas Libavius versus Tycho Brahe', *Isis*, 77 (1986), 585–610; S. Forgan, 'Context, image and function: a preliminary inquiry into the architecture of scientific societies', *British Journal for the History of Science*, 19 (1986), 89–113; S. Sheets-Pyenson, *Cathedrals of Science: The Development of Colonial Natural History Museums during the Late Nineteenth Century*, Kingston, Ontario, 1988; S. Forgan, 'The architecture of science and the idea of a university', *Studies in History and Philosophy of Science*, 20 (1989), 405–34; fascinating observations on the relations between layout of institutions, access to information, relations to the public, status and authority, and division of labour are to be found in E. Goffman, *The Presentation of Self in Everyday Life* [1959], London, 1967, ch. 3, and *Asylums*, London, 1968.

fication, adaptation and refurbishment of policies, instruments and housing.

In seeking to explain stability and change in disciplinary methods it is clearly important to consider the career patterns and social roles of their practitioners. A classic essay in explanation along these lines by Robert Westman concerns sixteenth-century astronomy.[42] Throughout the period many 'professional' mathematical astronomers evaluated astronomical hypotheses simply in terms of their predictive accuracy and convenience, either ignoring the issue of their truth or relegating it to natural philosophy. However, the latter part of the century saw an increased concern amongst astronomers with the truth or falsity of astronomical hypotheses, accompanied by an increasing preparedness to venture into natural philosophical territory in order to confirm or impugn them. Westman convincingly relates this methodological change to the establishment of a courtly context for the practice of astronomy in which the boundary between natural philosophy and 'mathematical' disciplines such as astronomy was less strictly maintained than in the universities, the traditional context for the study of astronomy. Turning to our chosen field of natural history, a strong case can be made out for a connection between the emergence of a repertoire of comparative methods in anatomy and physiology in the opening decades of the nineteenth century and the establishment of museums as sites of sustained employment of natural historians.[43] In the same period there is an evident connection between the development of methods for the study of plant and animal communities in relation to climate and geography and the opportunities of employment for naturalists offered by exploratory, colonial, missionary and mercantile expeditions.[44]

In connection with shifts of scene in natural history we have already had occasion to mention the importance of changes in the sources and types of material that accrue to museums and gardens and in the means of communication involved in the distribution of

[42] 'The astronomer's role in the sixteenth century: a preliminary study', *History of Science*, 18 (1980), 105–47; see also B. T. Moran, 'Christoph Rothmann, the Copernican theory, and institutional and technical influences in the criticism of Aristotelian cosmology', *Sixteenth Century Journal*, 13 (1982), 85–108.

[43] See e.g. Appel, *The Cuvier–Geoffroy Debate*, ch. 2.

[44] See J. Browne, *The Secular Ark: Studies in the History of Biogeography*, New Haven, Conn., 1983, ch. 2; M. Nicolson, 'Alexander von Humboldt, Humboldtian science and the origins of the study of vegetation', *History of Science*, 25 (1987), 167–94.

specimens, descriptions and illustrations. It has, for example, been argued by Scott Atran that the development of methods of systematic classification of plants at the end of the sixteenth century and in the opening decades of the seventeenth is to be seen in part as a response to the crisis engendered by the perceived misfits between the descriptions of plants inherited from the ancient Mediterranean and Near Eastern world and the specimens collected for medicinal and horticultural purposes in Northern Europe.[45] And we have endorsed the further suggestion that the development of ever more complex methods of classification of minerals, plants and animals in the course of the eighteenth century was a response to the almost exponential influx of new and exotic types occasioned by worldwide European colonial and commercial expansion. In the second half of the nineteenth century the establishment of specialist societies in the various branches of natural history is correlated with extensive enrolment and disciplined delegation of amateurs: in the collection and distribution of specimens; in the recording and mapping of distributions in relation to habitat; in the recording of climatic data; etc. Such recruitment was a major factor in the formation of the practices and methods of biogeography, ecology and meteorology.[46] Turning to the realm of communication, it is plausible to relate the substantial changes in the practice of anatomy in the first half of the nineteenth century, and, indeed, the consolidation of comparative anatomy as a discipline, to the opportunities for extensive comparative illustration opened up by the development of the steam press and the replacement of expensive copperplate engraving, first by the cheaper processes of lithography, then by the yet cheaper process of steel-plate engraving.[47]

Such flow of materials to and from 'centres of calculation'—museums, observatories, laboratories, research institutes, etc.—is

---

[45] *Fondements de l'histoire naturelle*, ch. 2.

[46] See D. E. Allen, *The Naturalist in Britain*, London, 1976, chs. 9–12. The importance of this recruitment in the formation of new disciplines was emphasized in unpublished papers delivered to the Cabinet of Natural History (Cambridge Group for the History of Natural History and Environmental Sciences) in the Michaelmas Term, 1989: J. Tucker, 'The Natural History of the Weather'; D. E. Allen, 'Formal Research Networks in Natural History: The Refining of a Technique'.

[47] See e.g. D. Knight, *Zoological Illustration*, Folkestone, 1977; L. Choulant, *History and Bibliography of Anatomic Illustration* [1852], trans. M. Frank, New York, 1962, 'Historical Introduction'.

a primary concern of the recently developed and now fashionable 'network theoretic' approach to the study of the sciences (to be discussed more fully in Chapter 9). In particular, Bruno Latour has written extensively on the patterns of enrolment and delegation which enable such centres of calculation to assemble, simplify and collate data from all over the world, and on the techniques by which they produce, replicate and distribute 'elaborated' materials—samples, illustrations, articles, tables, maps, etc.[48] Two aspects of Latour's network theoretic speculations on the cycles of accumulation and distribution controlled by 'centres of calculation' are of especial interest in the present context.

First there is his constant emphasis on the heterogeneity of the human and non-human agents and agencies whose enrolment and delegation make possible the reliable accumulation and effective distribution of facts and techniques by centres of calculation. Many of these 'actants' (as Latour calls them) operate at sites and in communities far removed from the spheres of activity of the practitioners of the discipline they affect. Thus, in the case of natural history Latour's approach would highlight the impacts on practitioners' methods and practices, and hence on scenes of inquiry, of the activities of collectors and their 'native' informants, their means of transport and livelihood, the devices they use to preserve dead or live specimens, etc. His approach would likewise give prominence to the effects on natural historical methods and practices of the expectations, requirements and tastes of the users of the products of natural history—physicians, horticulturalists and gardeners, agriculturalists and farmers, amateur enthusiasts.

Secondly, there is Latour's emphasis on the central role in the cycles of accumulation and distribution by centres of calculation of conventions and technologies of representation; in particular, of the 'cascades of representations'—involving descriptions and narratives, tables, graphs, diagrams, illustrations, etc.—whereby 'raw' information is progressively selected, simplified, collated and combined in the interests of amenability to analysis, of communicability, of aesthetic and literary effect and of didactic and polemical effectiveness.[49] Thus, following William Ivins and

---

[48] See e.g. B. Latour, *Science in Action: How to Follow Scientists and Engineers through Society*, Milton Keynes, 1987, ch. 6.

[49] 'Visualization and cognition: thinking with eyes and hands', *Knowledge and Society: Studies in the Sociology of Culture Past and Present*, 6 (1986), 1–40.

Stanley Edgerton, Latour draws attention to the magnitude of the impact on the sciences of the invention of linear perspective, whose 'optical consistency' makes possible images that can be transported, scaled up or down and variously combined without loss or distortion of crucial geometrical properties of the objects represented.[50] And, following Elizabeth Eisenstein and John Law, he details the impact on the sciences of printing, whose capacity faithfully to replicate texts and illustrations enhances the capacity of practitioners of the sciences to enrol and delegate distant allies, to wage paper war on distant enemies, and to devote their best efforts to the acquisition of new knowledge rather than to the preservation of existing knowledge.[51]

CONCLUSION

As noted at the beginning of this chapter, the diversity of the practices and social embodiments of the sciences provides grounds for circumspection in essaying generalizations about the sources of methodological innovation and consequent change in scenes of inquiry in the sciences. However, our discussion has provided a basis for some tentative hypotheses about factors that are of widespread efficacy in shifting scenes of inquiry.

First, two negative hypotheses: articulation of universally distributed 'common-sense' procedures probably does not play the substantial role with which it is often credited as a source of the methods of the sciences; and similar doubt attaches to claims for the power of pontifical disciplines—logic, epistemology, etc.—to dictate new methods to the sciences. In a positive vein I suggest that 'role model' disciplines, often disciplines that are not themselves counted as sciences, are frequent sources of new methods. A further important source is, I have argued, the articulation of tacit local practices.

With respect to remote factors affecting scenes of inquiry I have urged the importance of the changes in patterns of education and initiation into the sciences that arise in response to new demands,

[50] W. Ivins, *On the Rationalization of Sight*, New York, 1973; S. Edgerton, *The Renaissance Discovery of Linear Perspective*, New York, 1976.

[51] E. Eisenstein, *The Printing Press as an Agent of Change: Communication and Cultural Transformation in Early Modern Europe*, ii, Cambridge, 1979; J. Law, 'Les Textes et leurs alliés', in B. Latour and J. de Noblet, eds., *Les "Vues" de l'esprit, Culture Technique*, 14 (1985), 58–69.

new didactic fashions and ideologies, new patrons and new publics for the sciences. Equally important, I have suggested, are changes in local instrumental repertoires and in the administration and housing of the institutions of the sciences. Finally there is a range of factors connected with the flow of materials to and from the institutions of the sciences that I believe to be crucial as sources of change in the local methods and scenes of inquiry of the sciences. In this category are changes in the practices, interests and resources of the purveyors of materials, instruments and data to the sciences—surveyors, collectors, manufacturers of instruments and plant, architects, etc. Also in this category are changes in the interests and tastes of the users and consumers of the products of the sciences—practitioners of other disciplines, businesses, governments, interested amateurs, the general public, etc. And in this category too, vying in importance with changes in instrumental repertoires as instigators of shifts of scenes of inquiry in the sciences, are changes in the technologies and conventions of representation involved in the transmission, simplification, replication, communication and promotion of data, claims and techniques.

6

Legitimation and History

In the last chapter I considered the sites of origin and modes of diffusion and tradition of methods and practices in the sciences as well as certain of the technological and institutional opportunities and demands that may provoke methodological change, thereby shifting scenes of inquiry in the sciences. The concern of the present chapter is with the strategies of legitimation that may be used to promote and defend methods and practices. Strategies of legitimation play major roles in all scientific disciplines in securing compliance with new methods and continued adherence to old ones. They also play major roles, both direct and indirect, in stimulating change in the methods and practices of disciplines. Directly they may bring about change when critical attempts at the legitimation of methods and practices fail, thus creating pressure for their abandonment or modification. Indirectly they may affect methodological innovations because those who promote and articulate new methods or modify existing ones generally have an eye to their legitimacy by current standards, even if they do not offer explicit legitimations. (In many cases there is ample room for dispute about the role of legitimations—whether as genuine stimuli to methodological change or as *ex post facto* justifications for methodological innovations brought about by other means. This is an issue to which we shall return in Chapter 9.)

One primary context for the legitimation of established methods and practices is education. Thus, in textbooks we customarily find a wide range of legitimating strategies deployed in support of 'accepted' methods and practices—appeal to exemplary successes, to the authority of great scientists, to the practices exhibited in classic works, to conformity to 'the scientific method', etc. It is, indeed, no accident that exemplary successful applications of approved methods—Pasteur's refutation of Pouchet's demonstration of spontaneous generation; Semmelweis's establishment of the sources of puerperal fever; Bateson's replication of

Mendel's findings—are called 'textbook cases'. Through exercises on problems designed to yield tidy results given reasonable intelligence and a reasonable expenditure of effort the techniques of analysis and calculation standard in the 'exact sciences' are legitimated by their evident power to yield correct answers. Similarly, in the laboratory the standard experimental and instrumental methods are legitimated through replication of their performance on set-ups designed to ensure a confidence-inspiring success rate.

The strategies of legitimation that figure in the educational context are largely implicit, being built in to curricula, textbooks and laboratory routines rather than self-consciously deployed by teachers and demonstrators. For deliberate and explicit deployment of strategies of legitimation of methods the historian or sociologist is well advised to turn from the settled context of teaching to unsettled contexts of anomaly, polemic and conflict.

Methods and practices may be challenged at many different levels and on many different scales. Such challenges may arise locally when application of a method or technique yields results that are perceived as being at odds with those obtained by other methods or predicted on the basis of background theories accepted by proponents of a particular programme of research. They may arise from rivalry between individual practitioners in a given field. Consider, for example, the attempts to legitimate techniques of telescopic observation through calibration of long-focal-length refracting telescopes that was occasioned by the race between Huygens, J. D. Cassini the elder and Christopher Wren to solve the problem of Saturn's anomalous excrescences.[1] They may arise when experimental results obtained at one site of research cannot be replicated at others. Thus, to take an example that will be discussed in Chapter 9, failure of workers at other sites to replicate Joseph Weber's alleged detection of gravitational waves led to attempts to legitimate Weber's detection apparatus by calibration against 'surrogate' signals. Legitimation of methods may be provoked by conflict of factions within a discipline. Thus, as described below, conflict within the Royal College of Physicians in

---

[1] See A. van Helden, 'Eustachio Divini versus Christiaan Huyghens: a reappraisal', *Physis*, 12 (1870), 26–50; 'Saturn and his anses', *Journal for the History of Astronomy*, 5 (1974), 105–21; ' "Annulo cingitur", the solution of the problem of Saturn', *Journal for the History of Astronomy*, 5 (1974), 155–74.

the opening decades of the eighteenth century lay behind John Freind's attempts to legitimate a particular approach to the practice of medicine in his *History of Physick*. Finally, the conflicts which provoke legitimation of methods may involve entire disciplines or complexes of disciplines. Consider, for example, Claude Bernard's *An Introduction to the Study of Experimental Medicine*,[2] a work polemically directed against the 'medical empiricism' which elevated medical personality and tact over the 'independent and impersonal experimental method'. This famous defence of experimental method is to be seen, in part, as a response to the conflict between traditionalists in the French medical community and those who promoted the laboratory disciplines of histology, experimental pathology and general physiology as essential elements of medical training and practice.[3] Similarly, as we shall see, Kepler's attempt to justify a realist methodology in astronomy can be seen as one of a range of sixteenth- and seventeenth-century epistemological responses to the long-standing conflict between mathematical astronomy and natural philosophy, a conflict initially occasioned by the inconsistencies between orthodox Aristotelian cosmology and the planetary models used by astronomers for predictive purposes and greatly exacerbated with the advent of Copernican planetary models.

The types of legitimation of methods and practices are as varied as the contexts of legitimation. The following rough taxonomy makes no pretence at exhaustiveness.

First, there is rationalization, the legitimation of methods by appeal to explicit norms, whether commonplace or emanating from such pontifical disciplines as logic and philosophy. Then there is vindication, the legitimation of methods in terms of their reliability and power. The species of vindication with which we are mainly concerned in this work is calibration, vindication by testing of a method against precedents and standards. We shall also have occasion to mention 'causal vindication', in which a causal account of the operation of a method is used to demonstrate its reliability. A third category is that of invocation of authority: of a classic paper, a canonical text, a founding father, a governing

---

[2] Paris, 1865.

[3] On the institutional conflicts which motivated Bernard's defence of experimental method see e.g. J. E. Lesch, *Science and Medicine in France: The Emergence of Experimental Physiology, 1790–1855*, Cambridge, Mass., 1984.

institution, the judgement of men of *bon sens*, the decision of a
tribunal of experts, etc. A fourth category is that of appeal to
social, political, professional or factional interests. A fifth is that of
appeal to literary, poetic or aesthetic sensibilities. Rationalization
and vindication, as envisaged here, are second-order methods—
methods for the legitimation of methods. Appeal to authority,
interests and aesthetic or literary sensibility, however, may come
into play either as second-order methods for the promotion of
methods or, more typically, as first-order methods for the
promotion of factual claims, hypotheses and theories.

In this chapter I shall attempt only to illustrate the various types
of legitimation by concentrating on a major setting for their use,
the writing of histories of scientific disciplines. The legitimating
uses of history come into play in both the principal contexts of
legitimation, the educational and the polemical; and they are, I
believe, of great importance in explaining shifts of scene of
inquiry. Moreover, they are of special concern to us given our
interest in calibration of methods against precedents and standards;
for calibration is an intrinsically historical activity.

In Part II of this work I shall consider certain types of
legitimation—calibration, appeal to interests, appeal to literary
and aesthetic sensibilities—in greater detail; and I shall address
the question of the relative effectiveness of these types of
legitimation in shifting and stabilizing scenes of inquiry.

HISTORY IN THE SCIENCES

Present-day scientists tend to dismiss out of hand the suggestion
that historical inquiry and writing are important, indeed indispensable, components of scientific inquiry. They do not, of course,
deny that writing up scientific work involves retailing events in the
recent past, that in replicating experiments and calibrating
instruments past experimental performances have to be taken into
account, that in writing review articles it is customary to use the
'classic' books and articles of the past decade or so to provide a
context for current developments. Nor do they deny that under
special circumstances a scientist may have to engage in the more
remote history of a discipline; that the astronomer interested in
supernovae may have to consult ancient astronomical records; that
the taxonomic botanist may have to study obscure eighteenth-

century publications and their exact provenances in order to establish the names of plants valid under the International Code of Botanical Nomenclature; that the pharmacologist on the look-out for naturally occurring drugs may have to turn to the account of ancient Chinese herbal lore in Needham's *Science and Civilisation in China*. Scientists do, however, habitually disavow a regular involvement in historical reflections that extend beyond the realms of currently relevant data, arguments and hypotheses. History of science, they are apt to maintain, is an 'arts' subject. It has a modest role in the teaching of the sciences, it is dabbled in by popular science writers and it is suitable as a hobby for retired scientists, but it is certainly not an integral part of the pursuit of science itself.

This perception of the present-day role of history in science is, I think, quite mistaken. It is misleading even if we confine our attention to the kind of science that informs most scientists' self-images, that is, research-oriented science—in Ludwik Fleck's terminology 'Journal Science'. The most sedate and routine specialist papers often cite earlier works for reasons that have more to do with the persuasive power of precedents and authorities than with relevant data and arguments. Such concern with the past is especially marked when the claims and methods advanced are controversial ones. For example, in the early years of the 'plate-tectonic' revolution in geology and geophysics there was extensive discussion of the history of those disciplines, discussion that extended far beyond the realms of likely sources of relevant factual or theoretical information.[4] A comparable disposition on the part of practitioners to wallow in history is at present evident in the various disciplines affected by what many see as the imminent break-up of the neo-Darwinian synthesis in the life sciences. Equally remarkable in the extent to which they range outside the bounds of historical concern usually acknowledged by scientists are the historical writings occasioned by priority disputes. A striking recent example is provided by the dispute between Luc Montagnier and R. C. Gallo over priority in isolation of the AIDS virus. A series of partisan histories played an important role in the conduct in the dispute. Moreover, the

---

[4] See R. Laudan, 'Redefinitions of a discipline: histories of geology and geological history', in L. Graham, W. Lepenies and P. Weingart, eds., *Functions and Uses of Disciplinary Histories*, Dordrecht, 1983.

Local Reality*

settlement of the dispute, conducted at government ministerial level, not only partitioned the patent rights between the parties but sanctioned the deal with an 'official' history in which the intellectual spoils were shared out to the exclusion of third parties.[5] As argued in the last chapter, there is good reason in considering changes in disciplinary practices not to confine our attention to esoteric or 'Journal Science'. But when we consider present-day 'Textbook Science' and 'Popular Science', the centrality of history becomes obvious. Much popular science writing is explicitly historical. And narrative histories—of anticipations of present theories, of exemplary research leading to discoveries, of invention and refinement of instruments and techniques—are a crucial resource in the didactic repertoires of science textbooks at all levels.

The historiography of disciplines, like other brands of historiography, has undergone complex and radical changes since the emergence of disciplinary history as a widespread genre in the late Renaissance.[6] The account of these changes which follows is simplified in the extreme. In particular, it should be noted that whilst it is convenient to recognize 'epochs' of historiography—doxographic, erudite (or Humanist), pragmatic (or Enlightened), heroic (or Romantic), positivist (or Modern)—such a periodization imposes inevitable distortions.

The roots of late-Renaissance historiography of the arts and sciences are to be found in two classical genres, 'history of inventions' (heurematography) and doxography. In histories of inventions notable practical discoveries and their authors are listed, usually in chronological order. In doxographies the sayings, opinions, works and foibles of notable practitioners of a discipline are retailed. Often, on the classical precedent of Diogenes Laertius' much emulated *Lives of Famous Philosophers*, the practitioners of a discipline are assigned to sects, each with a founding father and a master–pupil succession.

Fifteenth- and sixteenth-century disciplinary histories are usually located in the prefaces to textbooks and epitomes. They generally

[5] A chilling account is in C. J. Tuckfield, 'Naming the AIDS virus: the AIDS dispute as science', M.Phil. thesis, Cambridge, 1987.

[6] My account owes much to the following synoptic works: D. von Engelhardt, *Historisches Bewusstsein in der Naturwissenschaft von der Aufklärung bis zum Positivismus*, Munich, 1979; L. Braun, *Histoire de l'histoire de la philosophie*, Paris, 1973.

attribute the origins of entire disciplines to the efforts of a few inspired heroes and sages of remote antiquity, though in the latter part of the century we find increased recognition of the gradual and painful nature of the growth of learning. Flourishing and decay in the history of a discipline are often associated with the rise and fall of empires and with celestial and climatic influences. In the great majority of such histories the emphasis throughout is on specific noteworthy opinions and on useful discoveries and applications, rather than on past hypotheses or theories.

In the course of the sixteenth century there emerges the more systematic and critical genre of erudite or 'philological' history of disciplines, a genre typified by Vossius's *De universae mathesios natura et constitutione liber* of 1650 and Riccioli's monumental *Almagestum novum astronomiam veterum novamque complectens* of 1651. Such histories show a minute and encyclopaedic concern with questions of chronology, attribution and provenance. They often venture judgements about the values of the views of past authors that they retail; and on occasion they take stands in the 'battle of the ancients and moderns', the then controversial issue of the superiority of ancient learning. However, theoretical progress and its causes rarely loom large in erudite histories.

Around the turn of the seventeenth century erudite histories of the arts and sciences come under widespread attack for their pedantry, their concern with learned men rather than learning itself, their lack of concern with the causes of the growth of learning, and, above all, their lack of relevance to the current practice of disciplines. All this is rectified in the 'pragmatic' histories of the sciences that play so central a role in the ideology of Enlightenment. Pragmatic history is typified by the splendid histories of astronomy and mathematics that emanated from the Académie des Sciences in the latter part of the eighteenth century. A fine specimen of pragmatic history in our chosen field of natural history is James Edward Smith's *Discourse on the Rise and Progress of Natural History* of 1788. All these works take for granted the victory of the moderns over the ancients. The history of the sciences is now confidently reconstructed as a progress towards their current superior status: in a famous definition of the period, pragmatic history is 'the science of the formation of the present'. Theoretical and practical development of disciplines, rather than the lives and opinions of their practitioners, become the central motifs. And there is much concern with the causes of progress in the sciences. In addition to discussion of such traditionally invoked stimuli as climate and national temperament we find extensive and varied treatments of the roles of education, learned academies and journals in the advancement of learning as well as reflections on the roles of genius, ambition and the pursuit of rational methods. Above all, pragmatic histories are openly didactic in intent, concerned to show how reason properly applied triumphs over superstition and fantasy to unveil truth.

At the end of the eighteenth century there is a widespread and radical shift in historical consciousness in the sciences. In the Romantic period all the central assumptions of pragmatic historiography are called in question. Where pragmatic histories had treated past beliefs as timelessly open to inspection and judgement, in Romantic historiography they figure as hidden treasures, to be excavated only by the historian capable of entering into the spirits of past ages and authors. Where pragmatic historians had regarded the doctrine of an ancient divinely inspired knowledge of the sciences as a mere superstition, Romantic historians appeal to an original intuitive understanding of nature concealed in folk-wisdom and the myths of the ancients. Pragmatic historians had presupposed a single line of progress culminating in the present. For Romantic historians the true and original ideas of the sciences have been variously elaborated by different nations at different times; since 'every age is immediate to God', it is both misguided and impious to attribute wholesale error to past ages. Pragmatic historians had treated progress as causally explicable, as the outcome of education, patronage and the application of sound methods. Where genius was invoked, it was genius controlled by rational procedure and discourse. For Romantic historians the growth and differentiation of knowledge is not to be accounted for in such mechanical ways; for what is at issue is the free creativity of genius through which ideas become articulated and embodied.

In Romantic historiography the connection between the sciences and their history assumes a special intimacy. Each science was supposedly built around certain 'original ideas' inherited from the depths of antiquity when mankind was more closely in harmony with nature; and its history consists in the varied elaboration and specification of those ideas. On this view study of the history of a science may, to the extent that it uncovers its original ideas, affect its most fundamental presuppositions. It is a further standard Romantic doctrine that the history of the human spirit, as manifested in cultural history, shows significant parallels with the developmental history of the cosmos as a whole, of the earth, and of living beings. Indeed, for Schelling and his disciples these histories are not ultimately distinct, but rather to be seen as inner and outer manifestations of one and the same history of *Geist*.

Full-blooded Romantic historiography of the sciences never achieved currency outside the German lands, and even there its reign was brief. By the 1870s it had perished in the onslaught on German idealism in general and *Naturphilosophie* in particular. However, certain themes of Romanticism live on. Thus in scientific biographies cast in the heroic mould, with their geniuses of humble origins triumphing over obstacles and prejudices to attain great discoveries and lasting fame, we may discern the plot structure of the Romantic folk tale. And in the organic metaphors of birth, growth, differentiation and decay of disciplines, movements and ideas we have an apparently ineradicable legacy of Romanticism.

The opening decades of the nineteenth century see the articulation of the current disciplinary category of 'natural science'. In the latter part of the century the ideological divide between natural sciences and human or 'moral' sciences (*Geisteswissenschaften*) becomes ever wider. In the 1850s and 1860s the first stages in the formation of history of science as an autonomous discipline are attested by the establishment of specialist societies and journals. At the same time we find natural scientists, often in explicit reaction against the historicism of *Naturphilosophie*, insisting on the irrelevance of history to the serious practice of the sciences. This is in striking contrast to philosophy and the human sciences, in which we find in the same period ever deeper immersion in history.

Both scientists' and historians' histories of science in the post-Romantic period show many continuities with the pragmatic historiography of the Enlightenment. In particular, the pragmatic obsession with progress persists. Indeed, there is an ever greater insistence on the inevitability and linearity of scientific progress.[7]

---

[7] On this *Fatalisierung* of the natural sciences see von Engelhardt, *Historisches Bewusstsein in der Naturwissenschaft von der Aufklärung bis zum Positivismus*, 166.

A further notable feature of much of the historiography of science in the post-Romantic period is its loss of the Romantic vision of the history of the sciences as an integral part of general cultural history. Along with this there is an almost total imperviousness to developments in general historiography. Thus, as von Engelhardt has noted, the vast debates on the methods, aims and cognitive status of history associated with the names of von Ranke, Droysen and Dilthey left the practice and theory of the history of science almost entirely untouched.[8]

STRATEGIES OF HISTORICAL LEGITIMATION

Despite the substantial changes of genre and presupposition just retailed, many of the legitimating uses of disciplinary history have persisted from the sixteenth century to the present day. By way of introduction to our four examples, let us consider some of these strategies in general terms. Though our primary concern is with the legitimation of methods, it behoves us to touch on a wider range of the uses of history; for, as will become evident from the examples, promotion of particular methods and styles of inquiry is often bound up with the advancement of other interests and causes—personal, factional, doctrinal and disciplinary.[9]

Most widespread and most straightforward is the use of history to legitimate a discipline as a whole. Standard strategies include appeal to its age, to the heroic status and achievements of its founders, to its record of practical utility, to its theoretical achievements and insights, to its contributions to other valuable disciplines, to its educational value and edifying power.

More specific, and often more devious, are the uses of history to legitimate within a discipline some particular practitioner, group, institution, methodology, style of inquiry, paradigm or research programme. Let us, for want of a better term, call such potentially competing components of a discipline 'factions'. One notable strategy (and the one that has the most legitimate claim to the title 'legitimation') is that of showing a faction to be the true heir to the

---

[8] On this *Fatalisierung* of the natural sciences see von Engelhardt, *Historisches Bewusstsein in der Naturwissenschaft von der Aufklärung bis zum Positivismus*, 220.

[9] Useful discussions of strategies of historical legitimation of disciplines and factions are to be found in Graham *et al.*, eds., *Functions and Uses of Disciplinary Histories*.

legacy of the founders or reformers of a discipline—to represent genuinely Hippocratic medicine, genuinely Newtonian natural philosophy, genuinely Darwinian evolutionary biology, genuinely Wundtian psychology, genuinely Freudian analysis. Often, there is dispute about the identity of the true founders or reformers of a discipline, about the nature of the founders' bequest, and about the identity of its beneficiaries. The strategy of affiliation is accordingly often backed up with characterizations of the putative founders or reformers designed to substantiate their authoritative status and the canonical standing of their works. Their mighty endeavours and discoveries are retailed, as are the great errors they opposed and vanquished. Their views, methods and works are, needless to say, so described as to highlight just those aspects that anticipate or prefigure the views, methods and works associated with the faction whose legitimation is being attempted. We have already, for example, had occasion to note the diversity of disciplinary factions that have constructed a Bacon, a Newton or a von Haller in their own images. Another striking instance is provided by the ways in which both protagonists of behaviouristic and positivistic approaches in psychology and protagonists of the new 'cognitive science' have sheltered under the mantle of Wundt, the acknowledged creator of psychology as a respectable experimentally based member of the natural sciences.[10]

An important related strategy of legitimation, to which Gaston Bachelard and Thomas Kuhn have drawn attention, may be called 'normalization'.[11] Here the history of a discipline is so reconstructed as to make the stance of a particular faction, however innovatory, revolutionary or aberrant it may in fact be, appear to be a matter of course, the natural or even inevitable culmination of the development of the discipline. Normalization may take many forms. The methods and concerns of major past practitioners may be represented as the same in substance as those of the faction in

[10] See M. G. Ash, 'The self-presentation of a discipline: history of pyschology in the United States between pedagogy and scholarship', in Graham *et al.*, eds., *Functions and Uses of Disciplinary Histories.* Other studies of diverse interpretations and appropriations of father-figures are L. S. Jacyna, 'Images of John Hunter in the nineteenth century', *History of Science*, 21 (1983), 85–108, and C. J. Lawrence, 'Cullen, Brown and the poverty of essentialism', in W. F. Bynum and R. Porter, eds., *Brunonianism in Britain and Europe, Medical History*, Suppl. 8, London, 1988.

[11] G. Bachelard, *L'Activité rationaliste de la physique contemporaine*, Paris, 1951; T. S. Kuhn, *The Structure of Scientific Revolutions*, ch. 11.

question, however much they may in fact have differed. Similarly, past hypotheses and theories may be retrospectively refurbished and tidied up so as to make them appear as anticipations or special cases of those held by the faction in question. The doctrinal and methodological normality of the faction being legitimated may be contrasted with the aberrations from sound tradition of rival factions. And so on.

Both affiliation to father figures and normalization are strategies designed to minimize the shock of the new. They are thus in potential conflict with strategies which attempt to justify a disciplinary faction by appeal to its breaks with past error, its reforming zeal, its unprecedented discoveries, its radical policies. This is by no means the only conflict that may have to be negotiated by one who would deploy history in the service of a faction. Further tensions may arise, for example, from the need to appear impartial and objective whilst avoiding giving credit to rival factions. They may arise too from the need to emphasize the beneficial practical consequences of a new programme without appearing to abandon the pure disinterested pursuit of knowledge.

DISCIPLINARY HISTORIES: FOUR EXAMPLES

The first of our four examples belongs to the genre of doxographic history described above. Tycho Brahe's *De disciplinis mathematicis oratio* (delivered in 1574, but not published in his lifetime) opens by praising the excellence, certainty, dignity, utility, educational value and edifying power of mathematical studies.[12] After a brief survey of the branches of mathematics, Tycho talks of origins. Geometry arose, as Herodotus tells, in Egypt where it was used after the annual flooding of the Nile to redetermine the field boundaries. The practical value of mathematics is further illustrated by Archimedes' marvellous devices used to repel the Roman naval attack on Syracuse. Astronomy, noblest of the progeny of mathematics, is of the greatest antiquity. It was invented by Adam, saved from the flood by Seth's descendants, who inscribed their astronomical lore on pillars of stone, and thence passed on to

---

[12] *Tychonis Brahe Dani opera omnia*, i, ed. J. L. E. Dreyer, Copenhagen, 1913. I discuss Tycho's oration in *The Birth of History and Philosophy of Science: Kepler's* A Defence of Tycho against Ursus *with Essays on its Provenance and Significance*, Cambridge, 1984, 262–4.

Abraham. From Abraham it passed to the Egyptians and thence to Pythagoras and the Greeks. Tycho then traces a succession of astronomers, Timocharis, Hipparchus of Rhodes, Ptolemy, al-Battani and, finally, Copernicus, whose system whilst physically absurd is mathematically superior to Ptolemy's. To Ptolemy and Copernicus all current knowledge in astronomy is owed.

We see here a use of history standard in the period, the promotion of a discipline by vaunting its age, dignity and utility. There is, however, a hint of a more subtle concern on Tycho's part to legitimate his own concerns and methodological stance within the discipline. It was very common in the period to consider mathematical astronomy as devoted entirely to the practical business of prediction of celestial phenomena, without regard to the issue of the physical truth of the hypotheses employed. Tycho's own commitment to the minority view of astronomy as concerned with the truth about the cosmos is indicated both by his castigation of Copernicus's system as physically absurd, and by his talk of contributions to knowledge. Further, the way in which Tycho juxtaposes Ptolemy and Copernicus creates a space for his own enterprise, that of constructing a system that reconciles the physical truth in Ptolemy's earth-centred system with the mathematical superiority of Copernicus's sun-centred system.

Our second example, Johann Kepler's *Apologia pro Tychone contra Ursum* (Defence of Tycho against Ursus) (written *c.*1601) is, on Kepler's own description, a specimen of 'philological' history.[13] It is, however, atypical of the genre in its concern with theoretical progress and the means whereby it comes about.

The work is a reply to a *Tractatus de astronomicis hypothesibus* published in 1597 by Nicolai Reymers Baer (Ursus), Mathematician to the Holy Roman Emperor, Rudolph II. Ursus's *Tractatus* is a violently polemical and scurrilous reply to Tycho Brahe's charge that he had plagiarized Tycho's new world-system. Ursus's riposte proceeds along curious lines. He does indeed deny the charge of plagiarism and make a counter-charge. But his primary strategy, reminiscent of the fable of the fox and the grapes, is to belittle the issue. Tycho's charge is, he claims, misguided because there is no question of priority, the system claimed for himself by Tycho

---

[13] Text and trans. in N. Jardine, *The Birth of History and Philosophy of Science*, ch. 5.

having been proposed in antiquity by Apollonius of Perga. Ursus argues further that the true disposition of the cosmos is inaccessible to us. Alternative astronomical hypotheses are to be judged simply in terms of their capacity to 'save the celestial phenomena'. Moreover, he claims, it is easy to devise a variety of hypotheses adequate for this purpose; so it is absurd of Tycho to make such a fuss as if a discovery of the true nature of the world were at issue. Ursus backs up these claims with a 'history of astronomical hypotheses'. In part, this is designed to substantiate the assertion that Apollonius of Perga had proposed the world-system claimed for himself by Tycho. Moreover, by presenting his history in jocular fashion as a sequence of predictive devices that are patently absurd if taken literally, Ursus evidently seeks to provide inductive support for his claim that the truth about the disposition of the cosmos is inaccessible to men.

The historical chapters of Kepler's refutation of Ursus treat the ancient history of astronomy in considerable detail, and contain substantial and original reconstructions of ancient astronomical hypotheses. Scattered throughout the work are reflections on the methods conducive to progress in astronomy and the factors that have fostered it. One manifest aim of Kepler's history of astronomy is to quash Ursus's suggestion that Tycho's system had been proposed in antiquity by Apollonius of Perga. A second principal aim is to vindicate against Ursus's scepticism the view that portrayal of the form of the cosmos is not only the proper aim of astronomy, but also an aim that it can achieve. As noted earlier, this 'realist' stance, held by Tycho, Kepler and Kepler's teacher, Michael Maestlin, was in the period a minority position amongst professional astronomers. Along with a variety of telling philosophical arguments Kepler mounts a historical defence of his position. The great theoreticians and practitioners of astronomy, Aristotle, Ptolemy, Copernicus and Tycho himself, are cited as proponents of the realist view of the task of astronomy. Moreover, the historical treatment as a whole is clearly designed to counter Ursus's pessimistic scepticism-inducing chronicle of absurd hypotheses with an optimistic account of astronomers' achievement of progressively more accurate depictions of the world.

Fifthly, [Ursus] despairs of true hypotheses in astronomy, holding everything to be uncertain in the Pyrrhonian manner. No one denies that there are still some flaws in even the best-constructed astronomy, and hence in the hypotheses also. That is why even today there is so much labour expended on repair. Let no one say that therefore all the rest is uncertain. Ptolemy discovered by means of astronomy that the sphere of the fixed stars is furthest away, Saturn, Jupiter and Mars follow in order, the sun is nearer than they, and the moon nearest of all. These things are certainly true and consonant with the form of the universe. He also postulated too great an ascent and descent of the moon. Regiomontanus and Copernicus discovered that from this hypothesis there follows something false and not in accord with the apparent magnitude of the moon. So they said that the moon does not make such great jumps up and down. And who doubts that this is the way things are in the heavens? And who, I ask, but a melancholic and despairing person would have doubts about the ratios of the diameters of the earth, sun and moon? Thus today there is practically no one who would doubt what is common to the Copernican and Tychonic hypotheses, namely, that the sun is the centre of motion of the five planets, and that this is the way things are in the heavens themselves—though in the meantime there is doubt from all sides about the motion or stability of the sun. Given that with the help of astronomy so many things have already been established in the realm of physical knowledge, things which deserve our trust from now on and which are truly so, Ursus' despair is groundless.[14]

In arguing for the attainability of knowledge of the form of the cosmos Kepler has to contend with a phenomenon of which Ursus had made effective use, the existence of inconsistent hypotheses about the real celestial motions that have exactly the same consequences in the realm of the apparent celestial motions. In reply Kepler argues that conformity to the apparent celestial motions is not the sole ground for choice between astronomical hypotheses.[15] In particular he refers to the dynamic and architectonic reasons he had adduced in support of a Copernican cosmology in his earlier work *Mysterium cosmographicum.* In his history of astronomy Kepler legitimates appeal to physical considerations by emphasizing the role that appeal to such consideration has in fact played in the development of astronomy.

As well as using the history of astronomy to vindicate his and Tycho's realist views on the status, aims and methods of astronomy, Kepler deploys it with considerable subtlety in support of his own Copernican convictions. Given that he is defending Tycho in a work that Tycho had in effect commissioned, he is understandably restrained. As the above quotation shows, he has

[14] Ibid. 147.   [15] Ibid. 140–3.

no hesitation in openly promoting the common ground between Tycho and Copernicus—'the sun is the centre of motion of the five planets'—as a culmination of progress in astronomy. The way in which he does so is a fine example of the strategy of normalization mentioned above, both in its glossing over of the disparities between Copernicus's and Tycho's systems and in its representation of what was in fact the view of a tiny minority as a general consensus. There are, however, passages that are clearly, if unemphatically, designed to validate the Copernican cosmology. There is the mention of the physical reasons that can be cited in its support. There is the sheer enthusiasm with which the Copernican system is described in the course of a demonstration of Ursus's misconceptions about it. And, perhaps most effectively of all by the 'philological' standards of the period, there is the painstaking translation and reconstruction of a problematic passage in Aristotle's *De caelo* that enables Kepler to attribute heliocentrism to the later Pythagoreans and thus to demonstrate the antiquity of the germs of the Copernican system.[16]

The third of our examples is John Freind's *History of Physick, from the Time of Galen to the Beginning of the Sixteenth Century: Chiefly with Regard to Practice* (1725–6). This is the first major history of medicine in English. Its central motifs, the master–pupil succession and the linking of the fortunes of the discipline with the rise and fall of empires, are typical of the genre of erudite history, as is the concern with questions of attribution and chronology. As with many erudite histories, it is at first sight hard to detect the motivation for the apparently haphazard compilation of learned material. The reader is apt to be further baffled by Freind's many digressions, with their often waspish comments on such diverse topics as the credentials of other scholars, the value of particular therapeutic practices, and the reports of werewolves in Ireland (which he appears to endorse). However, a fascinating recent paper by Julian Martin shows that read in the context of Freind's career and the controversies of the period within the medical profession the *History of Physick* emerges as a cogent polemical work.[17]

Freind had strong Jacobite sympathies, and a corresponding

[16] N. Jardine, *The Birth of History and Philosophy of Science*, 161–3.

[17] 'Explaining John Freind's *History of Physick*', *Studies in History and Philosophy of Science*, 19 (1988), 399–418.

respect for tradition, the lessons of history, and the sacred nature of the gift of healing (as manifest in Christ's and the apostles' miracles of healing and in the cure of scrofula by the Royal Touch of the Stuart monarchs). He was also a champion of the Newtonian medical theory of Archibald Pitcairne (1652–1713), in which the body was treated as a hydraulic machine. Associated with the Newtonian theory was a body of therapeutic practices whose efficacy was explained in terms of restoration of mobility to the bodily fluids. In the case of treatment of fevers, the prime focus of controversy in the period, the therapeutic regime included, on the one hand, procedures of 'evacuation' (bleedings, vomits, purges, sweats, etc.) designed to rid the body of 'morbific' matter and over-thick blood and, on the other hand, procedures of 'corroboration' (rests, baths, cordials, etc.) designed to fortify the patient against the disease and the debilitating side-effects of evacuation. This Newtonian medicine had only recently gained the ascendancy at the Royal College of Physicians after a prolonged and bitter battle in which Freind had played an active part. As Martin points out, the Jacobite and Newtonian commitments of Freind and his teachers at Oxford were not unrelated, both being founded on a belief in a universe and society uniformly governed by God's wise and incontrovertible laws.

In the *History of Physick* Freind reacts strongly against two of his main sources, Daniel LeClerc and J. K. Barckhausen.[18] LeClerc he denounces for having treated the Paracelsian system as the culmination of theoretical progress in medicine; Barckhausen is criticized for having concentrated on the history of medical theory at the expense of medical practice. Freind's contention is that the only progress to be discerned in the history of medicine is practical progress. Through judicious reading of the ancient authors combined with personal observation, learned physicians have been able to build on the therapeutic experience of their predecessors. This practical progress culminates in the therapeutic regimes associated with Newtonian medicine. At the level of theory, however, Freind denies any such progress. In his view all the theoretical speculations that preceded the certain and evident Newtonian system have yielded equally ill-founded and pre-

---

[18] D. LeClerc, *Histoire de la médecine*, Paris, 1723 (Freind's target is the account of post-classical medicine appended to this edition); J. K. Barckhausen, *Historia medicinae . . .*, Amsterdam, 1710.

sumptuous hypotheses. Thus Freind's history contrives to make the tradition of sound medical practice and the Newtonian medical theory appear complementary and mutually supportive.

Martin shows how Freind's historical legitimation of a particular medical theory and practice is reinforced by his promotion of a particular view of the physician's role. In keeping with his Jacobite sympathies, Freind's history emphasizes both the sanctity of the physicians' calling and the paramount role of tradition in the formation of a true healer. He repeatedly condemns 'free-thinkers', proponents of non-Newtonian medical systems, who base their theories on their own arrogant speculations without taking account of the accumulated wisdom and experience of the succession of learned physicians. Thomas Linacre, the founder of the Royal College of Physicians, figures in the *History of Physick* as the type of the wise physician deferential to the traditions of the ancients, and the subsequent history of the College is blandly presented as an uninterrupted learned succession. Thus the Newtonian faction is 'normalized' by glossing over the recent battles within the College. Instead of being a place of wrangling and dissent the College is made to appear as the current locus of the learned succession of physicians, a succession that goes back to Hippocrates and culminates in the persons of Freind and his Newtonian allies.

Our final example is a work that shows extraordinary variety and subtlety in its strategic uses of history. In 1803 the natural historian and comparative anatomist Georges Cuvier (aged only 26) and the astronomer and historian J.-B. J. Delambre were appointed Perpetual Secretaries to the First Class, *Sciences mathématiques et physiques*, of the Institut National. In 1808, on government orders, Cuvier presented to the Imperial Council of State his *Rapport historique sur les progrès des sciences naturelles depuis 1789*. Delambre presented the companion volume on *sciences mathématiques*. In terms of genre Cuvier's work may be regarded as a specimen of pragmatic history, though the attitudes to progress and rationality in the sciences are more uneasy and nuanced than is usual in the genre. The following account, much indebted to the work of Dorinda Outram,[19] teases out but a few of the strands in Cuvier's cunning web.

[19] *Georges Cuvier: Vocation, Science and Authority in Post-Revolutionary France*, Manchester, 1984.

At the most general and explicit level Cuvier is concerned to promote an image of the sciences and their institutions that will show them to be worthy objects of state support. Recent political history had rendered his task a delicate one. The speculative systems thrown up by savants were widely perceived in the period as having been a major incitement to the recent social and political disruptions. Moreover, the closure in 1803 of the Second Class of the Institut, *Sciences morales et politiques*, a stronghold of Napoleon's *idéologue* opponents, highlighted the need for a politically low profile.

Cuvier's presentation is admirably calculated to allay political fears and to encourage patronage. Throughout the work he denounces *hautes conjectures* of the kind that might be thought to encourage enthusiasm and free-thinking amongst the populace. Instead he emphasizes in the introduction the ever more accurate portrayal of nature that results from measurement and calculation in the case of *sciences mathématiques* and from collation of facts and cautious generalization in the case of *sciences naturelles ou physiques*. In the body of the work pride of place is given to the accumulation of accurate observations, and theoretical progress in the sciences is consistently presented as the fruit of extended observation and comparison. Further, there is much attention to the practical utility of recent theoretical discoveries. Cuvier's virtuosity in weaving together the potent themes of discovery, utility and neutrality is splendidly in evidence in the following passage:

If we were to address an ordinary prince, it is on these immediate advantages that we should most insist. Most governments believe themselves right to see and encourage in the sciences nothing but their day to day use for the needs of society; and doubtless the vast picture that we have to draw would appear to them, as to the vulgar, only as a series of speculations more curious than useful.

But Your Majesty, himself nurtured on the most sublime sciences, knows perfectly that all the operations of practice, sources of the commodities of life, are nothing but easy applications of general theories, and that there is not to be found in the sciences any general truth that might not be the germ of a thousand useful inventions.

One could say to him that no physical truth is indifferent to the amenities of society, just as no moral truth is indifferent to the order which should rule it.[20]

[20] *Rapport*, 15.

Cuvier's specific concern in the work is to promote the cause of the *sciences naturelles ou physiques*, 'the vast and fertile space' that lies between the exact sciences and the moral sciences. As Outram points out, Cuvier is in an awkward predicament.[21] On the one hand, he is out to claim full scientific status for the *sciences naturelles*: chemistry and natural history (in the broad sense including mineralogy, geology and the entire range of sciences of living beings). On the other hand, he is bound by his own doctrines to admit crucial differences between them and the paradigms of certainty and rationality, the *sciences mathématiques*: the phenomena of the *sciences naturelles* are rarely amenable to measurement; vital phenomena habitually violate the laws of physics and chemistry; and since intervention destroys the harmonious manifestations of the vital principle, experimental methods cannot uncover the laws that govern them. Though a close reading reveals a certain unease, there is considerable finesse in the ways in which Cuvier implies the scientific respectability of these inexact sciences. Despite the irreconcilability of the behaviour of living beings with the laws of physics and chemistry, and the inscrutability of the vital principle itself, Cuvier's history shows confidence in the capacity of the naturalist to arrive at laws and principles through meticulous comparison and analysis of phenomena pursued in accordance with an *esprit mathématique*. Deference to the certainty and rationality of the mathematical sciences, loudly proclaimed in Delambre's companion volume, is nicely combined by Cuvier with insistence on the autonomy of the methods and principles of the *sciences naturelles*.

Within the field of *sciences naturelles* Cuvier is out to legitimate a specific set of disciplinary practices, priorities and alliances. He is much concerned to demonstrate the inseparability of the disciplines which deal with life: botany, zoology, anatomy, physiology. Within this *étude de la vie* he highlights the importance of zoology, and in particular of his own discipline, the comparative anatomy of animals. A full exposition of the motives behind these disciplinary priorities and of the ways Cuvier seeks to legitimate them in his *Rapport* would require substantial digressions on Cuvier's views on structure, function and classification, and on his dominant role in the institutional career of natural history after the

[21] 'Uncertain legislator: Georges Cuvier's laws of nature in their intellectual context', *Journal of the History of Biology*, 19 (1986), 323–68.

Revolution. Here a few obvious points will have to suffice. Cuvier's promotion of comparative anatomy is related to his view that it provides the key both to physiology, the study of the harmonious correlation of functions that maintains life, and to *méthode*, the classification of plants and animals according to their natural affinities. In the *Rapport* Cuvier confidently presents his own comparative anatomy, and the insights into physiology and classification of animals that ensue from it, as the culmination of progress in these fields. At the institutional level certain of Cuvier's disciplinary priorities are readily explained.[22] It was only recently that zoology had obtained substantial recognition in French learned institutions. The old Académie des Sciences, replaced by the First Class of the Institut National, had had no separate zoology section. Indeed, only with the conversion of the old Jardin des Plantes into the Muséum d'Histoire Naturelle in 1793 did the study of animals acquire an institution; and only with the establishment of the *Annales* of the Muséum did it acquire an outlet for specialized publications. The Muséum was quite literally Cuvier's base, being the site both of his home and of the galleries of comparative anatomy that were arranged on the principles laid down in his monumental *Leçons d'anatomie comparée* (1800–5). The classification and ranking of disciplines that is used to structure the *Rapport*, and to which the *Rapport* gives the apparent sanction of a long historical standing, is in fact both in ideological terms and in institutional terms a recent arrangement. Moreover, it is an arrangement in whose creation Cuvier himself had played a major role. Here we see a masterly use of the strategy of normalization.

As already indicated, Cuvier uses the *Rapport* to advertise his own contributions, both substantive and methodological, to the disciplines that he presents as central to the *étude de la vie*. There is considerable subtlety in the way in which he contrives to do so whilst preserving an appearance of judicious impartiality. To start with, he has to be seen to deal fairly with competitors in the crucial fields of comparative anatomy and systematic classification—

[22] The following remarks are derived from T. A. Appel, *The Cuvier–Geoffroy Debate: French Biology in the Decades before Darwin*, Oxford, 1987, ch. 2 and apps. A–D. Much further information on French controversy in the period about the reform of natural history is to be found in P. Corsi, *The Age of Lamarck: Evolutionary Theories in France, 1790–1830*, trans. J. Mandelbaum, Berkeley, Calif., 1988, ch. 1.

Blumenbach, Étienne Geoffroy Saint-Hilaire and Lamarck, for
instance. Cuvier refrains from direct criticism. Instead rival
contributions are given due credit, but variously subordinated to
Cuvier's own. Blumenbach's treatise on comparative anatomy is
comparable in utility with his own, but less extensive.[23] Lamarck's
renaming of the *animaux à sang blanc* as *animaux sans vertèbres* is
justified by Cuvier's discovery of a class of red-blooded animals in
the old Linnaean group of *vers*; and in his treatment of these
animals Lamarck has used Cuvier's system of classes, with some
additions and modifications.[24]

In legitimating his own contributions as culminations of progress
Cuvier has to proceed with circumspection. On the one hand, he
must appear to do justice to the contributions to knowledge that
lead up to his own. On the other hand, to bring out the magnitude
of his contributions, he must emphasize his break with the past.
Two effective devices help him to carry off this feat of balancing.
One is the presentation of his own position as sifting the wheat
from the chaff in conflicting past positions. The other is the careful
avoidance of affiliation to any one precursor by citation of a
multiplicity of 'ancestors'.[25] A neat example of the combination of
the two strategies occurs in the course of his history of *physiologie
générale*. The progress in this discipline that has culminated in
Cuvier's own approach is said to lie along the *route intermédiare*
between the excesses of mechanism and Stahlian vitalism.[26] Cuvier
gives special mention to Friedrich Hoffmann as the first to follow
this middle way, and as having held views on the function of the
nervous system that were perhaps closer to the truth than those of
von Haller.[27] Thus Cuvier avoids affiliating himself and his style of
inquiry exclusively to the celebrated von Haller.

Methodological considerations are prominent throughout
Cuvier's *Rapport*. An empircist methodology for the *sciences
naturelles* is vindicated by pointing to its exemplary achievements.
And empiricist strictures are repeatedly invoked against speculative
doctrines that Cuvier holds to have no place in the sciences. In
discussing this aspect of Cuvier's use of history we face an obvious
difficulty. For all his loquacity on the issue, it is extremely difficult
to establish the actual content of Cuvier's methodology. The

---

[23] *Rapport*, 328.   [24] Ibid. 313–14.
[25] Cf. Outram, 'Uncertain legislator', 353–6.   [26] *Rapport*, 230.
[27] Ibid. 230.

difficulty is reflected in the extraordinary range of characterizations to be found in the secondary literature—Kantian empiricism, Lockean sensationalism, Condillacian analysis, proto-positivism, semiotic inference from signs. This is not the place to address this fascinating issue in detail. However, certain general observations are in order. To start with it should be noted that Cuvier himself is at pains to emphasize the differences between the methods proper to different *sciences*. Measurement and calculation are central to the mathematical sciences but largely inapplicable to the *sciences naturelles*. Experimental intervention, crucial to the discovery of laws in other domains of inquiry, is of limited use in the quest for the laws which regulate vital phenomena because it disrupts the harmony of functions which constitutes life. Cuvier's language does on occasion suggest that he views all the various methods of the sciences as forms of analysis, conceived in Condillac's manner as a process of isolation and naming of significant parts followed by establishment of significant correlations. But at the level of detail at which methodology is used to validate or invalidate specific hypotheses and explanations there is surely no such thing as *the* Cuvierian method. In the domain of *études de la vie* Outram is, I think, right in diagnosing a Kantian stance.[28] Certainly there is much common ground between the Blumenbach–Kant scheme of physiology and natural history that we outlined in Chapter 2 and the Cuvierian quest for the laws of relation and interaction of organs under the governance of an inscrutable 'harmony of functions'. Moreover, this diagnosis fits well with Cuvier's dismissal from natural history of all 'metaphysical' questions that are in principle unamenable to empirical investigation. Finally, it may be noted that throughout Cuvier's writings there is an insistence on the importance of exact and compendious description and meticulous and extensive comparison in the study of living beings. Whatever the precise brand of empiricism this may represent, it clearly reflects Cuvier's deep commitment to the value of museum-based inquiry.

The prime example in the *Rapport* of Cuvier's critical use of methodological considerations is the effective and well-informed attack on *Naturphilosophie*. Here is his opening gambit:

Moreover, if we continue thus to refer all our physical sciences to

---

[28] Outram, 'Uncertain legislator', 344–50.

generalized experience, it is not because we are unaware of the recent attempts of certain foreign metaphysicians to tie natural phenomena to rational principles, to demonstrate them a priori, or as these metaphysicians put it, to remove them from conditionality.[29]

Cuvier does not, of course, object to demonstration from rational principles *per se*: on the contrary, he repeatedly recognizes this as the glory of the mathematical sciences. His objection is rather that no such demonstrations are to be had in the *sciences physiques ou naturelles*, in which the only route to laws is generalization from *expériences*. Moreover, he takes specific exception to the kinds of principle invoked by the *Naturphilosophen* and to the means of demonstration that they employ.[30] Their principles are metaphysical principles of a sort that belong properly to the moral rather than the physical sciences. (In keeping with his general policy of avoiding comment on theological issues, Cuvier voices no theological objections to *naturphilosophische* principles. He does, however, set out a sample of them in a way clearly designed to highlight their theological heterodoxy.) Their demonstrations he finds objectionable because they employ metaphorical language and dialectical artifices, and because they pass 'without fixed rule' from abstract premises to concrete conclusions.

Cuvier presents his methodology of 'generalized experience' as being the only way in which controversy and the proliferation of speculative systems is to be avoided. Thus Cuvier outlaws speculative natural history in the style of Buffon, a genre which still had a substantial popular following in the period and whose conduciveness to popular enthusiasm and social disorder he has already insinuated.[31] However, Cuvier's primary mode of vindication of his empiricist methodology is display of the exemplary general truths that have been acquired through its observance, and of the miserable falsehoods that have resulted from its non-observance. Thus, in the *Resumé* of the *Rapport*, after rehearsing the major recent 'revolutions' or 'steps towards the truth' in the *sciences naturelles*, Cuvier offers the following glowing testimonial to the powers of *expérience*:

Such are the principal discoveries that have rendered our epoch illustrious and which open the century of NAPOLEON. What hopes they give rise to

---

[29] *Rapport*, 11.   [30] Ibid. 235–6.
[31] On the continued popularity of Buffonian works after the Revolution see Corsi, *The Age of Lamarck*, 20–3, 30–9.

in themselves! How they manifest above all the general spirit that has occasioned them and which promises so many others for the future! All those hypotheses, all those more or less ingenious suppositions that still had such vogue in the first half of the last century, are today rejected by true *savants*: they no longer obtain for their authors even fleeting glory. *Expérience* alone, precise *expérience*, formed with weight, measure, calculation and comparison of all the substances used and all the substances obtained, that today is the only legitimate way of reasoning and demonstration. So, though the *sciences naturelles* elude the applications of calculation, they glory in being submitted to the mathematical spirit; and by the wise course that they have invariably adopted they no longer show themselves to be a step behind: all their propositions are established with certitude, and become so many solid foundations for that which remains to be constructed.[32]

In sum, Cuvier's *Rapport* is a work of remarkable rhetorical force, exhibiting and combining in subtle and effective forms the full range of legitimations and vitiations of disciplines, methods and practices—appeals to authority, appeals to the norms of reason, appeals to interests, appeals to exemplary successes and cautionary failures. Moreover, it does so under the mask of the objectivity and disinterestedness that in the course of the nineteenth century became entrenched as fundamental values in the ideology of science.

[32] Ibid. 390.

7

A New Historiography

By way of a conclusion to this first part of my work I shall reflect briefly on the virtues and prospects of a new kind of historical study of the sciences, a historiography centred on scenes of inquiry.

First let me survey the principal claims, both positive and negative, that I have ventured concerning the factors that constrain, shift and stabilize scenes of inquiry in the sciences.

I have argued that of the immediate determinants of scenes of inquiry, namely, the presuppositions and methodological commitments of communities of inquirers, it is methodological commitment that is fundamental. I have suggested that though particular sciences have often been prosecuted under the aegis of general methodological precepts promoted by pontifical disciplines—logic, epistemology, philosophy of science, etc.—general methodology has rarely played a dominant role as a determinant of scenes of inquiry. Nor, I have argued, are the methods that determine scenes of inquiry to be seen as varied refinements of an underlying body of common-sense methods and practices. Instead, the primary determinants are methods of production, presentation and adjudication of claims local to particular disciplines, particular periods and particular communities and sites of inquiry.

I have suggested that the principal sources of methodological innovation are articulation, refinement and elaboration of practices local to particular disciplines, schools, institutions and factions together with the piecemeal import and adaptation of methods from role model disciplines, the donor disciplines often being ones that are not by any standards scientific. I have speculated more tentatively on the educational, institutional and technological factors that may shift and maintain local methods and practices and hence scenes of inquiry. In the educational domain I have emphasized the importance of canons of classic works and the control of their interpretation, of pedagogical methods and fashions, and, more generally, of modes of initiation into disciplines. With regard to institutions 1 have emphasized the importance of administration, of architecture and layout, of internal division of cognitive and technical labour. With regard to the machinery of the sciences I have emphasized the absolutely essential roles of, on the one hand, the practical and instrumental technologies that control material input to the sciences—specimens, samples, signals, data—and, on the other hand, the technologies of representation, replication and communication which control their visual, dramatic and literary output.

In my discussion of the strategies of legitimation that may serve both to stabilize and maintain methods and practices and to provoke methodological change, I have noted the diversity of the types of legitimation operative in the sciences—rationalization, appeal to authority, appeal to interests, appeal to literary and aesthetic sensibilities, calibration against precedents and standards; and I have emphasized the roles of anomaly, polemic and conflict as well as personal interests and ambitions as stimuli to attempts at legitimation and as determinants of strategies of legitimation. To illustrate the various strategies of legitimation I have offered a series of case-studies of their deployment in historical writing to promote and secure the methods and practices of particular disciplines and factions. In the second part of this work I shall devote much further attention to the various types of legitimation, and I shall argue (in the face of seemingly cogent objections) for the centrality of calibration against precedents and standards as a determinant of changes in the repertoires of local methods and practices in the sciences.

My overall contention has been pluralist. There is, I have suggested, an irreducible diversity in the factors, both immediate and remote, that have been responsible for the formation, maintenance and displacement of scenes of inquiry.

Study of past scenes of inquiry and of the factors that have determined them is proposed as the core of a new historiography of the sciences. But it by no means constitutes the whole programme. Outstanding among the issues not addressed here is that of the formation of research agendas, of the rosters of questions within a scene of inquiry that are deemed worthy of serious pursuit. (It is here, I believe that sociological 'interest theory', to be discussed in Chapter 9, finds one of its most fruitful fields of application.) Moreover, we have hardly even touched on a host of further issues concerning the content and structure of the negotiations through which communities of inquirers arrive at consensuses on factual and theoretical claims. (It is here, I shall argue in Chapter 9, that the recently developed 'network theoretic' approach to the study of the sciences finds a fruitful field of application.) Nor have we considered the interactions between agendas of inquiry, theoretical claims, and technological resources and products. In the context of a more complete programme our treatment of determination of scenes of inquiry as a well-defined field would doubtless appear as a simplification. For it is clear that formation of scenes of inquiry, of agendas for research, of substantive consensuses, of technological products, do not in general form a causal or chronological sequence. Rather we should expect to find complex interactions and feedbacks between these different levels of production.

Even within the somewhat artificial terms of reference to which we have confined ourselves, there remain serious incompletenesses in our discussions. On the issue of remote determinants of scenes of inquiry we have offered only the most tentative and bland of suggestions. Far more remains to be said, for example, about the ways in which the local practices of the sciences are conditioned by political and social interests, instrumental repertoires, experimental traditions and technologies of communication and representation. We shall consider these matters again in later chapters; but it is obvious that a much more detailed exploration of these issues is needed than is possible in the confines of the present work.

There are two methodological issues that are, I believe, of particular urgency in the development of the proposed new historiography of the sciences. The first concerns the proper level for the analysis of scenes of inquiry in the sciences. Should the primary focus be on complexes and alliances of disciplines, on disciplines, on fields of inquiry within a discipline, on factions, schools or research programmes, on particular institutions or sites of inquiry? We have, on the whole, tacitly taken as our communities of inquirers local traditions of inquiry within particular disciplines. But this choice is problematic on several scores. On the one hand, the suspicion arises that it may be too broad. For there is ample evidence of divergence in practices and 'institutional epistemologies' even between sites of inquiry that are closely allied in their agendas and theoretical commitments.[1] On the other hand, the suspicion arises that it may be too narrow. For, as highlighted by many recent sociological studies, the networks of agents involved in the practices of a given discipline are extraordinarily heterogeneous, involving practitioners of many disciplines and occupants of many social roles outside the community of accredited scientists.[2] (Given the diversity of the social and institutional embodiments of the sciences, it remains an open question whether any one level of analysis of scenes of inquiry is appropriate for all sciences in all periods.) Further problems concern the notions of tradition and discipline that we have invoked. Clarification of the notion of a tradition of inquiry requires much further investigation of the various social and institutional frameworks for the handing on of local methods, skills and practices from generation to generation. It is my hunch that such investigations would cast doubt on the ways in which large disciplinary categories—astronomy, chemistry, biology, science—are customarily employed, showing them to be in certain cases retrospective historiographical artefacts and in many other cases categories used in the legitimation and promotion of traditions of inquiry rather than genuine alliances of traditions united by common practices and agendas. The emphasis of the new historiography should, I believe, be on disciplines more narrowly conceived, constituted by single traditions of inquiry or groups of traditions showing substantial overlap in practices and agendas.[3]

The second problematic area is that of the roles to be assigned to individual agency, choice and strategic deliberation in shifting and stabilizing scenes of inquiry.[4] I have expressed reservations about a particular kind of appeal to individual agency and strategy, that characteristic of approaches which attach paramount importance

[1] On 'institutional epistemologies' see C. Salomon-Bayet, *L'Institution de la science et l'expérience du vivant: Méthode et expérience à l'Académie Royale des Sciences, 1666–1793*, Paris, 1978.

[2] See e.g. K. Knorr-Cetina, *The Manufacture of Knowledge: Toward a Constructivist and Contextual Theory of Science*, Oxford, 1981; B. Latour, *Science in Action: How to Follow Scientists and Engineers through Society*, Cambridge, Mass., 1987.

[3] I discuss the issue of demarcation of disciplines and traditions of inquiry in a forthcoming paper, 'What constitutes a discipline?'

[4] My thoughts on the roles of individual critical deliberations owe much to conversations with Michael Ben Chaim and to my reading of his thesis, 'The moral dimensions of scientific innovation'.

to the methodological innovations and pronouncements of 'great' scientists and philosophers. Such approaches are suspect on several scores. The supposed innovations are often in reality articulations, generalizations or refinements of existing local practices and methods. They may be unrepresentative of methods or practices actually employed, being interpretable instead as retrospective rationalizations of doctrines whose formation was in fact mediated by other means. Moreover, the attribution of methodological innovations to great men is often a product of uncritical acceptance, or indulgence in, a heroic and hagiographical style of historical narrative (a style which, as I suggested in the last chapter, owes much to the Romantic ideology of genius that was so prevalent at the time of formation of 'science' as an alliance of disciplines).

However, both in my case-study of German natural history and in my general speculations on the explanation of shifts in scenes of inquiry I have assigned central and irreducible roles to individual strategy and deliberation. One domain in which I have done so is that of the interpretation and reception of works and performances in the sciences: as I have argued in Chapter 3, these processes generally involve criticism, adaptation and appropriation by individuals to their particular circumstances, expectations and priorities. Another domain in which I have assigned a central role to individual strategy is that of legitimation of practices and methods. All the various types of legitimation of methods and practices—rationalization, appeal to authority, appeal to interests, appeal to literary and aesthetic sensibilities, calibration against precedents and standards—involve critical deliberations by individuals, often, as we have seen in the case of Cuvier's use of history to legitimate the methods and practices of *sciences physiques*, highly complex deliberations.

There are obvious dangers in downplaying the roles of individual deliberation and agency in explaining shifts of scenes of inquiry. Where the concern is with innovations in the sciences such downplaying is apt to make practitioners of the sciences appear as blind and unreflective agents of canons of rationality, genres and styles of writing, social interests, patterns of authority, etc., and, by the same token, apt to make such social conventions appear as impersonal forces rather than local products of human construction and criticism. Where the concern is with interpretation and reception of innovations it is students, emulators and adherents who are made to appear passive and uncritical victims. To put it bluntly, any historiographical approach which fails to do justice to the roles of individual criticism and deliberation in the sciences creates a world of dopes and suckers. In so doing it overlooks the manifest evidences of criticism and deliberation in the sciences. By arrogating to itself the critical stances that it denies to practitioners of the sciences it creates for itself obvious and serious problems of reflexivity. And, most damagingly of all, it systematically conceals the dependence of the scenes and doctrines of the sciences on contingencies, accidents and idiosyncracies—on the details of individuals' educations and employments; on their projects and ambitions; on the encouragements and opportunities, obstacles and challenges they happen to encounter; on the information available to them; on the specificities of their social circumstances; on their perceptions and interpretations of their own cognitive and social situations; on their self-images and self-projections; on their particular cognitive, moral and social priorities, commitments and reflections. In thus suppressing the contingency of developments in the sciences it makes a significant contribution to the 'fatal-ization' of the sciences whose dire consequences I shall bewail in the final chapter.

The emphasis on individual strategy and deliberation in the proposed historiography does, however, create serious methodo-logical and practical problems. To start with there are problems of attribution, problems that are by no means peculiar to the proposed approach. When is the historian justified in attributing specific deliberations and strategies to practitioners, performers, interpreters and recipients in the sciences? How much imaginative reconstruction is in order? How is the historian to adjudicate the often conflicting claims of authorial declaration, testimony of others, evidence from deeds, argument from plausibility in the light of prevailing conventions, etc.? These standard problems of historical interpretation are greatly exacerbated by the emphasis in the proposed historiography on local and often inarticulate practices and conventions and on the local adaptation of received practices and conventions. At the end of Chapter 4 I reflected briefly on the problems of access to local and inarticulate methods. But those reflections fall far short of adequate guide-lines for the investigations of the strategies, deliberations, perceptions, interpretations and reflections of obscure persons that are required for a·fully fledged historiography of scenes of inquiry.

In the Introduction I suggested that by concentrating on the formation, maintenance and displacement of scenes of inquiry in the sciences we may hope to overcome the confrontation between 'intellectualist' and 'praxis-oriented', 'internalist' and 'externalist' approaches in which the historical study of the sciences is at present locked. By focusing on scenes of inquiry we can arrive at an understanding that does full justice to intellectualist and internalist insistence that historians keep sight of the contents of the sciences. For scenes of inquiry, the ranges of questions valid for communities of practitioners, constitute the most fundamental level of content, the content that underlies both the research agendas of the sciences and the factual and theoretical doctrines of the sciences. In attempting to explain formation, maintenance and displacement of scenes of inquiry we do equal justice to the insistence by externalist historians and praxis-oriented sociologists that we keep sight of the local practices, institutions and technologies of the sciences and of the ways in which those practices, institutions and technologies form and are transformed by society. For it is precisely the local practices, institutions and technologies of the sciences that constitute, so I have argued, the primary determinants of scenes of inquiry.

The proposed historiography centred on scenes of inquiry overcomes a related historiographical confrontation as well, that between 'individualist' history of science centred on the careers of particular practitioners and 'collectivist' history of science centred on the careers of institutions, traditions and research schools. On the one hand, as we have just noted, it does full justice to the 'collectivist' insight that practices, interests and conventions local to particular institutions and traditions are major determinants of the content of the sciences; on the other hand, as argued earlier, it assigns central and irreducible roles to reflection on and criticism of social practices and conventions by individual practitioners of the sciences.

Much remains to be done, both in the way of methodological reflection and in the way of detailed and local case-studies, before this new historiography can be counted as a going concern. But I trust that I have done enough to inspire excitement, perhaps even confidence, about its prospects.

II

ABSOLUTE REALITY

8
Absolute Reality and Dissociation

ABSOLUTE REALITY

So far we have invoked only the local reality of questions, reality in a community of inquirers. To define global or absolute reality we must drop all reference to communal beliefs and dispositions. Moreover, we must specify more tightly the kinds of evidential consideration relevant to the resolution of questions. For in order to do justice to the diversity of cognitive goals and values that have been pursued by practitioners of the sciences our account of local reality admits considerations held to be indicative of virtues of answers other than truth. The time has come to declare our conviction that truth is the proper goal of the sciences. Accordingly we confine our attention to evidential considerations reliably indicative of truth. Thus we obtain:

> Question $Q?$ is (absolutely) real just in case there is an evidential consideration E reliably indicative of the truth of some straight answer to $Q?$

Is it reasonable to suppose that a substantial proportion of the questions addressed by our sciences are not only real for particular communities of scientists, but also real absolutely? My concern in this chapter is with a line of argument from the history of the sciences, set out by Ian Hacking, which strongly suggests that this may not be a reasonable supposition.[1] In the next chapter I shall discuss a variety of sociological considerations which likewise threaten the absolute reality of many of the questions addressed by current sciences.

HACKING'S CHALLENGE

Hacking's argument is premised on the prevalence in the history

[1] 'Language, truth and reason', in M. Hollis and S. Lukes, eds., *Rationality and Relativism*, Oxford, 1982. My interpretation of Hacking's argument may well be a strong appropriation, in the sense introduced in Ch. 3.

of the sciences of agendas of inquiry and bodies of belief that are, by our lights, largely unreal—that are, in Hacking's terminology, 'dissociated' from our present-day agendas and beliefs. Such prevalence may be inferred from observed instances. Thus Hacking adduces as a typical example of dissociation the relation between present-day scientific beliefs and the beliefs of the sixteenth-century physician and alchemist, Paracelsus, concerning analogies and sympathies between earthly and heavenly bodies and between the macrocosm of nature and the human microcosm.[2] The account of developments in German natural history in Chapter 2 of the present work provides further striking examples of agendas of inquiry and bodies of belief dissociated from our own. Hacking relates local reality ('positivity' in his terminology) to the ability of inquirers (in principle) to 'get to grips' with questions.[3] He is thus able to strengthen his case by inferring the prevalence of dissociation from the historical diversity of styles of inquiry. Given the way in which we have related local reality to methodology, this is an inference that we cannot but endorse.

Faced with past agendas of inquiry and bodies of belief dissociated from our own, how are we to justify the claim that it is reality from our standpoint rather than reality from the past standpoint that has the better claim to constitute absolute reality? On our account of absolute reality the obvious way is to show the methods which constitute our style of inquiry to be more reliable than those which constituted the relevant past style of inquiry. How is such a vindication of our methods to be achieved?

In the last chapter we distinguished two types of vindication of methods, calibration and causal vindication. In vindication by calibration the case for the reliability of a method, technique or practice rests on its performance on 'bench-mark' questions, questions whose answers are independently attested. In a causal vindication it is shown that when the method at issue is correctly applied the causal ancestry of its deliverances implies that those deliverances are reliably indicative of the relevant 'worldly' states of affairs.

Elsewhere I have argued at length that causal vindication of methods is far more problematic both in theory and in practice

[2] M. Hollis and S. Lukes, eds., *Rationality and Relativism*, 60.
[3] Ibid. 55.

than is generally supposed.[4] Here it suffices to indicate grounds for
holding that its actual role in the sciences is limited and that the
prospects for an increased role are dim. It must, of course, be
conceded that, at the levels of direct observation and the use of
instruments, we have to hand some of the materials for causal
stories of the kinds needed for causal vindication. Thus the current
state of research in psychology and neurophysiology allows the
formation of hypotheses about causal processes that eventuate via
events in the sense organs in psychological states that are, under
appropriate circumstances, reliably discriminant of, for example,
pitches, reflectances of surfaces, relative distances, etc. And there
are many instruments of whose mode of operation we have a
causal understanding that enables us to make a case for their
reliability under appropriate conditions of use. However, it should
be noted that we do not have even the makings of causal
vindications for many of the specialized observational and instrumental techniques on which major bodies of present-day theory
depend for their credibility. Moreover, even in the case of
perceptual and instrumental methods of which we do have a
measure of causal understanding, full vindication remains highly
problematic. For a full vindication does not require only a
specification of causal chains leading from worldly states of affairs
to psychological states or instrument readings. Rather, what is
needed are causal stories linking worldly states of affairs to
consensuses about those states of affairs reached on the basis of
the observational and instrumental methods at issue. We have
already emphasized the fact that even in the case of the most
straightforward observational and instrumental methods the processes that lead to consensus—processes of replication of findings,
debate on the reliability, competence and credibility of observers
and experimenters, selection and presentation of findings for
publication, etc.—are much more complex than one might be led
to believe by the standard textbook accounts of famous and crucial
observations and experiments. When we move from observational
and experimental methods to methods for the formation, presentation and adjudication of theories the difficulties are greatly
magnified. We have simply no idea what form causal vindications

---

[4] *The Fortunes of Inquiry*, Oxford, 1986, ch. 8; 'Science, ethics and objectivity',
in J. E. J. Altham and T. R. Harrison, eds., *World, Mind and Ethics: Essays on the
Moral Philosophy of Bernard Williams*, Cambridge, forthcoming.

of such methods might take. Indeed, the whole metaphor of users of reliable methods as 'detectors' of states of affairs appears to break down. For resolution of theoretical questions is generally a holistic affair involving adjudication of whole complexes of hypotheses.

The fact that even partial causal vindications of methods are rarer than might be supposed is grounds for pessimism about the prospects for causal vindication of our methodologies against divergent methodologies. Further grounds for pessimism arise from the involvement in causal vindications of very substantial bodies of background theory, physical, physiological and psychological. In cases of drastic dissociation of style of inquiry such theoretical considerations will very rarely fall into the common ground of agreed reality, let alone of agreed truth. Even in those relatively rare cases in which at least partial causal vindications of our methods are available, we are most unlikely, on pain of begging the question in our own favour, to be able to appeal to those causal vindications in defence of our own styles of inquiry against radically divergent styles.

Calibration of methods against precedents and standards provides, at first sight, a more promising approach to the vindication of our styles of inquiry against alien styles. By way of illustration of the prevalence and flexibility of this type of vindication let us consider some of the techniques for demonstrating the reliability of instrumental methods that are retailed in an excellent recent survey by Allan Franklin.[5] All the techniques reviewed by Franklin involve calibration in the above sense either in isolation or, in a minority of cases, in combination with considerations concerning the functioning of instruments which provide partial causal vindications. Doubtful instrumental methods may be calibrated, for example, by comparing the results obtained with those obtained using instruments whose reliability is not in question. Alternatively, they may be calibrated by comparing the results obtained with the predictions of well-corroborated theories. More subtly, there is a variety of types of what may be called 'conditional calibration'. For example, Franklin points out that the reliability of an instrument as a detector of phenomena of a certain type is substantiated if using the instrument the phenomena are

---

[5] 'The epistemology of experiment', in D. Gooding, T. Pinch and S. Schaffer, eds., *The Uses of Experiment: Studies in the Natural Sciences*, Cambridge, 1989.

shown to behave as would be expected of such phenomena on independent grounds, rather than as would be expected of instrumental artefacts. Thus, Galileo's demonstration that the supposed moons of Jupiter behaved in the manner to be expected on general astronomical grounds of a small planetary system (showing phases, regular orbits, etc.) vindicated his otherwise highly questionable claim that his telescope was a reliable detector of celestial bodies invisible to the naked eye. Here the use of the instrument is vindicated because, on the assumption that it is a reliable detector of objects of a certain type, its deliverances match independently warranted claims whereas those deliverances are virtually inexplicable on the assumption that they are instrumental artefacts. Another important category of evidence of reliability of instruments discussed both by Ian Hacking and by Franklin may likewise be classed as conditional calibration in our sense. Here the reliability of the instrument as a detector of objects or phenomena of a certain kind is corroborated not by its recording of behaviour to be expected of objects or phenomena of those kinds on theoretical grounds, but rather by its recording of behaviour induced by the experimenter's intervention. Hacking cites, for example, the continued trust in the reliability of microscopes in the face of Ernst Abbe's demonstration in 1873 of the role of diffraction in their operation, a demonstration that one might have expected to induce severe doubt about their reliability.[6] This continued trust he attributes to the capacity of the microscope to record in predictable ways experimental interventions: staining, injection of fluids and other kinds of manipulation of the material under examination. When we turn from instrumental methods to other kinds of method, methods for the choice of hypotheses and theories, for example, we find an equal variety and flexibility of strategies of calibration, both direct and conditional.[7]

Alas, as in the case of causal vindication, it seems that attempts to use calibration to vindicate our methods against alternative methods will generally be question-begging whenever we are faced with drastic cases of dissociation in which past and present scenes of inquiry and systems of belief are underwritten by radically divergent methodologies. For there will, it seems, be few or no questions real from both standpoints, let alone answers acceptable

---

[6] *Representing and Intervening*, Cambridge, 1983, ch. 11.
[7] I discuss calibration of methods more fully in *The Fortunes of Inquiry*, ch. 7.

from both standpoints. The independently warranted claims which we habitually use to calibrate our own methods cannot, it seems, on pain of begging the question of reliability in our own favour, be appealed to in order to vindicate our methods against the methods and practices of a radically divergent style of inquiry.[8]

It is this apparent impossibility of vindicating present styles of inquiry against radically divergent past styles of inquiry that I take to constitute the challenge to the absolute reality of the questions posed by the sciences that is at least implicit in Hacking's reflections on dissociation and the historical diversity of practices and methods in the sciences.

IMPLICATIONS OF DISSOCIATION

Before attempting to meet this challenge, let us consider briefly the consequences should we have to concede it. At first sight it appears that we should have to concede that few of the questions addressed by our sciences are likely to be absolutely real; and *a fortiori* that few of the answers delivered by them are likely to be true.

It may be that this dire conclusion could be avoided by retreat to a relativist position. The form of relativism at issue would deny the applicability of the notion of absolute reality to substantial ranges of the questions addressed by present-day sciences, while claiming for those questions reality relative to the styles of inquiry of the sciences at issue. It would similarly relativize claims about the truth of answers to those questions, denying that they have absolute truth values, but insisting that many of them are true relative to the relevant present-day styles of inquiry.

Unlike familiar forms of relativism, this position appears to be tenable in the face of the standard objections. Since it is a partial relativism, one which relativizes the reality of some but not all questions and assertions, it avoids the knock-down argument that relativism is self-subverting. One who claims that certain questions and assertions in the sciences have reality only relative to styles of inquiry can coherently answer in the affirmative the catch reflexive question: Is your claim itself real not only relative to your style of inquiry but absolutely?

---

[8] Cf. Hacking, 'Language, truth and reason', 65.

A second kind of incoherence with which relativists are commonly charged concerns the identity of assertions. How can it ever be one and the same assertion that is true relative to one style of inquiry but false relative to another?[9] Proper estimation of the force of this type of objection requires an account of the content of assertions. However, for our purposes it is quite safe to concede the objection. For the form of relativism at issue here does not allow assertions to take different truth values relative to different styles of inquiry. The claim is rather that an assertion that has a particular truth value from the standpoint of one style of inquiry may from the standpoint of other styles of inquiry not even be a candidate for a truth value, because relative to them it is not real.

Of course, these defensive remarks do not suffice to show that a partial relativism about the reality of questions is a viable option. For this we should at least have to provide some principled basis for the partition of questions into ones to which the absolute notion of reality is applicable and ones to which it is not. However, if this form of relativism is, as I suspect, coherent, Hacking's challenge is reinforced. Faced with a cogent case for an unmitigated scepticism about the sciences, we may well react complacently, supposing that even though we cannot see what is wrong with the argument, there must be something wrong simply because the conclusion is absurd. We can no longer react in this way if there is a coherent relativist refuge from the sceptical conclusion.

MEETING HACKING'S CHALLENGE

Can Hacking's challenge in fact be defeated?

Hacking himself moots the possibility that, unable to show the superiority of our style of inquiry on grounds of reliability, we might nevertheless vindicate it against past styles of inquiry on the grounds of the greater open-endedness of the domain of questions it opens up.[10] There is something in this suggestion. Hacking's criterion might well be wielded to good effect against past styles of inquiry that generated limited scenes of inquiry and that were repetitive and unreflective in their practices. But there are plenty

[9] See e.g. C. Swoyer, 'True for', in J. W. Meiland and M. Krausz, eds., *Relativism, Cognitive and Moral*, Notre Dame, 1982; L. Stevenson, 'Can truth be relativised to kinds of minds?', *Mind*, 97 (1988), 281–4.

[10] Hacking, 'Langue, truth and reason', 65–6.

of past styles of inquiry which generated diverse and elaborate scenes, which were reinforced by reflective accounts of the sources of knowledge and error, but which are radically dissociated from our own styles of inquiry. The Paracelsian approach to medicine and natural philosophy, cited by Hacking, is one notable instance. Another is the Kant–Blumenbach scheme for inquiry in natural history that we outlined in Chapter 2. It is hard to see how our styles of inquiry could be vindicated against such rich and powerful alternatives by the proposed criterion.

The second line of resistance is that of simply denying the need for a vindication of the reliability of our styles of inquiry against the past styles of inquiry that have yielded agendas and beliefs radically dissociated from our own. Such denial may be based on the complacent view that the current scenes and doctrines of the sciences provide our only available standards of reality and truth. Or it may be premissed on the scarcely less complacent view that all styles of inquiry dissociated from our own, along with the questions and doctrines to which they gave rise, were unscientific.

Such refusal to face Hacking's challenge is not, I think, an option. Elsewhere I have argued that there are general grounds on which it is always incumbent on seekers after truth to attempt to resolve conflicts between their own agendas and doctrines and those of other inquirers.[11] Here it suffices to note a couple of more parochial reasons for dissatisfaction with the response. Tempting though it may be to dismiss the medical and natural philosophical agendas and doctrines of Paracelsus and his followers as unscientific, such dismissal is hardly appropriate in the case of many of the more recent scenes of inquiry and bodies of belief dissociated from our own, for example, the German natural historical scenes and doctrines discussed in Chapter 2. For here we are dealing with relatively recent disciplines directly ancestral to our current scientific enterprises.

Let us consider some more strenuous attempts to meet Hacking's challenge. One line of resistance would be to argue for the existence of a substantial common methodological ground between all systematic inquiries. It has, for example, been argued that attribution to others of a measure of conformity to basic principles of reasoning is a necessary condition for the adequate

[11] *The Fortunes of Inquiry*, ch. 7.

interpretation of their utterances.[12] If so, we cannot correctly convict past inquirers of habitual violation of these basic principles: a modicum of common methodological ground between them and us is assured. Further common ground is assured if there is any substance in the claim that the specialized methods of the sciences are to be seen as elaborations and refinements of culturally universal common-sense procedures. It has been supposed that some at least of these allegedly universal methods are innate, and moreover that they are likely to be reliable because they are the products of natural selection. Were this so, the case against Hacking's challenge would be further strengthened. Not only would there always be a substantial methodological common ground to facilitate the calibration of styles of inquiry, but, in addition, there would be special scientific grounds for confidence in the truth of the answers generated by those universal methods.

Alas, this line of defence is suspect at every stage. First, the claim that attribution of conformity to some particular canon of rationality is a necessary condition for interpretation is dubious. At best, it may be that establishment of some methodological common ground or other between interpreter and interpretee is a necessary condition for adequate interpretation.[13] Secondly, such a minimal common ground is scarcely likely to suffice for the calibration of scientific styles of inquiry. Thirdly, as argued in Chapter 5, the claim that there is a substantial and powerful body of common-sense methodology common to all sciences is exceedingly dubious. Finally, the 'biological' case for the reliability of common-sense methods is notoriously weak. It may well be that there are analogies between certain scientific methods and certain innate processes—for example, Helmholtz may have been right in thinking that the unconscious processes of formation of perceptual beliefs show significant parallels with scientific methods of hypothesis formation and assessment.[14] But it is a far cry from this to the claim that there are innate scientific methods—that we are, for example, literally programmed to form and assess scientific

[12] M. Hollis, 'The limits of irrationality', *Archives Européennes de Sociologie*, 7 (1967), 265–71.

[13] See e.g. Steven Lukes's discussion of Hollis's and related arguments, 'Relativism in its place', in Hollis and Lukes, eds., *Rationality and Relativism*, 262–71.

[14] Helmholtz, *Treatise on Physiological Optics*, trans. J. P. C. Southall, New York, 1962.

hypotheses in specific ways. Moreover, even if the innateness of certain scientific methods were established, the argument from natural selection would be of dubious efficacy. Doubtless natural selection would have eliminated innate procedures so unreliable as to frustrate the four Fs fundamental for survival—fighting, fleeing, feeding and fucking. There is good reason to suppose, however, that natural selection would not in general have optimized the reliability of innate procedures. Rather, one would expect it to have optimized trade-offs between reliability, power and speed. As Alvin Goldman has shown, unreliable methods may be integral components of 'packages' that optimize such trade-offs.[15]

A much more promising line of resistance focuses on the historical status of claims about disparity of styles of inquiry. There are, I think, several good reasons for supposing that such claims are often the product of historiographical biases.

One such bias is the 'hagiography' which leads historians to concentrate on great innovators and discoverers, paying relatively little attention to the less celebrated figures active in the protracted and intricate processes that have mediated consensus and closure in the sciences. Let us call 'original' the reasons that are used by innovators to promote their claims, 'consensual' the reasons that mediate eventual acceptance or rejection of those claims in the relevant disciplines. That consensual reasons are likely to be less diverse in their methodological presuppositions than original reasons is obvious. When the peer group or public to be persuaded of the veracity of a new finding or hypothesis is homogeneous in its methodological commitments, successful promotion of the finding or hypothesis will often require a replacement of idiosyncratic or aberrant original reasons by reasons more in line with the prevailing methodology. And when the peer group or public to be persuaded is heterogeneous in its methodological commitments success will often require an even greater reduction in aberrancy and idiosyncrasy of reasons so as to appeal to whatever modicum of common ground there is between the various methodological factions. In its concentration on great innovators and original reasons hagiographical history is, therefore, apt to exaggerate the methodological instability and discontinuity of the sciences.

---

[15] A. Goldman, *Epistemology and Cognition*, Cambridge, Mass., 1986, pt. 2.

Even in historical accounts which deliberately avoid hagiography there is often a tendency in charting the progress of the sciences to concentrate unduly on about-to-be victorious doctrines, ignoring or prematurely writing off doctrines doomed to ultimate defeat. Such 'triumphalism', like hagiography, may exaggerate methodological instability by focusing on original reasons at the expense of consensual reasons.

Most insidious of all in its tendency to generate spurious epistemological breaks is intellectualism. It is intellectualism that leads historians of science to concentrate on high theory at the expense of the practical and empirical bases and applications of theories. Again, the result is apt to be an exaggeration of doctrinal discontinuities. For dissociation at the level of high theory may often conceal substantial agreement at the level of the questions which arise at the practical and empirical levels. Intellectualism also leads historians to pay heed to general methodological pronouncements rather than to investigate the minutiae of practices and procedures local to particular disciplines and communities of inquirers. Instability and discontinuity in the sciences at the level of general methodology is extremely well documented.[16] However, as we have already argued, it is not general methodology but rather procedures local to particular disciplines and communities that constitute the primary determinants of scenes of inquiry in the sciences. Discontinuity at the local level cannot, however, safely be inferred from discontinuity at the general level. For, as pointed out in Chapter 5, general methodological pronouncements by practitioners of the sciences are often to be read not as bona fide attempts to articulate the practices of their inquiries, but rather as rationalizations designed for didactic or promotional ends. Moreover, by virtue of their very generality and openness to variant interpretations, general methodologies rarely place tight constraints on real activities. Once we turn to specific practices local to particular disciplines, we may expect to find a much greater degree of historical continuity

[16] See e.g. E. Madden, ed., *Theories of Scientific Method from the Renaissance through the Nineteenth Century*, Seattle, 1960; G. Buchdahl, *Metaphysics and the Philosophy of Science*, Cambridge, Mass., 1969; L. Laudan, 'Theories of scientific method from Plato to Mach: a bibliographic survey', *History of Science*, 7 (1968), 1–63; *Science and Hypothesis: Historical Essays on Scientific Methodology*, Dordrecht, 1981.

than might be inferred from the vagaries of fad and fashion at the level of general methodology. In particular we may expect to find methodological continuities of long duration associated with the use of particular types of instrument and with particular routines of observation and description. There are, for example, remarkable continuities over several centuries in the traditions of practices and competences associated with microscopes, telescopes and surveying instruments.[17] And it is surprising how little effect on the routine descriptive practices of natural historians was produced by the dramatic theoretical and general methodological shifts in natural history that we retailed in Chapter 2: for all their massive divergences on issues of general method and theory, there is extensive overlap in the routine methods of naming, ordering and describing living beings in evidence in the textbooks of such doctrinally opposed figures as Blumenbach, Cuvier and Oken; and many of these routine practices remain in force amongst present-day natural historians.

The above considerations call in question the assumption of the prevalence in the sciences of radical dissociation between past and present agendas and bodies of belief. However, there undoubtedly are cases in which radical dissociation has to be conceded. Even then Hacking's challenge can be resisted. For the argument crucially involves a further questionable assumption—namely, that to vindicate a present style of inquiry M against a past one M' it is necessary to locate a common ground of agreed answers against which M and M' may be calibrated for reliability. Is such direct calibration the only way in which M may be vindicated against M' on the score of reliability? I think not.

Consider the case in which style of inquiry M' is ancestral to M: that is, M has arisen from M' through successive modifications in the body of local methods and practices of a discipline. We may then attend to the historical question of the precise way in which M arose from M'. Suppose it can be shown that the outcomes of attempts at calibration have prompted the successive refinements, displacements and replacements of methods that have transformed M' into M. Under these circumstances we have a prima-facie case for supposing M to be more reliable than M', because derived (or

---

[17] See e.g. S. Bradbury, *The Microscope, Past and Present*, London, 1968; S. Butler, R. H. Nuttall and O. Brown, *The Social History of the Microscope*, Cambridge, 1986; H. C. King, *The History of the Telescope*, London, 1955.

largely derived) from M' by a sequence of reliability-enhancing steps. For this kind of vindication the existence of a common ground of questions real from the standpoints of both M and M' is unnecessary. Provided the right kind of historical derivation can be demonstrated, the extent of the dissociation between the agendas and beliefs generated by M' and M is immaterial.

In sum, my suggestion is that to meet Hacking's challenge we need to concentrate on the local disciplinary practices and procedures that are generally ignored by intellectualist historians of the sciences. For it is these local methods that are the primary determinants of local validity of questions. Hacking's challenge is weakened if we can demonstrate substantial continuities in such local practices. The prospects for this are, I believe, excellent, at least in the case of disciplines grounded in observation and experiment. The challenge is further weakened if, in addition, we can show that attempted calibration of methods against precedents and standards has generally played a major role in bringing about changes in the local methods and practices of the sciences.

Has calibration in fact been a predominant, or even a major, agent of methodological change in the sciences? We have already discussed the rival claims of rationalization, that is, legitimation of methods by appeal to explicit norms of pontifical disciplines— logic, epistemology, etc. In the next chapter we shall consider other strategies for the legitimation of methods and beliefs whose prevalence and effectiveness appear to cast doubt on the primacy of calibration against precedents and standards as arbitrator of methods and practices in the sciences.

9
The Sociological Challenge

Suppose that many of the methods and practices effective in bringing about consensus in a discipline should turn out to be unreliable. We would then have grounds for doubting or denying not only the (absolute) truth of many of the answers delivered by that discipline but also the (absolute) reality of many of the questions posed in it.

In the last chapter we distinguished two basic ways in which a method or practice may be vindicated, that is, shown to be reliable. In vindication by calibration the method or practice in question is shown to perform well when tested against independently warranted precedents. In causal vindication a causal story is told which shows the answers delivered by the method or practice to be reliable indicators of the relevant 'worldly' states of affairs. It was argued that causal vindications are unavailable in practice, and perhaps in principle, for the methods and practices that govern consensus on theoretical issues in the sciences and, moreover, that even in the case of the observational and instrumental methods and practices that govern consensus on factual issues the available causal vindications are both incomplete and rarer than might be supposed. Calibration, on the other hand, appears to play a substantial role in the routines of many scientific disciplines. It is on the prevalence and effectiveness of calibration of methods and practices that we must rest our hopes for real questions and true answers in the sciences.

My concern in this chapter is with recent findings in the sociology and social history of the sciences that suggest that the methods that are in fact effective in securing consensuses in the sciences are generally neither calibrated nor such that they would survive genuine attempts at calibration.

I shall start by considering a direct attack on the prevalence of genuine calibration in the sciences. Combining philosophical reflections on the nature of rule-following in the sciences with

case-studies of attempts to replicate new experimental findings,
Harry Collins has argued that even in the central case of
instrumental methods attempts at calibration of disputed procedures are inevitably circular and that the issue of acceptability is
in fact always decided on other and, in respect of reliability,
decidedly fishy grounds.[1] I go on to consider two sociological
approaches to the study of closure of debate in the sciences,
interest theory and network theory. According to the interest
theory, the primary determinants of closure in the sciences—both
on first-order issues and on issues of method and practice—are the
professional, social and political interests of participants in debate
and of the parties whose acquiescence they seek. According to the
network theory, closure of debate in the sciences is mediated by
highly heterogeneous agencies, many of them operating far
outside the confines of scientific institutions and communities of
scientists. Protagonists of the interest theoretic approach—notably
Steven Shapin, Simon Schaffer, Trevor Pinch and Andrew
Pickering—have produced findings that threaten the view that
consensuses in the sciences are achieved through methods that are
calibrated, or at least amenable to calibration.[2] And the threat to
the prevalence of genuine calibration posed by recent network
theoretic studies—notably in the writings of Bruno Latour—is
equally, if not more pressing.[3]

Before embarking on accounts and assessments of these
sociological threats, it is worth indicating two related features
common to Collins's approach, interest theory (at least in its more
sophisticated recent manifestations) and network theory.

In contrast to the concerns of much of the earlier historiography
and sociology of science with the historical, social and psychological backgrounds of new techniques, doctrines and theories,
these new approaches are concerned above all with the transmission, modification and application of scientific innovations.

[1] *Changing Order: Replication and Induction in Scientific Practice*, London,
1985.
[2] See e.g. S. Shapin and S. Schaffer, *Leviathan and the Air-Pump: Hobbes,
Boyle and the Experimental Life*, Princeton, NJ, 1985; T. Pinch, *Confronting
Nature: The Sociology of Solar Neutrino Detection*, Dordrecht, 1986; A. Pickering,
Constructing Quarks: A Sociological History of Particle Physics, Edinburgh, 1984.
[3] See e.g. B. Latour, *Science in Action: How to Follow Scientists and Engineers
through Society*, Milton Keynes, 1987; *The Pasteurization of France*, trans.
A. Sheridan, Harvard, 1988.

There is a common emphasis on the ways in which innovations are selectively interpreted and adapted *en route* to consensual acceptance or rejection, and on the social transformations that are inextricable from the formation of such consensuses. In the jargon of literary criticism these are all reception theoretic approaches.

To explain the second common feature it is convenient to invoke a distinction of Latour's between primary and secondary 'mechanisms of legitimation'.[4] Primary mechanisms include all the arguments, strategies, recruitments, etc. involved in the formation of a consensus. Secondary mechanisms are the retrospective claims that legitimate and maintain a consensus once formed. (In this terminology most of the historical strategies for the legitimation of disciplines and methods discussed in Chapter 6 belong to the secondary mechanism of legitimation.) Underlying all the sociological approaches with which we shall be concerned is a provocative claim about the relationship between the primary and secondary mechanisms. It is supposed that it is the secondary mechanism that provides the context of application of the central terms of scientific approbation—'discovery', 'priority', 'validity', 'truth', 'fact', 'crucial experiment', 'reliability', 'calibration', 'rationality', 'scientific status', etc. The tendency of historians and philosophers to apply them in the context of the primary mechanism, the means by which consensus is reached, is alleged to bear testimony to the effectiveness of the secondary mechanism at work in scientists' published accounts of their discoveries and breakthroughs.

In these terms the general challenge with which we shall be concerned is readily stated. The apparent prevalence of calibration in the sciences is an illusion generated by a mechanism which conceals the actual methods and practices effective in bringing about consensuses in the sciences, methods and practices that are often neither calibrated nor amenable to calibration.

COLLINS: CALIBRATIONS FAIR AND FOUL

The charge of inevitable circularity in principle has not uncommonly been levelled at all attempts at the vindication of methods. In the case of vindication by calibration the charge is, I

<hr />

[4] Latour, *The Pasteurization of France*, 42 and *passim*.

think, unfounded. Of course, routine precautions must be observed. In particular, the precedents and standards against which a method is tested must not be dependent for their warrants on the reliability of the method itself.

This condition does indeed place limits on the applicability of vindication by calibration. We cannot, for example, hope to calibrate an entire methodology in the face of sceptical appeals to malicious demons and malevolent neurosurgeons. For then there would be no independently warranted claims acceptable to us and the sceptic as bases for the calibration. And as we have seen in the last chapter, we may run into the same difficulty if we attempt to calibrate present styles of inquiry against very different past styles of inquiry. The charge of circularity levelled by Collins, however, applies not to vindication by calibration of whole methodologies in the face of radically divergent methodologies, but to the calibration of the particular and local instrumental techniques that yield new and contentious findings in the sciences.

Collins argues from linked philosophical claims about the nature of rules and rule-following in the sciences.[5] The rules which govern scientific practice cannot be fully articulated as foolproof algorithms. However tightly scientists seek to specify the rules, they remain open to variant interpretation and application. This is evident in the diversity of application of rules according to the varied tacit skills and competences associated with local communities of researchers and particular sites of inquiry. It is in evidence too in disputes concerning the competence of applications and performances of rules; for judgements about competence depend not only on explicit local theoretical assumptions, but also on 'prejudices' and similarity judgements that are again tacit and local to particular communities of researchers and sites of inquiry.

The rules on which Collins concentrates have to do with the validation of experimental findings: namely, that they should be replicated and that the instruments which yield them should be calibrated. When the findings and instruments at issue are uncontroversial, tacit agreements about the nature and conditions of competent performance render replication of findings and calibration of instruments unproblematic. When, however, novel and controversial instruments and findings are at issue—the very

---

[5] Collins, *Changing Order*, ch. 1.

cases in which one might suppose replication and calibration to have a crucial role in bringing about consensus—both replication and calibration turn out to be deeply problematic.[6]

Collins takes as his central example Joseph Weber's highly controversial claim in the early 1970s that he had constructed an apparatus that had detected gravitational waves. To check Weber's claim other physicists attempted to replicate his experiments, acting in accordance with the replication rule. Collins insists, however, that in this case, as generally in the case of contentious claims, replication proved an ineffective procedure, because the issue of what constituted a genuine and competent replication was wide open to variant interpretation.

A number of scientists set out to repeat Weber's experiment in order to test the claim. It was not clear at the outset whether a properly designed experiment should detect gravity waves or should not detect gravity waves because their detectability was the very subject of the dispute. To settle this question, experimenters needed to know whether or not gravity waves existed, and to find this out they needed to do some well-performed experiments. But to know whether their experiments were well performed they needed to see if their experiments produced the 'correct' results, and to determine this they needed to know whether gravity waves existed—and so on. This is the Experimenter's Regress. The Regress prevents scientists knowing whether an experiment is a satisfactory copy of another before they know what result it should produce. It prevents them from using the rule of replication to demarcate genuine results from spurious claims unless they already know the answer by other means.[7]

Collins considers a variety of ways in which experimenters may try to escape the Experimenter's Regress, including the use of surrogate phenomena to calibrate their instruments. In the case of gravity wave detectors the calibration method involved injection of pulses of energy via an electrostatically energized 'end-plate'. However, Collins argues, in such attempts at calibration the Experimenter's Regress is merely iterated in a new guise. For the rule that to establish the reliability of an instrument it should be calibrated is no less open to variant interpretations than is the rule that to establish the validity of an experimental finding it should be

[6] Ibid., chs. 2 and 4.

[7] H. Collins, 'The meaning of experiment: replication and reasonableness', in H. Lawson and L. Appignanesi, *Dismantling Truth: Reality in the Post-Modern World*, London, 1989, 88.

replicated. In particular, it is always open to the experimenter to reject the competence of the calibration on the grounds that the surrogate phenomena used in that calibration are not sufficiently similar in kind to the phenomena whose reliable detection is at issue.

Calibration is the use of a surrogate signal to standardize an instrument. The use of calibration depends on the assumption of near identity of effect between the surrogate signal and the unknown signal that is to be measured (detected) with the instrument. Usually this assumption is too trivial to be noticed. In controversial cases, where calibration is used to determine relative sensitivities of competing instruments, the assumption may be brought into question. Calibration can only be performed provided this assumption is not questioned too deeply. In fact, the questioning is constrained only by what seems plausible within the state of the art of the science in question. But the very act of using a calibration surrogate may help to establish the limits of plausibility.[8]

Weber did not in fact challenge the use of an electrostatic surrogate. He did, however, raise *ad hoc* objections to the algorithm used to process the incoming signal, suggesting hypothetical pulse profiles for gravitational waves for which his own non-linear algorithm would be appropriate. These hypothetical profiles were generally held by others in the field to be grossly implausible on cosmological grounds.[9]

Collins goes on to suggest that agreement by the relevant community of accredited scientists—the 'core-set', in his terminology—on whether or not a controversial instrument has been successfully calibrated is consequent on rather than antecedent to their agreement on the validity of the controversial findings it yields, the latter agreement being reached on quite different grounds.[10] In Latour's terminology calibration of controversial instruments belongs not to the primary mechanism of generation of consensus but to the secondary mechanism of legitimation and fixation of an achieved consensus. Precisely when calibration is really needed it doesn't in fact take place, but is merely at a later date said to have done so.

In attempting to answer Collins's arguments, we are well advised to concede his premisses. Indeed, we have already conceded his general premisses in earlier chapters when we endorsed the central

---

[8] Collins, *Changing Order*, 105.   [9] Ibid. 105–6.   [10] Ibid. ch. 6.

role of local and tacit competences in the sciences. We concede also the facts of the controversy over Weber's claims as Collins retails them. Collins himself presents his findings about replication and calibration as a special case of the so-called 'Duhem–Quine thesis', the claim that 'any statement can be held true come what may if we make drastic enough adjustments elsewhere in the system'.[11] And his examples of disputed replications of experiments and calibrations of instruments do indeed vividly illustrate ways in which what might at first sight be taken as secure judgements directly based on experiment may be challenged by revising either the theoretical assumptions used in the analysis and interpretation of experimental outcomes or assumptions about the competence of particular experimenters and their performances. Thus, Collins makes a cogent case for the inconclusiveness of replications and calibrations: no replication or calibration is proof against all possible challenges and objections. Collins is surely right to consider claims to the effect that there has been a conclusive replication of once controversial experimental findings or a conclusive calibration of once controversial instruments to be components of the secondary retrospective mechanism of legiti-mation and celebration of consensus rather than of the primary prospective mechanism of consensus formation.

None of these concessions is damaging to our view that genuine calibration of doubtful methods is prevalent in the sciences and that it plays a substantial role in the achievement of consensus both about the methods of the sciences and about the deliverances of those methods. Let us consider again what is needed for the fair calibration of a method or practice in the face of objections. On pain of begging the question one way or the other, protagonists and antagonists of the method or practice that is challenged need to find a common ground of questions of agreed reality and answers of agreed truth in order to establish precedents and standards against which calibration is to be carried out. In the case of instrumental methods this will typically involve finding or negotiating a measure of theoretical agreement about the func-tioning of the instrument and about the phenomena to which it is supposedly applicable. Moreover, as Collins shows, it will typically involve finding or negotiating a measure of practical agreement on

---

[11] Collins, 'The meaning of experiment', 88.

the issue of competence and credibility of experimenters and their performances. Provided that such common ground can be established a fair calibration can be carried out. Its results, of course, will never be conclusive. For, as Collins argues and as we have conceded, it will always be open to antagonists of the method at issue to withdraw from the common ground or to come up with further objections. It will, however, be a fair calibration, one which does not beg the question in favour of either the protagonists or the antagonists of the instrumental procedure at issue.

There are, indeed, certain occasions on which claims for the successful or unsuccessful calibration of instruments are made and widely accepted, but on which conditions for a fair calibration are not met, because the very findings allegedly produced by the instrument are taken as sufficient to discredit its reliability and/or the competence of the experimenters. This is quite commonly the case when the instruments and findings involved are in the domain of marginal or crank science. More strikingly, Shapin and Schaffer have produced detailed evidence which convincingly suggests that this is what happened in the case of the famous air-pumps of Boyle and Huygens.[12] Although after prolonged negotiations they and the witnesses before whom they demonstrated their machines reached agreement that successful calibrations had been achieved, no fair calibrations were in fact ever carried out. Indeed, the disagreements between Boyle and Huygens concerning the working of the instruments, the interpretation of the devices used to calibrate the instruments, and, above all, each other's competence were so great as to make it very hard to see how fair calibrations could possibly have been achieved.

(Faced with Shapin and Schaffer's account it is tempting to observe that even though no fair calibration of the air-pump was achieved prior to consensus on its reliability, there must have been at least the possibility of fair calibrations at later dates when the technology of air-pumps had been standardized and consensus on a theoretical understanding of the relevant phenomena had been achieved. So even though genuine calibration did not figure in the achievement of consensus, it may have played a role in the preservation of consensus on the reliability of the instrument.

---

[12] Shapin and Schaffer, *Leviathan and the Air-Pump*, ch. 6.

Alas, the career of the original air-pumps was too short. By the time the requisite consensuses on interpretation of the relevant phenomena had been achieved air-pumps had changed out of all recognition. And even the fair calibration of a reconstructed Boylean or Huygensian air-pump is blocked in practice by the irrecoverability of the fine details of construction of the instruments—concerning washers, stoppers, lubricants, etc.—and the irrecoverability of the skills involved in their manufacture and operation.)

However, when we turn to Collins's account of the calibration of Weber's gravity wave detectors a quite different pattern emerges. On the crucial issues of the validity of use of electrostatic signals as a surrogate and the competence of Bell Laboratories, who carried out the tests, Weber and his opponents were in agreement. On the evidence presented by Collins the calibration was a fair one. Collins makes play with the fact that the calibration would not have been fair had Weber not conceded the analogy between electrostatic signals and gravity waves. And he suggests that even when Weber had made this, in Collins's view unwise, concession he could have gone on indefinitely finding new grounds for objection to the negative results of the calibrations. These are surely genuine might-have-beens. They show that this calibration like other calibrations was not conclusive. But they do not show that it was an unfair calibration.

I suggest that cases like that of the air-pump, in which consensus is reached on the fair calibration of an instrument without a fair calibration having occurred, are rare in the annals of mainstream scientific disciplines. The pattern revealed by Collins's study of the calibration of gravity wave detectors, that of fair but inconclusive calibration, is, I suggest, a typical one.

There is a marked discrepancy between Collins's trenchant deconstruction of standard scientists' and philosophers' accounts of the processes of consensus formation in terms of 'discovery', 'replication', 'calibration', etc., and his tentative metaphorical account of the processes genuinely responsible for termination of debate over contentious experimental techniques and findings. His metaphor is that of a web or network whose links are at once conceptual and social.[13] Novel claims may produce 'reverberations' in the web. Often the reverberations die away, a negative

13 Collins, *Changing Order*, ch. 6.

consensus being reached which preserves much or all of 'the web of prior agreements and alliances'. More rarely the web is disrupted and a new positive consensus is reached through formation of a new network of agreements and alliances. Achievement of a positive consensus requires the acquiescence of the core-set, the community of accredited experts in the relevant discipline. The innovator's ability to secure this will depend upon success in pitching the novel claims in such a way as to appeal to the interests of members of the core-set and members of other communities, both scientific and non-scientific, to which the core-set is linked.

The two following sociological approaches to consensus formation can be regarded as variant specifications of Collins's compelling but vague programme.

INTEREST THEORY

The central claim of interest theory is that professional, factional, social and political interests play primary roles both in innovations in the sciences and in the acceptance or rejection of those innovations.

Unsurprisingly, given that it is the approach that has dominated English-language sociological studies of the sciences since the early 1970s, interest theory comes in a variety of brands. Our discussion of the interest theoretic approach will be highly selective, for much of the earlier work has little relevance to our concerns with consensus formation, concentrating as it does (under the influence of functionalist anthropology) on the alleged reflection by scientific theories of social and political structures, rather than on the reception of scientific innovations. In these earlier studies little attention was paid to the 'hard case' for interest theory, that of the attainment of consensus on observational and experimental claims. The notion of interest employed was often broad to the point of vacuity, admitting such dubious items as interest in preserving the status quo and interest in prediction and control. (As Steve Woolgar asked in a witty critique: Why not include such items as 'interest in being bloody-minded'?)[14] Society was often treated as a stage on which the

---

[14] S. Woolgar, 'Interests and explanation in the social study of science', *Social Studies of Science*, 11 (1981), 365–94, 381.

sciences are performed against a fixed backdrop of social and political interests, overlooking the ways in which scientific controversies may modify existing interests and create entirely new ones. And, most damagingly of all, there was a tendency to ignore practitioners' own perceptions and attributions of interests, so that they appear as passive and unreflective agents of established interests, as 'interest dopes', in Harold Garfinkel's phrase.[15]

In the more recent manifestations of interest theory—notably in the writings of Shapin, Schaffer, Pinch and Pickering—these weaknesses are overcome. The focus is on reception of innovative claims, especially claims concerning observations and experimental findings. The interests attributed are generally both specific and local. Due account is taken of the ways in which new interests may be generated and old ones transformed in the course of debate. And there is scrupulous attention to the perceptions and attributions of interests by participants in controversy.

The *loci classici* of this sophisticated interest theory are the papers by Shapin on the career of phrenology in early nineteenth-century Edinburgh and the major work by Shapin and Schaffer on Robert Boyle's air-pump experiments and the controversies which attended them.[16]

The science of phrenology, consolidated in Vienna and Paris in the first decade of the nineteenth century, was premised on a strict identification of mind with brain, backed up by a partition of the brain into organs (thirty-five on the standard account) whose size was taken to be indicative of particular types of intellectual and perceptual capacity and of emotional and moral disposition. The size of the cerebral organs was supposedly accurately reflected in the shape of the skull, so that careful observation and measurement could yield a precise diagnosis of character and temperament. Shapin considers the reception of phrenological

---

[15] H. Garfinkel, *Studies in Ethnomethodology*, Englewood Cliffs, NJ, 1967, ch. 2.

[16] S. Shapin, 'Phrenological knowledge and the social structure of early nineteenth-century Edinburgh', *Annals of Science*, 32 (1975), 219–43; 'Homo phrenologicus: anthropological perspectives on an historical problem', in B. Barnes and S. Shapin, eds., *Natural Order: Historical Studies of Scientific Culture*, Beverly Hills, Calif., 1979; 'The politics of observation: cerebral anatomy and social interests in the Edinburgh phrenology disputes', in R. Wallis, ed., *On the Margins of Science: The Social Construction of Rejected Knowledge*, Keele, Staffs., 1979; Shapin and Schaffer, *Leviathan and the Air-Pump*.

doctrines in Edinburgh in the first four decades of the nineteenth century. He shows how these doctrines were opposed by the 'cultural élite', centred on the Royal Society of Edinburgh, who saw in them a threat to the existing educational and social establishment, and, in the case of moral philosophers and medics, to their professional interests and authority as well. By contrast, 'disaffected mercantile groups', centred on the Phrenological Society, saw in phrenology a means to social reform.

Phrenologists claimed that a reliable observation-based (and therefore 'scientific') system of character-diagnoses was a prerequisite to *shifting* human nature in a desired direction; for the size of the 35 cerebral organs subserving each distinct mental faculty indicated the traits an individual would come to display, *other things being equal*. Things could be made 'unequal' by a whole array of interventionist environmental techniques; education, public health, even, over generations, what later came to be called 'eugenic' marriages. British (and American) phrenology thus developed into one of the most important naturalistic resources deployed by bourgeois social reformers.[17]

Shapin is at pains to forestall the objection that conditioning of reception by interests operates only at the level of theory. He shows in detail how the Edinburgh disputants' selection, preparation and interpretation of anatomical data were no less informed by their interests.[18]

Throughout his account of the Edinburgh career of phrenology Shapin is concerned to emphasize the inextricability of the 'intellectual' and the 'social': to exhibit the intimacy of the links between, on the one hand, dispute concerning the principles, methods and data of phrenology and, on the other hand, social and political confrontation on the issues of authority, public accountability, and reform in the educational and moral spheres.

In Shapin and Schaffer's *Leviathan and the Air-Pump: Hobbes, Boyle and the Experimental Life* the themes of the inextricability of social and cognitive dispute and of the penetration by interests of the entire body of practices which constitute a discipline are developed in unprecedented detail. In addition to their exemplary avoidance of the salient objections to early interest theoretic studies, two features of this work lend it a special relevance to our

[17] S. Shapin, 'History of science and its sociological reconstructions', *History of Science*, 20 (1982), 157–211, 185.
[18] Shapin, 'The politics of observation'.

concerns. One is the exhaustiveness of its treatment of the methods and practices that led to consensus on the reliability of the instrument, on the proper ways to use it and on the admissible modes of interpretation of its deliverances: methods of construction, operation and calibration of the air-pump ('material technologies' in their sense), methods of communication of experimental findings ('literary technologies') and methods of assessment of natural philosophical and experimental claims and claimants ('social technologies'), all are exposed in the most scrupulous detail. The other is the richness and specificity of the interests, many of them at play outside the immediate circles of the operators and critics of the air-pump, whose workings are exhibited: interests in the demarcation and integrity of experimental natural philosophy, of its competent practitioners and its proper places of public performance; interests in the control of interpretation and explanation of experimental findings; interests in the preservation or renegotiation of the boundaries and statuses of existing disciplines and forms of knowledge; interests in the institution and enforcement of standards of moral decency in dispute and criticism; interests in the recruitment of potential allies and in the isolation of implacable opponents; interests in the preservation of structures of moral, religious, social and political authority against sectarianism and popular enthusiasm.

Before we consider the impact of the sophisticated versions of the interest theory on our claims for the prevalence of fair calibration as a source of consensus in the sciences, it is as well to dispose briskly of two lines of thought, of which one would make the interest theory trivially true, whilst the other would make it trivially false. The trivial proof of the interest theory rests on the assumption that formation of beliefs, or at least acceptance of beliefs, can be modelled on rational action. On standard accounts of rational action (ignoring certain technical epicycles) premises of the form 'X believes that doing Y will bring about Z' and 'X desires Z' always figure in the explanation of action Y. So, if belief or acceptance is modelled on rational action, it seems that interests must figure in all explanations of belief. The corresponding trivial refutation rests on the converse assumption that belief formation (and/or acceptance) cannot be modelled on rational action, because it is conceptually impossible to decide to believe. An agent's perception that holding a belief would serve his or her interests is not an item of the right kind to serve as a premiss in the explanation of his or her holding of the belief in question. We need not enter here into the analytic niceties of these conflicting models of belief formation. Even if we accept the, in my view entirely implausible, rational action model of belief formation or acceptance, interest theory is not proved. For this account leaves room for formation or acceptance of beliefs on any grounds whatsoever, provided only that the agent wants to have beliefs that are thus grounded. Thus proved, the interest theory becomes vacuous. Conversely and more interestingly, insistence that belief is not a matter of decision does very little to undermine the interest theory. Even if we leave aside cases of the kinds beloved of analysts—injection of belief-inducing drugs, hypnotic suggestion, etc.—there remains a host of ways in which interests can nevertheless play central roles in formation and acceptance of beliefs: they may predispose the interested party to seek out or attend to certain kinds of evidence rather than others (as Shapin shows in the case of the anatomical data invoked in the Edinburgh phrenology disputes); they may motivate the interested party in seeking to tailor an 'interesting' hypothesis to fit his or her criteria of acceptability; they may motivate agnostics or unbelievers to so present claims that others will come to believe them; etc.

A further preliminary remark concerning scientific rationality is in order. Many of the earlier interest theoretic studies of the sciences were concerned to show how interests motivate the formation and acceptance of beliefs in ways that are at odds with present-day standards of scientific rationality. (Ironically, many of these earlier studies, by appealing to philosophical theses concerning underdetermination of theory by data in order to provide leeway for the operation of interests in the determination of theoretical beliefs, display an implicit commitment to current empiricist standards of scientific rationality.) In the more sophisticated recent studies considerations of rationality often enter in a different manner, the concern being to exhibit the conditioning of formation and acceptance of beliefs by interests in ways that are at odds with the standards of rationality publicly espoused by the interested parties themselves. For our present purposes such divergences between interest-motivated choices and strategies and general standards of scientific rationality, whether present or past, are of little concern. For we have already argued that general standards of scientific rationality rarely play substantial roles as determinants of scenes of inquiry. Our prime concern is with the local and specific methods and practices that are, so we have argued, the primary determinants of scenes of inquiry in the sciences. In particular, we are concerned with their reliability as manifested by their fair calibration, or at least their fair calibrability: whether or not the methods possess the additional conceptually dubious attribute of rationality is a matter of little concern to us.

Another favourite target of interest theoretic studies is that form of naïve realism that treats observational and experimental findings as 'transparent' indicators of wordly states of affairs. It may well be objected that this is a doctrine which no self-respecting present-day realist would entertain for a moment, a horse flogged to death in the 1960s. However, this form of naïve realism is not quite the unworthy target it might appear, being at least implicit in much scientific writing and in much standard historiography of science. Opposition to such realism has been one of the primary motivations of sociologists of science in seeking to uncover the often tacit and devious practices and the prolonged and strategically complex negotiations that mediate consensus on observational and experimental findings. Given our concern with the calibration of such practices and strategies, we may happily join forces with the interest theorists in opposing the naïve realism which serves to conceal them.

These preliminary provisos do little to mitigate the challenge to the prevalence of methods amenable to calibration that is posed by the more sophisticated applications of the interest theory. For these studies purport to show the operation of specific professional, social and political interests over the entire range of the methods and practices that mediate closure of debate in the sciences.

One line along which we may seek to soften the impact of these findings has to do with time-scale. A genuine threat to the effectiveness of calibrated and calibrable methods in bringing about consensus arises when interests are shown to play a dominant role in the formation not of local and temporary consensuses, but of a stable and general consensus. Thus one might, for example, seek to escape the threat posed by Shapin's study of the Edinburgh phrenology disputes by insisting that a genuine challenge would have to be based not on a study of reception of phrenological doctrines and techniques in the opening decades of the nineteenth century at a single site, but rather on a study of the interests at play in the eventual Europe-wide rejection of phrenological claims in the 1850s and 1860s.

A second and potentially powerful line of resistance concerns the conditions under which appeals to interests are effective. It is a widely observed precept, perhaps even a cultural universal of capitalist societies, that one should not buy a pig in a poke. There is a substantial class of appeals to interests that are unlikely to secure stable consensus on theories, hypotheses and methods amongst those observant of this precept unless backed up by convincing demonstrations that the cognitive goods in question yield an adequate pay-off of predictive and technological successes. The substantial role of appeals to interests of this kind does not *per se* militate against the effectiveness of calibrated or calibrable methods in securing consensus. Rather, the problem is displaced. There is an onus on the interest theorist to show that acceptance of the relevant demonstrations of predictive and technological success was itself conditioned by interests; and a corresponding onus on the defender of the efficacy of calibration to show that the demonstrations employed methods that were calibrated, or at least calibrable.

A similar displacement of onus is often in order when the interests shown to be effective in securing consensus are the professional interests of some discipline or of some school, institution or research tradition within a discipline. Here the crucial issue is that of the status of the doctrines, methods and practices of the relevant discipline or faction. The onus is on the interest theorist to show that these doctrinal and methodological commitments are themselves to be explained in terms of interests; the corresponding onus on the defender of the prevalence and effectiveness of calibration is to demonstrate the role of calibration in securing stable commitment to those doctrines and methods.

Finally, there is a charge of *tu quoque!* that can, on occasion, be levelled at the findings of interest theorists. It is widely assumed amongst interest theorists that whereas agents' claims about the roles of rationality, reliability, calibration, proof, fact, etc. in the formation of their beliefs are suspect, being likely to belong to the secondary mechanism of legitimation, their claims about the roles of interests may be taken on trust. Given the widespread human disposition to back winners and hunt with the hounds, there is

ample room for the suspicion that many of the declarations of
interest assigned by sociologists to the primary mechanism of
consensus formation belong in fact to the secondary mechanism
of legitimation of already formed consensuses.[19] There is, indeed,
much in the findings of Shapin and Schaffer to reinforce this
suspicion. In showing how natural philosophical doctrines and
methods have been exploited as resources in moral, social and
political conflict, they emphasize again and again the flexibility of
interpretation that allows one and the same theoretical construct
or methodology to serve divergent interests. (Shapin even claims,
unguardedly, that 'any sort of ideas may come to serve any sort of
social function. The link between ideas and social purposes is a
contingent matter.'[20]) Thus, as Shapin points out, phrenological
doctrines were associated with conservative political stances in
Europe, but with liberal reform in Britain and America. Likewise,
Schaffer has demonstrated the diversity of the political and
religious factions that were able to selectively interpret, adapt and
exploit Newtonian cosmology in their own interests.[21] In such
cases of adaptation of a given body of doctrine in the service of
divergent interests, and of divergent bodies of doctrine in the
service of a given interest, further explanatory factors must be
invoked if the espousal of the doctrines in question by the
interested parties is to be fully explained. With respect to these
other explanatory resources it is the interests in question that will
appear as secondary legitimations of doctrinal affiliations brought
about by other means.

Even when mitigated by the above considerations, there is one
particular claim, well documented in the studies of Shapin and
Schaffer as well as in recent works by Bruno Latour and Peter
Galison, that seems particularly threatening to the effectiveness of
calibrated and calibrable methods in bringing about closure of
debate in the sciences.[22] This is the claim that a substantial role in

[19] Bruno Latour has criticized interest theory along these lines: 'Clothing the
naked truth', in Lawson and Appignanesi, *Dismantling Truth*; 'Post-modern? No,
simply *a*modern! Steps towards an anthropology of science', *Studies in History and
Philosophy of Science*, 21 (1990), 145–71.

[20] Shapin, 'Phrenological knowledge', 242.

[21] S. Schaffer, 'Newtonian cosmology and the steady state', Ph.D. thesis,
Cambridge, 1980.

[22] Shapin and Schaffer, *Leviathan and the Air-Pump*; Latour, *The Pasteurization
of France*; P. Galison, *How Experiments End*, Chicago, Ill., 1987.

securing and maintaining consensus on innovations is played by the interests of groups and communities far removed from the sites of inquiry and communities of experts of the disciplines in which those innovations are proposed. Such remote interests include, for example: the interests of collectors of specimens and samples; the interests of makers and vendors of scientific instruments; the interests of planners and architects of the institutions of the sciences; the interests of patrons, sponsors and fund-giving and -raising bodies; the interests of popularizers, publishers, media men and advertisers; the professional interests of disciplines that threaten or are threatened by the innovations in question; the interests of entrepreneurs, businesses, corporations and 'the public', whose profits and lives are transformed by technological innovations; the interests of religious, social and political factions whose ideologies can exploit, or are threatened by, new methods, findings and theories. The role of appeals to remote interests is peculiarly threatening because such appeals will often be invisible to practitioners of the discipline in question and hence immune against criticism by them.

NETWORKS AND MULTIPLE CONSTRAINTS

The network theoretic approach to the study of the sciences, pioneered by Michel Callon, Bruno Latour and John Law, is, in my view, an approach of the greatest interest and fruitfulness, one that is at present transforming the sociology and history of the sciences.[23] However, in expounding the network theory and its implications for our claims about the roles of calibration in the sciences we face certain difficulties. The theory is of extraordinary generality, purporting to provide a framework for the analysis of the entire complex of processes whereby 'the production of knowledge and social structure is mediated through practice'. It is cast in a forbidding and largely French (or Franglais) technical terminology. And its most prolific exponent, Latour, is a genuinely funny writer, given to marvellous word-plays, paradoxes,

---

[23] See e.g. M. Callon, 'Some elements of a sociology of translation: domestication of the scallops and the fishermen of St Brieuc Bay', in J. Law, *Power, Action and Belief: A New Sociology of Knowledge?*, London, 1986; J. Law, 'On the methods of long-distance control: vessels, navigation and the Portuguese route to India', in *Power, Action and Belief*; Latour, *Science in Action*; *The Pasteurization of France*; 'Clothing the Naked Truth'; 'Post-modern? No, simply *a*modern!'

ironies and speculative extravaganzas that make interpretation hard going for prosaic philosophers and historians. My brief treatment of the theory will be humourless and, as with interest theory, highly selective.

We have noted how in the more sophisticated versions of the interest theory there is a recognition of the inextricability of the processes whereby, on the one hand, the social interests and social and institutional structures associated with the sciences are transformed and, on the other hand, consensus is achieved on scientific and technological claims. The network theory goes a step further, claiming that the processes of production of knowledge and technology and the processes of production of social structure are identical. In so doing, it sets itself up in opposition to 'sociologism', the view that social structures and interests can be taken as antecedently given resources in explaining the acceptance of beliefs and technological artefacts in the sciences (a view which is somewhat unfairly attributed by the network theorists to sociologists of science across the board). Equally, it is opposed to the 'realism' and 'technologism' which take the factual and technological deliverances of the sciences as antecedently given resources in explaining transformations of social structure and interests.

Callon has illustrated the principles of the network approach by an elegantly crafted study of the interactions between the fishermen of St Brieuc Bay, the scallops which at the outset of the study they were overfishing to extinction, and a group of scientists concerned with the possibility of increasing production of scallops of the local species using techniques of controlled cultivation and harvesting that had proved effective on a Japanese species.[24] He examines the ten-year negotiations and interactions between fishermen, scientists and scallops that yielded: scientific knowledge of the life cycle of the scallops; an efficient technology of controlled cultivation and harvesting; the organization of a community of specialists in the biology and breeding of the scallops; and an association of fishermen with exclusive scallop-fishing rights and an agreed, though not always observed, practice of scallop farming. Callon's account of these negotiations and interactions is in terms of the forging of links between agents and

---

[24] Callon, 'Some elements of a sociology of translation'.

agencies ('actors' or 'actants' in the network theoretic jargon): the scientists, the fishermen, the scallops, the containers in which the scallops are bred, and the records, descriptions, graphs and tables which represent the scallops' population sizes, life cycles, etc. Here is his summary of the network formation which instituted the new knowledge, technology and social structure of Breton scallop farming. It proceeded, he claims, in four stages:

(a) problematisation: the researchers sought to become indispensable to other actors in the drama by defining the nature and the problems of the latter and then suggesting that these would be resolved if the actors negotiated the 'obligatory passage point' of the researchers' programme of investigation; (b) interessement: a series of processes by which the researchers sought to lock the other actors into the roles that had been proposed by them in that programme; (c) enrolment: a set of strategies in which the researchers sought to define and interrelate the various roles that they had allocated to others; (d) mobilization: a set of methods used by the researchers to ensure that supposed spokesmen for the various relevant collectivities were properly able to represent those collectivities and not betrayed by the latter.[25]

Two features of Callon's and others' network studies deserve special mention. First, there is in operation a principle of 'free association'. No prior limits are imposed upon the kinds of entity that can be linked into networks. Secondly, there is a principle of symmetry. No prior limits are imposed on the kinds of thing that may dominate others in a network: humans may be enrolled and delegated by non-humans (scallops, containers, graphs, etc.) and conversely; scientists may be enrolled and delegated by non-scientists (scallops, fishermen, etc.) and conversely; and so on.[26]

Though scientists and scientific institutions have no a priori privileged rights of delegation and mobilization on the network theory, nevertheless the network theorists have devoted much of their attention to the peculiar capacity of a particular class of scientific institutions, 'centres of calculation', to enrol, delegate and mobilize heterogeneous and distant 'actants'.[27] From centres of calculation—laboratories, observatories, research institutes, museums, etc.—the world is colonized by mobilized delegates—

---

[25] Ibid. 196.
[26] Ibid. 221–3. See also B. Latour, 'Mixing humans and non-humans together: the sociology of a door-closer', *Social Problems*, 35 (1988), 298–310.
[27] See e.g. Latour, *Science in Action*, ch. 6.

informants, collectors with their vehicles and equipment, mechanical probes, field stations, etc. To centres of calculation there accrue traces of the world—specimens, samples, and representations in the form of descriptions, tables, graphs, etc. At centres of calculation these traces are further simplified, superimposed, combined. The products of such calculations—replicated in the form of images, articles, books, etc.—are published and distributed enabling centres to recruit and mobilize further allies and to isolate and disable opponents. Thus are established 'cycles of accumulation' whereby centres of calculation consolidate their dominion over the world and its inhabitants.

To date the only large-scale study of consensus formation within the framework of the network theory is Latour's *The Pasteurization of France*. Here Latour charts the careers of Pasteurian techniques, right through from the initial experiments on anthrax to the eventual deployment of inoculation throughout the French Empire. His primary concern is with the processes whereby the Pasteurians recruited allies, packaging and demonstrating their claims so as to establish community of interests with hygienists, farmers, agriculturists, vets, statisticians, military doctors and colonial administrators. In this way, he argues, they succeeded in establishing Pasteurian techniques and the Institut Pasteur as indispensable 'obligatory passage points' for those diverse groups. Latour revels in the heterogeneity of the linkages thus forged, finding them 'refreshing' because they 'play havoc with any definition of society or nature by unexpectedly tying microbes with God, heat with Academies and flasks with commission reports'. And he shows in detail how the formation of those links entailed not only the transformation of existing social structures and, especially in the French colonies, the formation of entirely new ones, but at the same time the transformation *en route* to consensus of Pasteur's initial claims and methods as the recipients selectively interpreted and modified them, adapting them to their own interests, practices and expectations.

Certain features of Latour's study make it a less than fully satisfactory illustration of the powers of the network theoretic approach. Partly because of the peculiar nature of this historical episode, and partly because the story is told entirely from a French standpoint, it provides relatively little evidence of the mechanics of all-out conflict in the sciences. (In particular, the conflict with

Robert Koch and the Berlin Academy of Sciences, in network theoretic terms a clear case of warfare between rival centres of calculation, is hardly mentioned.) Obstacles to the Pasteurian triumph of other sorts—the constraints posed by recalcitrant instruments, recalcitrant agricultural and medical practices, re-calcitrant weather, lack of funds, etc.—do indeed play a substantial role in Latour's story. But there is surprisingly little detailed discussion at the technical level of the ways in which they were eliminated or circumvented; indeed (as Shapin remarks in a critical review of Latour's *Science in Action*) it is easy to form the impression that Latour supposes that such obstacles were simply 'talked away' by the Pasteurians.[28]

However, I believe that network theory, with its basically agonistic model of the processes of production of knowledge and society, has ample resources for dealing with the roles in consensus formation of obstacles—both the obstacles posed by rival insti-tutions and schools and the obstacles posed by constraints on cost and availability of resources and skills, as well as the countless 'spanners in the works' that disrupt tests and demonstrations. Thus, in connection with conflict between 'centres of calculation' Latour has offered fascinating, if programmatic, speculations on the roles of 'proof-races' and competitive publication.[29] And the schema of enrolment and delegation of heterogeneous actants provides an effective framework for the treatment of attempts to assimilate, bypass or suppress material and technical obstacles.

A recent review by Latour indicates how little adjustment is needed to retell in network theoretic terms Shapin and Schaffer's account of the controversies surrounding Boyle's air-pump.[30] In this connection it is worth considering two other historically and sociologically detailed accounts of major controversies, Martin Rudwick's *The Great Devonian Controversy*[31] and Peter Galison's *How Experiments End*. The general pictures of consensus forma-tion that these authors take their studies to substantiate could hardly be more different—'social contructivism' in the case of Shapin and Schaffer; moderate realism and empiricism in the cases of Rudwick and Galison (tempered by recognition of the pervasive

---

[28] S. Shapin, 'Following scientists around', *Social Studies of Science*, 18 (1988), 533–50, 545.   [29] Latour, *Science in Action*, ch. 6.

[30] Latour, 'Post-modern? No, simply *a*modern!'

[31] Chicago, Ill., 1985.

roles of conventions, especially conventions of representation, in Rudwick's case; tempered by recognition of the role of historically contingent constraints in Galison's case). Nevertheless, their stories of consensus formation have much in common. They are stories in which conformity to current general canons of scientific rationality plays little part; in which local practices, skills and interests, often in sites and communities far removed from the centres of inquiry and expertise, are of crucial importance; in which initial claims are selectively interpreted, compromised and adapted to new interests and concerns *en route* to consensus; in which authority to adjudicate controversial issues is debated and redistributed in the course of the dispute rather than being vested from the outset in a privileged community of experts; in which the obstacles to consensus formation—cost, availability of resources and technical skills, barriers to communication, objections from allied disciplines, etc.—are strikingly heterogeneous; in which central roles are played by techniques and conventions of data processing and representation. Here we have stories apparently tailor-made for retelling in network theoretic terms, in terms of centres of calculation, of delegation and mobilization of hetero-geneous actants, of cascades of representations, etc.[32]

Network theoretic accounts of consensus formation pose a range of challenges to our claims for the predominant role of calibrated methods in the resolution of questions in the sciences.

First, it should be noted that despite the opposition to interest theory voiced by its proponents, the network theory assigns fundamental roles to interests in consensus formation. Interests, indeed, lie at the heart of the network theory: the basic mechanism of network formation which supposedly underlies all change in the

---

[32] In considering the potential of network theory to deal with constraints or obstacles it is of interest to read Galison's *How Experiments End* alongside Latour's 'Post-modern? No, simply *a*modern!' Galison (ch. 5) draws a distinction betweeen long-, middle- and short-term constraints on experimentation. The middle- and short-term constraints operate on time-scales comparable with that of consensus formation on disputable experimental findings, but the long-term constraints—imposed by standard instruments and traditional practical routines, by established professional interests, entrenched theories, etc.—are securely in place at the outset of controversy. In his review, Latour replaces the simple network model for the joint production of knowledge and social structure by an account in terms of cycles of production, the products of earlier cycles serving as 'givens' in later cycles of production. Latour's 'givens' match well with Galison's 'long-term constraints'.

cognitive and social domains is one of establishment of mutual interests; the basic strategy for promotion of claims is that of appeal to interests; and the basic mechanism of transformation of initial findings and claims *en route* to consensus is one of adaptation to interests.

As well as enchancing the threat posed by interest theory, the network theoretic accounts challenge the role of calibrated and calibrable methods in consensus formation on two further scores. Firstly, they assign crucial roles in consensus formation to methods and practices that are at once of questionable reliability and operative at sites far removed, spatially, cognitively and socially, from the communities of competent researchers and assessors in the relevant disciplines. This is threatening because it appears that such methods and practices will often be invisible to expert practitioners of the discipline in question and hence immune to criticism and calibration by them. Secondly, they assign very substantial roles to strategies of rhetorical and aesthetic appeal in the recruitment and mobilization of allies that lead to victory in controversy. This is threatening because these are strategies, it might be thought, that are bound to fail attempts at calibration, being as well suited to the advertisement and marketing of unreliable methods and false claims as they are to the promotion of reliable methods and true claims.

In attempting to meet these challenges a point already made in the connection with the interest theory bears repetition. The issue with which we are concerned is not the conformity of the processes that eventuate in consensus to canons of rationality, but their reliability as evinced by their amenability to fair calibration in the local historical and disciplinary contexts of their use. The fact that many of the methods and practices whose operations are brought in evidence by the network theory are either, by current scientific standards, irrational or such that the question of their rationality appears ill posed is irrelevant to our concerns.

On the pressing issue of remote methods and practices, lying at the ends of long chains of delegation, two considerations may somewhat mitigate the threat. First, we should beware of prejudicial contrasts between the sciences, on the one hand, as loci of criticism and calibration of methods and non-scientific activities, on the other hand, as loci of unreflective and uncritical practices. The fact that a method or practice has its primary sphere of operation outside the domain of the sciences by no means implies the indifference of its agents to its calibration against precedents and standards. Secondly, it may be observed that for practitioners of a discipline to be able to calibrate a remote practice or method neither constant surveillance nor even awareness of the existence of the method or practice in question is necessary. What is required is satisfaction of a 'traceability' condition. Suppose that the operation of a remote method or practice were in fact responsible for results at odds with findings or claims independently warranted in the discipline in question. Provided that under these circumstances practitioners of the discipline would be able to track down and diagnose those methods or practices as the sources of the anomaly, the possibility of calibration remains open. Alas, even with these provisos the threat posed by questionable but unquestioned remote methods and practices remains a serious one. For a host of cases spring to mind in which remote methods are so 'black-boxed' into machines or tacit routines as to be both beyond the range of criticism by their agents and unlikely to satisfy the traceability condition. The other major threat posed by the network theory, namely, the substantial roles in consensus formation that it assigns to rhetorical and aesthetic strategies, deserves a chapter of its own.

10
Rhetoric, Aesthetics and Reliability

INTRODUCTION

My concern in this chapter is with the roles in the sciences of the various forms of appeal to literary and aesthetic sensibility. Earlier chapters have given scattered indications of the importance of such appeals. For example, in our discussions of changes of scene of inquiry in natural history we have had occasion to mention the link between general shifts in aesthetic sensibility and the collecting crazes—for shells, for insects, for ferns, for monstrosities, etc.— which swept Europe in the eighteenth and nineteenth centuries and which had major impacts on the anatomical and classificatory practices of natural history. We have mentioned also the role of dramatic narratives of human and sacred history as models for histories of the earth and of the three 'kingdoms of nature'— minerals, plants and animals—that proliferated in the wake of Buffon's *Époques de la nature* of 1779. And we have suggested that a common aesthetic methodology underlies Goethe's ventures into art criticism and his new science of morphology. Likewise, in our discussion of the legitimating uses of histories of the sciences, we have touched on strategies of appeal to literary sensibility—for example, in the employment of histories as myths in which heroic scientists triumph over error and superstition to make great discoveries and achieve lasting fame. Yet further roles of literary and aesthetic appeal are implied by our emphasis on the importance of effective didactic methods in fixing and controlling the interpretation of the methods and practices of the sciences.

The pervasiveness in the sciences of strategies of literary and aesthetic appeal has been well documented in recent 'microsociological' studies of laboratory life and of the behaviour of scientists in contention. Thus, following Latour and Woolgar's pioneering *Laboratory Life* a host of studies have shown how in the processing of experimental outcomes for publication scientists

select, simplify, decontextualize and recontextualize those outcomes, by eliminating references to failures and accidents, by
removing qualifications and complexities, by strategic use of
references designed to place findings in a progressive history of
discoveries, and so on.[1] Michael Lynch has shown how similar
processes operate in the selection, preparation and enhancement
of photographic images for public presentation.[2] Nigel Gilbert and
Michael Mulkay in *Opening Pandora's Box* have shown how
scientists adopt different rhetorical repertoires in assessing and
interpreting, on the one hand, what they regard as valuable and
successful work and, on the other hand, work of which they
disapprove: in the one case they use an 'empirical repertoire',
ascribing discoveries to sound use of experimental techniques; in
the other they resort to a 'contingent repertoire' which airs
mistakes, accidents, incompetences, personal ambitions and
biases.[3] In the same work Gilbert and Mulkay indicate the
importance of joking and satire in scientists' treatments of
scientific practices: their emphasis is on the gentle humour through
which scientists habitually expose their own practices to ironic
reflection;[4] other sociologists have detailed the rhetorically
aggressive and dismissive humour that is often used to discredit
and marginalize opponents and dissidents.[5]

The interest and network theoretic approaches to the sociology
of the sciences discussed in the previous chapter provide more
general grounds for ascribing substantial roles in consensus
formation to literary and aesthetic strategies. Both approaches
imply the fundamental importance of the processes whereby a
community of interests is established between promoters and
recipients of claims and techniques. Literary and visual strategies
for the advertisement of advantages accruing from acceptance of
claims and techniques play obvious parts in the establishment of

[1] *Laboratory Life: The Construction of Scientific Facts*, Berkeley, Calif., 1979,
chs. 3 and 4. See also the papers cited in n. 25, below.
[2] *Art and Artifact in Laboratory Science: A Study of Shop Work and Shop Talk
in a Research Laboratory*, London, 1985, ch. 4.
[3] *Opening Pandora's Box: A Sociological Analysis of Scientists' Discourse*,
Cambridge, 1984. [4] Ibid., chs. 7 and 8.
[5] See e.g. G. D. L. Travis, 'On the construction of creativity: the "memory
transfer" phenomenon and the importance of being earnest', in K. D. Knorr,
R. Krohn and B. Whitley, eds., *The Social Process of Scientific Investigation*,
Dordrecht, 1980; also the papers cited in n. 28, below.

such mutual interests. And in the case of promotion of instrumental techniques and experimental findings, an equally important part is played by strategies for the effective and dramatic staging of demonstrations. Network theory prescribes further important roles for strategies of literary and aesthetic appeal: for according to network theory the processes of enrolment and delegation on which the production of consensus depends involve the casting of agents into social roles and the control of their activities in those roles. Again, literary devices are crucial. The terms and strategies of address of texts imply readerships of particular kinds, armed with particular competences and commitments.[6] Moreover, the modes of appeal to precedents and authorities in texts and the modalities and qualifications with which claims are made are means whereby bounds may be set on the reader's freedom to question, interpret and appropriate.[7] In network theory central roles in the attainment of consensus are assigned to the 'chains of command' whereby data accrue to and emanate from 'centres of calculation', that is, labs, museums, research institutes, etc. Such chains involve 'cascades of representations' in which descriptions and depictions of phenomena are progressively abstracted, simplified, scaled up or down, in the interests of impact, comprehensibility and amenability to combination, replication and analysis.[8] Aesthetic and literary appeal and sensibility clearly play major parts in the operation of such cascades of representations.

By way of further illustration of the roles of literary and aesthetic strategies in the sciences, let us consider briefly some recent historical studies which are suggestive of their major importance in the constitution of new scientific disciplines and agendas and the transformation of existing disciplines and agendas. The first group of studies to be considered concerns the literary strategies used to promote new conceptions of the nature and

[6] The 'reader in the text' is a major concern of the brand of literary criticism called 'reception theory': see e.g. W. Iser, *The Implied Reader*, Baltimore, Md., 1974, and the articles in S. R. Suleiman and C. Inge, eds., *The Reader in the Text: Essays on Audience and Interpretation*, Princeton, NJ, 1980.

[7] On control of interpretation in scientific texts see B. Latour and F. Bastide, 'Writing science—fact and fiction', in M. Callon, J. Law and A. Rip, eds., *Mapping the Dynamics of Science and Technology: Sociology of Science in the Real World*, London 1986; B. Latour, *Science in Action: How to Follow Scientists and Engineers through Society*, Milton Keynes, 1987, ch. 1.

[8] On 'cascades of representations' see B. Latour, 'Visualization and cognition: thinking with eyes and hands', *Knowledge and Society*, 6 (1986), 1–40.

status of experiments in early seventeenth-century natural philosophy. The second is concerned with the formation and transformation of the discipline of chemistry.

PLACING EXPERIMENTS IN NATURAL PHILOSOPHY

The experiments reported by Galileo in his *Dialogue Concerning the Two Chief World-Systems* of 1532 and *Discourses Concerning Two New Sciences* of 1638 have long occasioned acrimonious dispute amongst historians and philosophers. As Alistair Crombie has said: 'Philosophers looking for a historical precedent for some interpretation or reform of science which they are themselves advocating have all, however much they have differed from one another, been able to find in Galileo their heart's desire.' Crombie's observation is strikingly confirmed by the diverse interpretations of Galileo's uses of experiment. For Ernst Mach, Galileo figures as the prototypical Machian, using experiment to chart the relations between phenomena without regard to underlying causes; for Alexandre Koyré, committed to the importance of metaphysics in the sciences, he is a Platonist whose experiments are thought-experiments designed to induce an anamnesis in his readers; in the writings of Stillman Drake he appears as a former-day practitioner of a commonsensical hypothetico-deductive approach; for Paul Feyerabend, Dadaist and methodological anarchist, his appeals to experiment are of a piece with his general methodological opportunism.[9]

Recent studies by Naylor, Wisan, Dear and Cantor have cast the issue in an entirely new light.[10] Winifred Wisan makes out a solid case for supposing that the primary role of the reports of

[9] E. Mach, *Die Mechanik in ihrer Entwickelung historisch-kritisch dargestellt*, Leipzig, 1883; A. Koyré, 'Galileo and Plato', *Journal of the History of Ideas*, 4 (1943), 400–28; S. Drake, *Galileo at Work: His Scientific Biography*, Chicago, Ill., 1978; P. K. Feyerabend, *Against Method: Outline of an Anarchistic Theory of Knowledge*, London, 1975, chs. 9–11.

[10] R. Naylor, 'Galileo: real experiment and didactic demonstration', *Isis*, 67 (1973), 398–417; 'Galileo's experimental discourse', in D. Gooding, T. Pinch and S. Schaffer, eds., *The Uses of Experiment: Studies in the Natural Sciences*, Cambridge, 1989; W. Wisan, 'Galileo's scientific method: a re-examination', in R. E. Butts and J. C. Pitt, eds., *New Perspectives on Galileo*, Dordrecht, 1978; P. Dear, 'Jesuit mathematical science and the reconstitution of experience in the early seventeenth century', *Studies in History and Philosophy of Science*, 18 (1987), 117–34; G. Cantor, 'The rhetoric of experiment', in Gooding *et al.*, *The Uses of Experiment*.

experiments in Galileo's mature works is demonstration: they are designed to render the principles of his new sciences 'evident to the senses'. In terms of the prevalent theories of demonstration of the period this is a highly contentious strategy. For the experiments at issue are singular occurrences, artificial, and requiring expert skills. By contrast, the standard, loosely speaking 'Aristotelian' view required that for experience to be demonstrative it should concern general occurrences, be natural, and be available to all who make proper use of their senses. Further, in proposing quantitative experiments as demonstrative of explanatory principles, Galileo was breaching the traditional boundary between mathematics and natural philosophy.

Against this background it is possible to understand the rich body of literary and didactic strategies Galileo employed to secure assent to the demonstrative force of his experiments. As Ron Naylor has argued in a series of convincing articles, Galileo's published experiments, whilst certainly not performed or performable in the forms in which he describes them, are derived from experiments he did perform by processes of simplification and embellishment in the interests of dramatic power, comprehensibility and generality.[11] Galileo's mature masterpieces are cast in the form of vernacular dialogues. This genre, brilliantly developed at the hands of Italian humanist writers of the preceding century and a half, is peculiarly suited to Galileo's purposes.[12] It is well adapted to his attempt to appeal to fellow virtuosi over the heads of hostile and prejudiced academic natural philosophers and theologians. It allows free play for his virtuosity in rhetoric and dialectic (persuasion using 'probable' auguments).[13] And it enables him to employ a persona (literally 'mask'), Salviati, to represent his views, thus creating a distance between himself and the Copernican cosmology—a sensible, though as it turned out

---

[11] R. Naylor, 'Galileo: real experiment and didactic demonstration'.

[12] On Italian humanist dialogues see D. Marsh, *The Quattrocento Dialogue: Classical Tradition and Humanist Innovation*, Harvard, 1980; L. Russo, 'Novellistica e dialoghistica nella Firenze dell' 500', *Belfagor*, 16 (1961), 261–83, 535–54.

[13] On rhetoric and dialectic in Galileo's writings see J. D. Moss, 'Galileo's *Letter to Christina*: some rhetorical considerations', *Rennaissance Quarterly*, 36 (1983), 547–76; B. Vickers, 'Epideictic rhetoric in Galileo's *Dialogo*', *Annali dell'Istituto e Museo di Storia della Scienza di Firenze*, 8 (1983), 69–102; N. Jardine, 'Demonstration, dialectic and rhetoric in Galileo's *Dialogue*', in D. R. Kelley and R. H. Popkin, eds., *Shapes of Knowledge in Early Modern Europe*, forthcoming.

ineffective, precaution given that he had been warned by the
ecclesiastical authorities not to hold, teach or defend it. Galileo
makes subtle use of the genre in prompting the reader's assent to the
demonstrative force of his experiments. The reader is by implication invited to identify with Sagredo (the reader in the text in
modern literary jargon), the intelligent middleman between
Galileo's protagonist, Salviati, and Simplicio, the Aristotelian
dolt. As objections, designed to be neatly and wittily met, are
raised and answered, and as Sagredo is in each case gradually
convinced, the reader is led along a 'literary road to consensus'.[14]
But should the reader remain unconvinced, the implied cost is
identification with the much reviled and mocked Simplicio.

In an important recent article Peter Dear looks at the ways in
which Jesuit mathematicians of the period sought to pre-empt the
above-mentioned objections to the demonstrative force of the
outcomes of particular quantitative experiments.[15] The context of
the Jesuit treatises Dear examines is a didactic one. The
unorthodoxy of the means of demonstration promoted is disguised
by the use of the didactic genres standard in the Aristotelian
tradition—the commentary or exegesis, the treatise on a specialized
topic in the form of *quaestiones* and *objectiones*, etc. Disguises of
other sorts play important roles in the Jesuits' promotion of
experimental demonstrations. Thus, the artificial nature of experiments is often concealed through emphasis on their links to
naturally given experience, their particularity by suppression of
circumstantial detail and specificities of performance. Moreover,
far from rampaging across the disciplinary divide between natural
philosophy and mathematics as does Galileo, many of these
authors emphasize the purely mathematical nature of these
demonstrations; and, especially in the case of optical experiments,
they often describe the experimental set-up and its outcome in
strictly geometric terms, thus creating the impression of the
demonstrative force proper to a classical geometrical *problema*.

Genre, implied audience and polemical stance could scarcely be
more different in Boyle's *New Experiments Physico-Mechanical,
Touching the Spring of the Air*. The genre is that of the discursive
essay, prolix, convoluted and, to the modern reader unapprised of

[14] Cantor, 'The rhetoric of experiment', 172.
[15] Dear, 'Jesuit mathematical science'.

Boyle's strategy, apt to appear rambling and inconsequential. Boyle is out to establish competently witnessed experimental matters of fact, and in particular the phenomena revealed to gentlemanly audiences by his air-pump, as the sole object of certainty (or, at least, 'moral certainty') in the domain of natural knowledge. In so doing he stands opposed, on the one hand, to 'dogmatists' and system builders in natural philosophy who hold that it is possible to achieve demonstrative knowledge of physical principles and, on the other hand, to alchemical 'secretists' and 'enthusiasts' who claim authority for experiments privately performed in their closets. (Another target is the 'methodical' chemistry of Libavius and his emulators, discussed below.) In a fine article Steven Shapin has analysed the literary devices Boyle uses to convey both the credibility of his own experiments and the pattern of conduct he holds to be proper to a community of experimental natural philosophers dedicated to the production of experimental matters of fact.[16]

Shapin characterizes Boyle's basic strategy in giving credence to experimental findings as that of 'multiplication of witnesses'. Boyle constantly emphasizes the public character of his experiments, listing the witnesses of each performance and (on the precedent of legal procedure) indicating their gentlemanly social status. His essay is cast in the form of a letter which will give the procedural details that are required for the recipient to replicate the experiments or at least (given the great practical difficulties of replication) to believe in their replicability. Moreover, Boyle is much concerned to bring about 'virtual witnessing', that is, to induce in the reader the impression of having been present. To this end he self-consciously avoids 'not alone all ceremony and compliment, but even all rhetoric and care of language'; he provides a meticulous depiction of a particular air-pump; and he offers wordy and circumstantially detailed accounts of particular experiments complete with frank admissions of false starts and failures. To enhance his own credibility Boyle emphasizes his 'modest and sober' approach, in which 'reflections' on causes are offered only tentatively, confidence being reserved for the witnessed matters of fact. In adopting the unsystematic style of an essay he is at pains also to demonstrate the unprejudiced nature of

[16] S. Shapin, 'Pump and circumstance: Robert Boyle's literary technology', *Social Studies of Science*, 14 (1984), 481–520.

his enterprise, his lack of prepossession by any natural philosophical system. In so doing, Shapin shows, Boyle is promoting a model for the conduct of experimental natural philosophy, a discipline that was as yet insecurely established in Restoration England. The community of experimental natural philosophers envisaged by Boyle would be one devoted to the production and discussion of experimental matters of fact and committed to basing their physical speculations on them alone. By concentrating on 'indisputable' facts and offering reflections on causes only tentatively the community would avoid dangerous and divisive disputation and sectarianism. Moreover, in the controversies occasioned by his essay, Boyle was much concerned to lay down and illustrate rules for the peaceable literary conduct of experimental natural philosophy, a conduct that would avoid disharmony whilst preserving freedom of opinion by following him in his resolve 'to speak of persons with civility, though of things with freedom'.

Shapin's account is of particular interest for its demonstration of the extensive and varied roles of strategies of literary appeal in the formation and consolidation of an entire new discipline. The same interest attaches to two recent studies in the history of chemistry, Owen Hannaway's *The Chemists and the Word* and Wilda Anderson's *Between the Library and the Laboratory*.[17]

DISCOURSES OF CHEMISTRY

In 1597 Andreas Libavius published his *Alchemia*, in Hannaway's words 'the first text which conceives of chemistry as an independent and integral discipline divorced from its applications and which seeks to organize the techniques and prescriptions of the subject in such a way that they can be taught'.[18] As Hannaway shows, Libavius's text is to be seen in part as a reaction against the alchemical writings of Paracelsus and his followers, with their disrespect for authority and tradition in natural philosophy, their subordination of alchemy to the healing art, their obscure, vernacular and unsystematic presentation and their heterodox claims of personal revelation and 'astral cognition'. Instead,

[17] O. Hannaway, *The Chemists and the Word: The Didactic Origins of Chemistry*, Baltimore, Md., 1975; W. C. Anderson, *Between the Library and the Laboratory: The Language of Chemistry in Eighteenth Century France*, Baltimore, Md., 1984.

[18] Hannaway, *The Chemists and the Word*, 142–3.

Libavius sets out to create a *chymia vera* respectful of tradition, theologically unexceptionable, systematic, presented in Latin and generally worthy to be taught alongside other philosophical disciplines. Hannaway shows how the organization and exposition of Libavius's *Alchemia* follows the precepts of the revolutionary humanist dialectician and pedagogue Ramus (Pierre de la Ramée) as mediated through the teachings of the conservative Lutheran educational reformer Philipp Melanchthon. The Ramist method of presentation of an art or science starts with a definition of the entire discipline, then divides it by successive dichotomies into sub-disciplines, each concerned with a particular field of practical operations. Such a procedure is, Ramus had claimed, both didactically effective and philosophically sound—didactically effective because it covers the subject in an orderly manner; philosophically sound because it ensures completeness and exclusion of irrelevant material and because philosophical knowledge is implicit in the tradition of practical operations and techniques. Libavius endorses these claims, whilst concealing his affiliation to the radical Ramus, choosing rather to emphasize the grounding of his *chymia vera* in the orthodox tradition of natural philosophy. Libavius's rhetorical strategy in setting up a philosophically sound, orthodox and teachable chemistry was remarkably successful. His *Alchemia* gave rise to an extensive tradition of didactically oriented chemical texts lasting well into the eighteenth century.[19]

Anderson's studies are concerned with the relations between the experimental and literary practices of eighteenth-century 'philosophical chemistry' typified by the writings of Pierre Joseph Macquer, and the experimental and literary practices of the new chemistry of Lavoisier.[20] Particular interest attaches to her examination of the ways in which in his *Mémoires* on the nature of water (1770) and the decomposition and recomposition of water (1781) Lavoisier sets out to discredit past 'philosophical chemistry' and promote a new type of experimental practice, one which is to address new types of question using a new type of experiment and requiring a new type of chemical competence. In place of an ontology of invisible principles whose operations are inferred from

[19] Ibid., ch. 7. See also J. R. R. Christie and J. V. Golinski, 'The spreading of the word: new directions in the historiography of chemistry 1600–1800', *History of Science*, 20 (1982), 235–66, 242–3.

[20] Anderson, *Between the Library and the Laboratory*, chs. 5 and 6.

visible qualitative changes, Lavoisier proposes an ontology of material elements detectable by quantitative means. In place of a philosophical chemistry whose practitioners abstract from experiments hypotheses about the operation of principles and affinities, Lavoisier promotes an analytic chemistry whose practitioners use experiments to establish 'natural facts'. In place of open experiments subject to a variety of interpretations, Lavoisier proposes closed experiments, designed to control all variables except the one relevant to the question at issue and thus to force acceptance of an unambiguous answer.

Anderson starts with a close reading of the historical first part of Lavoisier's *Mémoire* on the nature of water. She shows how in describing earlier experiments which purported to demonstrate the transmutation of water into earth Lavoisier is at pains to tease apart experimental data (which he generally concedes) and hypothetical interpretations (which he generally calls in question). In retailing a chronological sequence of earlier experiments Lavoisier presents the move from open experiments to closed ones as a progress. And in charting this progress Lavoisier gradually insinuates his own views: that preservation and transmutation of elements is not to be inferred from observed qualities of chemical systems; that identity and persistence of elements can be detected only by quantitative physical means; and that only closed experiments in which all but the unknown variable are controlled can yield unambiguous and definite answers to questions, that is, 'natural facts'. Thus Lavoisier cultivates in his readers the expectations and habits of interpretation required by the second part of his *Mémoire*, the part in which he presents 'objective' descriptions of his own experiments and of the natural facts about the composition of water that they yield. In her account of the 1781 *Mémoire* on the decomposition and recomposition of water Anderson further analyses the literary techniques Lavoiser uses to gain the reader's acquiescence in the power of his closed quantitative experiments to yield 'natural facts'. She examines the ways in which Lavoisier exploits the distinction between chemical and physical agents—the one material in nature and subject to confinement and manipulation in a properly controlled experimental apparatus, the other able to enter and leave the experimental apparatus and providing the quantitative indices for detection of chemical phenomena. In particular, she shows how

Lavoisier uses this distinction in his critical discussion of the experiment in which Priestley claimed to have isolated phlogiston. In his reinterpretation of the experiment Lavoisier imposes his own conception of a closed chemical system measured by physical parameters and in so doing educes from the experiment a 'natural fact' diametrically opposed to Priestley's interpretation. She brings out also the way in which by judicious selection of the factors which figure in his descriptions of his own experiments Lavoisier creates the impression of closure, thus compelling the reader's assent to the 'natural facts' established by measurement of the single unknown factor. It is worth adding that in Lavoisier's descriptions we have none of the detailed circumstantial documentation conducive to 'virtual witnessing' of the kind elicited by Boyle's descriptions. Rather, Lavoisier's descriptions are authoritative, objective and highly simplified. Lavoisier displays no doubt that readers will believe that matters transpired as he says. Instead, there is a concern to induce in the reader what may be called 'virtual analysis': the experiments are described step by step in terms of the measures taken to control each potentially interfering chemical variable, leaving only the unknown at issue to dictate the outcome, in such a way that the reader is invited to re-enact the experimental analysis that leads inevitably to the natural fact.

Anderson's study is of special importance in the context of the present work. It is specifically concerned with a transformation of chemistry in which the scene of inquiry shifts, old questions being invalidated and new ones validated. Moreover, she explicitly relates this shift to changes in existential presuppositions (concerning principles and elements) and explanatory presuppositions (concerning the form of a proper explanation of experimentally demonstrated facts) as well as to changes in experimental practice (from open to closed experiments) and, above all, to changes in the practices of interpretation of experiments (concerning the relevance of experimental findings to theoretical issues and the kinds of 'reading' of experimental findings that are permissible). Anderson's claims concerning the central roles of rhetorical use of history in legitimating the new presuppositions and methods and concerning the literary strategies used to promote new experimental practices and modes of interpretation of experimental findings are therefore of peculiarly direct concern to us.

THE CHALLENGE OF LITERARY AND AESTHETIC
STRATEGIES

These demonstrations of the effectiveness of aesthetic and literary
strategies in the establishment of new disciplines and practices are
challenging on several scores to our claims for the predominant
role of calibrated and calibrable methods and practices in
determining scenes of inquiry in the sciences.

To start with, common sense is apt to suggest that literary and
aesthetic strategies are inevitably unreliable, being deployed with
equal ease to package true and false doctrines, reliable and
unreliable methods. On this score common sense is apparently
reinforced by present-day 'official' antipathy amongst scientists to
rhetorical and aesthetic strategies.[21] Such antipathy has, at least in
the case of rhetorical strategies, a long history typified by Galileo's
disparagement of the 'little flowers of rhetoric', Boyle's pleas for
rhetoric-free communication in natural philosophy and Kant's
dismissal of rhetoric as the merely entertaining treatment of
serious matters.[22]

A challenge to the very possibility of calibration of rhetorical
strategies is posed by the studies of Hannaway and Anderson. For
they appear to substantiate a Foucaultian view of rhetorical
conventions as the epistemes which validate, or make possible, the
ranges of questions that constitute entire fields of inquiry. Were
this so, calibration of those practices would be impossible for want
of independently warranted precedents.

There is a further ground for doubting the amenability to
calibration, let alone the prevalence of calibration, of literary and
aesthetic strategies. For they so pervade the discourse of practitioners of a given discipline in a given period that it is hard to see
how, in practice, specific findings and hypotheses are to be

---

[21] On present-day scientists' attitudes to aesthetics see M. Lynch and
S. Y. Edgerton, 'Aesthetics and digital image processing: representational craft in
contemporary astronomy', in G. Fyfe and J. Law, eds., *Picturing Power: Visual
Depiction and Social Relationships*, London, 1988.

[22] On past programmes for the exclusion of rhetoric from the sciences see e.g.
B. Vickers, 'The Royal Society and English prose style', in *Rhetoric and the Pursuit
of Truth: Language Change in the Seventeenth and Eighteenth Centuries*, Los
Angeles, Calif., 1985 (on promotion of a 'plain' and 'naked' prose style in the early
Royal Society); W. Lepenies, *Das Ende der Naturgeschichte: Wandel kultureller
Selbstverständlichkeiten in den Wissenschaften des 18. und 19. Jahrhunderts*,
Munich, 1978 (on 19th-cent. reactions against the ornate Buffonian style in natural
history).

attributed to their operation. It appears harder still to envisage, let alone carry out, controls in which more 'neutral' methods of presentation are substituted for them: often the only way to set such strategies in abeyance would, it seems, be to remain silent.

MEETING THE LITERARY AND AESTHETIC CHALLENGE

We should not, I think, be unduly impressed by the common-sensical view that rhetorical and aesthetic strategies provide mere packaging in which the true and the false, the reliable and the unreliable, may equally well be packaged. For the common sense in operation here is surely not the native and original brand, but rather a common sense informed by current standards of objective and disinterested presentation in the sciences. In the absence of independent argument we may well dismiss this view as a prejudice, and, moreover, one that is in the present context question-begging.

The challenge posed by Foucaultian claims for the total determination of scenes of inquiry by discursive strategies is less pressing than it may at first sight appear. For all their Foucaultian resonances, Hannaway's and Anderson's studies of consolidation and transformation in the discipline of chemistry do not in fact substantiate such claims. On the contrary, these studies show in detail how concerned were the reformers of chemistry, Lavoisier no less than Libavius, to assimilate from past chemical and alchemical practice what they took to be the sound elements—effective techniques and operations in Libavius's case, experimental findings uncorrupted by philosophical systems and hypotheses in Lavoisier's case. Thoroughgoing though their reforms of the literary practices of chemistry may have been, these reformers did not attempt to constitute anew the entire field of real chemical questions. Further, it should be noted that on the account of the reality of questions defended here it is almost inconceivable that the scene of inquiry of any discipline involving experimental practices should be determined by literary and aesthetic strategies alone. For in such disciplines there will be a range of questions whose reality is primarily determined by traditions of experimental practice that are themselves relatively unaffected by current literary and aesthetic standards (however large a role such standards may have played in their original constitution).

The calibration of literary and aesthetic strategies is apt to appear unfeasible in practice, if not in principle, if those strategies are thought of in terms of the styles and genres of presentation and representation familiar from literary and art history. For it is indeed difficult to see how particular findings could be attributed to such large-scale practices or how controls may be applied by suspending them. The difficulties are less in evidence, however, if more specific literary and aesthetic strategies are considered and if due account is taken of the diversity of the strategies within disciplines according to the subject matter, the kind of audience addressed, the author's education, the polemical target, etc.

In considering the extent of occurrence of calibration of literary and aesthetic strategies we may learn a lesson from interest theory. Just as the cruder versions of the interest theory were wont to portray practitioners of the sciences and their audiences as 'interest dopes', so there is a danger of considering them as 'style dopes', uncritically and unreflectively addicted to current conventions and fashions of representation. The view of scientists as 'style dopes' is encouraged by the declared avoidance by many present-day scientists of all forms of rhetoric and aesthetics, together with the presence in all scientific communications of strategies of persuasion that are indisputably rhetorical or aesthetic in nature. There are, I believe, genuine grounds for supposing that many present-day sciences are unreflective in their rhetorical and aesthetic practices—a point to which I shall return in the final chapter. However, it should be noted that the term 'rhetoric', and to a lesser extent the term 'aesthetics', have acquired distinctly pejorative connotations in the sciences, being often associated with popular scientific writing and the more blatant forms of advertisement and promotion. Scientists' reluctance to apply these terms to their strategies of persuasion by no means proves that they are unaware of, or unreflective about, what are in fact strategies of rhetorical and aesthetic appeal. There is, indeed, in standard manuals of scientific style and presentation a modest level of reflection on the rhetorical and aesthetic strategies appropriate to the sciences.[23] Explicit reflections by scientists on

[23] See e.g. R. A. Day, *How to Write and Publish a Scientific Report*, Philadelphia, Pa., 1979; E. R. Tufte, *The Visual Display of Quantitative Information*, Cheshire, Conn., 1983. For an analysis of the rhetorical content of the

the roles of aesthetic criteria in the formation and choice of theories and hypotheses are by no means rare. And at least one influential critique of standard practices of scientific writing, Peter Medawar's 'Is the Scientific Paper a Fraud?', is the work of a scientist.[24] Moreover, the historical studies by Shapin, Hannaway and Anderson, discussed above, give ample evidence of past critical reflections on specific rhetorical and aesthetic strategies in the sciences.

It must, I think, be conceded that certain of the rhetorical and aesthetic strategies prevalent in the sciences, especially in polemical contexts, are deeply suspect. To this category belong the strategies denounced by Medawar whereby experimental work is written up in the form of a fictional narrative in which the original performances and the inferences drawn from them have been selected, tidied up and chronologically reordered so as to make it appear that they were carried out in strict accordance with an acceptable methodology. Lavoisier's experimental reports, mentioned above, well instantiate such procedures and there is a large recent sociological literature in which its present-day prevalence is documented.[25] In the domain of aesthetics strong suspicion attaches to certain widespread practices of selection, sequencing, processing and enhancing of images in the interests of publishable standards of neatness and clarity and of convincing visual impact.[26] Equally suspect is the common practice of citation and acknowledgement designed to lend authority to claims even when what is cited or acknowledged is irrelevant, or relevant only under highly selective interpretation, to those claims.[27] And,

American Psychological Association's *Publication Manual* see C. Bazerman, *Shaping Written Knowledge*, Madison, Wis., 1989, ch. 10.

[24] *Saturday Review*, 1 Aug. 1964, 42–3.

[25] See e.g. G. N. Gilbert, 'The transformation of research findings into scientific knowledge', *Social Studies of Science*, 6 (1976), 281–306; S. W. Woolgar, 'Discovery, logic and sequence in a scientific text', in Knorr *et al.*, eds., *The Social Process of Scientific Investigation*; M. Lynch, E. Livingston and H. Garfinkel, 'Temporal order in laboratory work', in K. D. Knorr-Cetina and M. Mulkay, *Science Observed: Perspectives on the Social Study of Science*, London, 1983; J. Law and R. J. Williams, 'Putting facts together: a study of scientific persuasion', *Social Studies of Science*, 12 (1982), 535–58.

[26] See e.g. Lynch, *Art and Artifact in Laboratory Science*; Lynch and Edgerton, 'Aesthetics and digital image processing'; G. Bowker, 'Views of the subsoil 1939', in Fyfe and Law, eds., *Picture Power*.

[27] See e.g. G. N. Gilbert, 'Referencing as persuasion', *Social Studies of Science*, 7 (1977), 113–22; Latour, *Science in Action*, ch. 1.

perhaps most suspect of all on the score of reliability, there is the whole range of strategies of innuendo—concerning scientific competence, professional training and standards, personal and political motivation, etc.—designed to discountenance and marginalize opponents, rivals and dissidents whilst preserving an appearance of objectivity and disinterestedness.[28] Cuvier was, as we have seen in Chapter 6, a master of such veiled attack and similar strategies in respectable present-day scientific publications have been unveiled with relish by sociologists of science.

However, in assessing the implications of the rhetorical and aesthetic strategies of the sciences it is, I believe, seriously misleading to concentrate as is the wont of many sociologists of science on the strategies that are most obviously suspect on the score of reliability. For there are, I am convinced, many rhetorical and aesthetic strategies that have solid claims to reliability. In the case of rhetorical strategies defence of my conviction would be a major undertaking requiring treatment of issues of genre, authorial voice and stance, narrative and dramatic techniques, strategies of placement and control of readers, etc. that lie beyond the scope of this work. In the case of aesthetics I shall, however, make a modest attempt to substantiate my conviction, by indicating certain aesthetic strategies whose reliability is, prima facie, not implausible and by pre-empting certain arguments drawn from aesthetic theory which appear to militate against the very possibility of reliable aesthetic strategies.

THE VERY POSSIBILITY OF A RELIABLE AESTHETICS

Aesthetic appeal and response are, we have argued, deeply involved in all aspects of inquiry in the sciences: in the marshalling and deployment of evidence; in the promotion of new methods and practices; in the presentation and adjudication of factual and

---

[28] See e.g. H. M. Collins and T. J. Pinch, 'The construction of the paranormal: nothing unscientific is happening', in R. Wallis, eds., *On the Margins of Science: The Social Construction of Rejected Knowledge*, Keele, Staffs., 1979; Travis, 'On the construction of creativity'; T. Gieryn, 'Boundary-work and the demarcation of science from non-science: strains and interests in professional ideologies of scientists', *American Sociological Review*, 48 (1983), 781–95; Gilbert and Mulkay, *Opening Pandora's Box*; L. J. Prelli, 'The rhetorical construction of scientific ethos', in H. W. Simons, ed., *Rhetoric in the Human Sciences*, London, 1989.

theoretical claims. I shall concentrate on the involvement of aesthetic criteria in the choice of theories and hypotheses.

In discussing the various types of aesthetic appraisal that may be counted in favour of a theory or hypothesis, I shall call the aesthetic qualities held to be indicative of truth 'aesthetic virtues'. The three types of aesthetic appraisal that I shall consider are as follows:

Type 1. These attribute aesthetic virtues directly to theories or hypotheses. The choice procedure is that of opting, other things being equal, for theories or hypotheses that possess certain aesthetic virtues.

Type 2. These attribute aesthetic virtues to phenomena viewed in the light of a theory or hypothesis. The choice procedure is that of opting, other things being equal, for theories or hypotheses which 'bring out' certain aesthetic virtues in the phenomena that they explain.

Type 3. These attribute aesthetic virtues to representations of phenomena—descriptions, illustrations, diagrams, maps, etc.—viewed in the light of a theory or hypothesis which explains those phenomena. The choice procedure is that of opting, other things being equal, for theories or hypotheses which bring out certain aesthetic virtues in representations of the phenomena that they explain.

Recent philosophical literature on the role of aesthetics in the sciences has focused almost exclusively on Type 1 appraisals. I shall focus primarily on Type 2 and 3 appraisals. I do so for two reasons. First, I believe these types of appraisal to be major determinants of the consensuses that scientists actually achieve, so that the issue of their reliability is a pressing one. Secondly, I take it that their status as *aesthetic* appraisals is relatively secure. It is arguable that even the allegedly central cases of Type 1 appraisal of theories can be assimilated to other categories: appraisal in terms of intelligibility, inductive support, analogy with established theories, etc. In the case of Type 2 and 3 appraisals such assimilation is much less plausible.

Since Type 2 and 3 appraisals are relatively unfamiliar, let me offer some examples. The first is a very simple example of Type 2 appraisal. Here are Paul Churchland's instructions for perceiving the Copernican cosmology in the night sky—for seeing the earth and planets as orbiting the sun.

In addition to a familiarity with the Copernican view, two elements are sufficient to effect the shift. First, one must learn to recognise the several solar planets by sight. This is a two minute job, for they stand out in the night sky like beacons, and the differences between them in colour and relative brightness make them easily identifiable. And second, one must learn to reconceive all positions and motions in a novel (but natural) coordinate system for visual space, a coordinate system in which the permanent 'horizontal floor' of visual space is defined not by the local horizon, but by the *plane of the ecliptic*, the more or less common plane in which the solar planets and the Moon revolve. Let me illustrate with some sketches. Fig. [10.]1 represents a kind of configuration not uncommon to the western sky shortly after sundown in the northern hemisphere. Aside from the Moon, the four brightest objects in sequence away from the horizon are Mercury, Venus, Jupiter, and Saturn. As can be seen, all five objects lie roughly along the same line, a line which also intersects the recently set Sun. Now the average person, though a convinced Copernican, will find this arrangement little more than curious, if it is noticed at all.

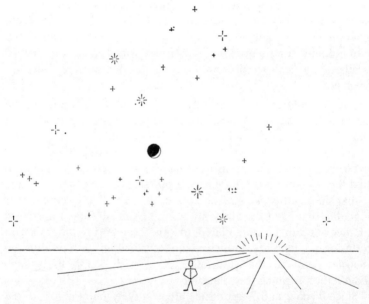

Fig. 10.1 The chaotic 'Ptolemaic' experience of the night sky just after sunset.

Source: P. M. Churchland, *Scientific Realism and the Plasticity of Mind* (Cambridge, 1979), 31.

But that roughly linear arrangement will become the dominant feature of the scene if it is viewed from a slightly different perspective. In order to see the situation 'as it really is', what the observer (in Fig. [10.]1) must do is *tilt his head* to the right so that the relevant line (the ecliptic, in fact) becomes a horizontal in his visual field. This will help him fix his bearings within the frame of reference or coordinate system whose horizontal plane is the plane of the ecliptic, whose origin or centre point is at the Sun, and in which all of the stars are reassuringly motionless. If this can be achieved—it requires a non-trivial effort—then the observer need only exploit his familiarity with Copernican astronomy to perceive his situation as represented in (Fig. [10.]2) . . . I urge the reader not to judge the matter from my own spare sketches. Judge it in the flesh some suitably planeted twilight.[29]

Suppose one follows Churchland's instructions and achieves the Copernican experience. For most people this experience is both

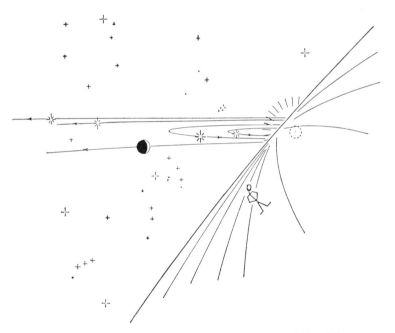

Fig. 10.2. The harmonious 'Copernican' experience of the night sky.
Source: Churchland, *Scientific Realism and the Plasticity of Mind*, 33.

[29] P. M. Churchland, *Scientific Realism and the Plasticity of Mind*, Cambridge, 1979, 32–4.

uncanny and pleasing. The Copernican cosmology reveals a harmony and dynamic order in the night sky which is sadly lacking in our usual earth-centred experience of it. This is surely an aesthetic experience. Moreover, it is an aesthetic experience that might well be appealed to in support of the Copernican cosmology.

In terms of complexity of imaginative projection this is an artificially simple case. For an instance which involves more strenuous exercise of the imagination consider the famous and moving passage with which Charles Darwin closes *The Origin of Species*.

It is interesting to contemplate an entangled bank, clothed with many plants of many kinds, with birds singing on the bushes, with various insects flitting about, and with worms crawling through the damp earth, and to reflect that these elaborately constructed forms, so different from each other, and dependent on each other in so complex a manner, have all been produced by laws acting around us. These laws, taken in the largest sense, being Growth with Reproduction; Inheritance which is almost implied by reproduction; Variability from the indirect and direct action of the external conditions of life, and from use and disuse; a Ratio of Increase so high as to lead to a Struggle for Life, and as a consequence to Natural Selection, entailing Divergence of Character and the Extinction of less-improved forms. Thus, from the war of nature, from famine and death, the most exalted object which we are capable of conceiving, namely, the production of the higher animals, directly follows. There is grandeur in this view of life, with its several powers, having been originally breathed into a few forms or into one; and that, whilst this planet has gone cycling on according to the fixed law of gravity, from so simple a beginning endless forms most beautiful and most wonderful have been, and are being, evolved.

Here the imaginative projection is exceptionally bold and complex. The bank is to be seen as locus and product of war, famine and death; but also as the site of harmonious coexistence and the evolution of higher forms. Moreover, the grim and serene aspects are to be envisaged not at odds, but reconciled: in this lies the grandeur of the 'view'. Again, the aesthetic judgement is supposed to count in favour of the theory which underlies it.

A nice example of a Type 3 aesthetic appraisal—attribution of an aesthetic virtue to a representation of a phenomenon viewed in the light of a theory—is provided by the 'beautiful vindication of Garcia-Bellido's theory' described in the following extracts from a newspaper report. I have quoted from this excellent article at length because the example cannot be appreciated without some understanding of the theoretical issues involved.

It started in the late 1960s in the Madrid laboratory of Antonio Garcia-Bellido, a professor at the Institute of Genetics. He was studying the common fruit fly, Drosophila melanogaster . . . Using a special irradiation technique, Garcia-Bellido was studying the fate of certain cells in the fruit fly embryo—he followed them as they divided and subdivided, to see which part of the adult fly they formed. His technique enabled him to follow not just the initial cell which he marked, but all its 'daughter cells' which formed colonies when the original one subdivided. And he found that, under certain circumstances, the colonies behaved very oddly indeed. He paid particular attention to the wing, which is a relatively simple structure, easy to examine. He found, to his surprise, that however small or large the colonies of cells were, they never occupied more than half the wing. There appeared to be no rule as to which part of the wing the colonies formed—some formed the anterior part and some formed the posterior part. But Garcia-Bellido's important observation was that at some point in the middle of the wing was an invisible line separating the front half from the back half. Colonies never crossed the line. Garcia-Bellido was well aware that his discovery was important. He had discovered an invisible something in a living organism, a structure—for want of a better word—which no one else had any idea existed. It was a totally new biological phenomenon. He had evidence, he believed, for the fact that animals—or at least the fruit fly—are divided into a number of normally invisible 'compartments' and that cells in the embryo 'know' from very early on which compartment they are destined for. . . .

Around 1982 two techniques had become available which enabled biologists to 'see' genes acting on embryos. The techniques are complicated but essentially they are like staining techniques where, if something is present in a cell, the cell stains one colour and if it is absent the cell does not stain at all. The Basle team were investigating a gene with an exotic name: fushi taratsu. It was discovered by a Japanese who gave it the name, which means 'not enough segments'. In its mutant form the fly never has enough segments so fushi should, if the theory is correct, help the normal fly have 14 segments. Using the new 'staining' techniques the Basle team treated a number of embryos with fushi and, using embryos five hours old, they produced a wonderful photograph. This showed the embryo striped like a zebra—with seven black stripes and seven white ones. This was the most beautiful vindication of Garcia-Bellido's theory. Here was a photograph of a gene acting on the embryo, in effect giving the individual cells 'instructions' as to which segment they belonged to. Clearly throughout development, genes act in series giving cells one set of instructions after another until the adult is formed. Some act on compartments, some on segments. But after the beautiful Basle experiment, no one could be in any doubt as to the basic mechanism.[30]

Note how natural it is in this report to talk of the photograph, which is literally of a sectioned embryo, as 'a photograph of a gene acting on the embryo'. To the untutored eye the photo is hardly worth a glance; but seen as an enactment of Garcia-Bellido's theory about the role of 'compartments' in the development of the embryo it becomes wonderful and beautiful.

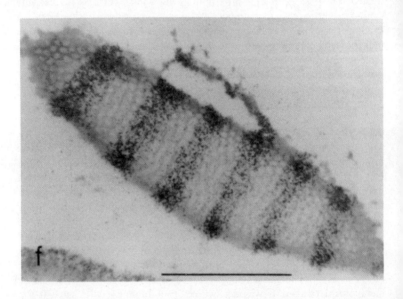

Fig. 10.3. From E. Hafen, A. Kuroiwa and W. J. Gehring, 'Spatial distribution of transcripts from the segmentation gene *fushi tarazu* during Drosophila embryonic development', *Cell*, 37 (1984), 833–41, 838. © Cell Press.

[30] P. Watson, 'The great Cambridge genetics race', *The Observer*, 7 Feb. 1988, 19–20.

Sometimes the aesthetic experience involved in Type 3 appraisals is vicarious. The aesthetic experience of the photo of the fruit-fly embryo reflects a possible aesthetic experience of a fruit-fly embryo viewed through a microscope. Very often, however, the aesthetic experience in question is of a kind peculiar to representations, and includes no transposition of an experience that might be afforded by the original phenomena or data represented. Consider a geological section which beautifully suggests the processes of deposition, faulting, etc. that have given rise to some present stratification. Only under exceptional circumstances—for example, when the section is derived from the face of a canyon or sea-cliff—will there be a corresponding possible aesthetic experience of the original phenomena on which the section is based. When we come to the aesthetic experience of graphs, tables and diagrams all connection with possible aesthetic experience of the original phenomena is lost.[31]

What rationales can be given for the possibility of reliable procedures for the choice of hypotheses and theories based on these types of aesthetic appraisal?

In each case the most obvious rationale involves the assumption that the aesthetic virtues to which appeal is made are virtues of natural processes or states of affairs. In the case of Type 1 appraisals the truth of theories is held to be indicated by their aesthetic virtues because true theories reflect the aesthetic virtues of nature herself. It need not, it should go without saying, be supposed that only true theories can possess those virtues; for that would make aesthetic virtues not merely indicative but demonstrative of truth.

The rationale is more complicated in the case of Type 2 appraisals. Here the natural account involves the assumption that aesthetic virtues are genuine properties of observed natural processes or states of affairs. The perception of these aesthetic properties is in each case enabled or facilitated by imaginative projection of a true explanatory theory or hypothesis. In other words, cognizance of the relevant explanatory or organizing theory or hypothesis is taken to contribute to an aesthetic competence. Grasp of the Copernican cosmology contributes to an

---

[31] The range of aesthetic qualities of graphs and tables is splendidly illustrated in Tufte, *The Visual Display of Quantitative Information.*

aesthetic competence to experience the dynamic harmony and unity of plan in the night sky. Cognizance of the theory of evolution through natural selection contributes to an aesthetic competence to experience the grandeur of Darwin's entangled bank. And so on.

The natural rationale in the case of Type 3 appraisals is similar. Again it is supposed that the grasp of true explanatory theories or hypotheses contributes to an aesthetic competence, in this case an aesthetic competence that makes possible or, at least, facilitates perception of aesthetic virtues in representations of data or phenomena.

These are surely not the only coherent rationales for the possibility of reliable methods of theory and hypothesis choice based on aesthetic appraisal. Alternative rationales are, for example, readily contrived by appeal to a pre-established harmony between mind and nature. But these are certainly the most obvious rationales. However, current aesthetic theory raises a series of apparently cogent objections to these rationales.

Secondary qualities

This objection is premissed on the view that the fabric of the world contains only primary qualities, the 'bloodless' entities of which we can form fully objective conceptions—conceptions that involve no thought of the responses of sentient subjects.[32] Aesthetic virtues, like other secondary qualities, are not in this sense objectively conceivable. So we cannot consider them as real properties 'out there' in the world.

The right response to this is, I think, a flat rejection of the premiss. But I shall not try to substantiate this here, since many others have ably defended the claims of secondary properties to world citizenship. It is worth noting, however, that this sledge-hammer objection, if successful, achieves an overkill; for it calls in question not merely the possibility of reliable methods based on aesthetic appreciation, but also the possibility of reliable methods based on empirical data. The cost of making the world so exclusive a club is evidently a high one.

---

[32] Cf. J. McDowell, 'Aesthetic value, objectivity and the fabric of the world', in E. Schaper, ed., *Pleasure, Preference and Value: Studies in Philosophical Aesthetics*, Cambridge, 1983, 2.

Illegitimate transposition[33]

I take it that the primary applications of aesthetic predicates are to perceptible objects. So Type 1 aesthetic appraisals involve transposition of aesthetic predicates from perceived tokens of theories to the theories themselves. And the proposed rationale for the possible reliability of methods of theory choice based on Type 1 appraisals depends on the further transposition of aesthetic virtues from true theories to the natural processes and states of affairs they describe. Similarly, the proposed rationale for the possible reliability of methods of theory choice based on Type 3 appraisals depends on the transposition of aesthetic virtues from perceived representations of often imperceptible natural states of affairs to the natural states of affairs themselves. The objection is that such transpositions are illegitimate.

Again, the right response is surely a flat denial of the premiss of the objection. There are absolutely central uses of aesthetic vocabulary in which such transposition of aesthetic virtues is quite obviously in order. Consider, for example, the attribution of aesthetic qualities to musical compositions on the basis of aesthetic appraisals of their performances. Of course, we are not always entitled to such transpositions. The verve of the conducting may not be transposable to the music performed. And in the passage from Darwin cited above, the aptness with which the tangled syntax mirrors the entanglement of the bank is certainly not transposable to the bank itself. Further, there is wide variety in the pattern of transposition from representation or performance to what is represented or performed. If one representation of a natural phenomenon is awesome, another serene, we may well suppose both qualities to be aspects of the phenomenon itself. We would, however, rarely react in the same way to different representations of a theory, one simple, the other complex. Here we are inclined to transpose only the simplicity, taking the charitable line that the simplicity of a theory is to be identified with the simplicity of its simplest representation. A general account of the patterns of legitimate transposition of aesthetic qualities from objects of perception to other entities would be a major undertaking. But it is quite clear that not all such transpositions are illegitimate.

The remaining objections are less easily met.

[33] On transposition of aesthetic properties see R. Wollheim, *Art and its Objects*, New York, 1968, §§35–7.

The aesthetic stance

This objection threatens Type 2 and 3 appraisals, the types with which we are mainly concerned. It arises from the view that attribution of aesthetic qualities to natural objects requires the adoption of an 'aesthetic stance' towards them, a stance that is at odds with our proposed types of aesthetic appraisal and with our rationale for regarding them as reliable indicators of the truth of theories and hypotheses. For instance, many nineteenth-century aesthetic theorists insisted that the aesthetic stance involves a deliberate suspension of belief in our customary interpretations of the sights and sounds that nature affords. Only thus, it was suggested, can we concentrate on the proper sources of aesthetic pleasure on 'beautiful appearances' and, reflexively, on the responses they evoke in us. Equally widespread amongst present-day aestheticians is the view that adoption of an aesthetic stance towards natural objects involves a pretence—involves viewing them as if they were works of deliberate art.

There are two lines along which we may seek to counter this type of objection. One is to attempt to relieve the apparent tension between these accounts of aesthetic stance towards natural objects and our proposed types of aesthetic appraisal. Thus it may be noted that the alleged involvement of bracketing or pretence in the aesthetic stance does not in itself imply that we cannot strictly predicate aesthetic qualities of natural objects. It may be that such indirection contributes to the reliable detection of the aesthetic qualities of those objects. After all, there are plenty of cases in which bracketing or pretence is just what is needed to enable one to see what is 'really there'. Consider, for example, the Copernican view of the night sky discussed above: perception of the true disposition of the planets is achieved by pretending that the visual horizon is in the plane of the ecliptic. However, a more specific threat is posed by the view that the aesthetic stance involves consideration of natural objects as if they were artefacts. Surely we cannot simultaneously envisage natural objects as works of deliberate art and at the same time perceive them in the light of a theory about the natural processes that gave rise to them: at least, Ruskin could not—he complained that reading Darwin had destroyed his ability to respond to the beauties of nature.[34] But

---

[34] I was told this by Professor Anthony O'Hear.

even here I am not convinced that we are faced with an insuperable conflict. Surely Ruskin could have continued in his aesthètic enjoyment of nature had he taken the line of many of his contemporaries, that of considering the natural processes that have given rise to the diverse beauties of nature as the secondary causes through which the Architect of nature works. Whether these conflicts can in fact be overcome will, of course, depend crucially on the precise ways in which these accounts of the aesthetic stance are elaborated.

The second line of resistance, my own, is yet again a flat denial of the premiss of the objection. These accounts of the aesthetic stance towards nature are, I believe, refuted by ordinary experience of the beauties of nature, experience which involves no pretence or shying away from our everyday ways of seeing.

Diversity of response

A consideration very commonly levelled at a realist construal of aesthetic properties is the liability of aesthetic judgement to the vagaries of fashion. Such liability may be inferred from fluctuations in the sales and prices of art works. At the level of cultural élites it may be inferred from instability in the canons of the various types and genres of art works. It may be inferred from the discontinuities between the critical vocabularies and theories of different ages. For example, Michael Baxandall's exemplary study of fifteenth-century Italian vocabularies for the gauging and valuation of paintings reveals sensibilities and priorities that are startlingly dissociated from those of such latter-day arbiters of aesthetic response to Renaissance painting as Walter Pater and Bernard Berenson.[35] Most striking of all, however, are the discontinuities in aesthetic response not of *cognoscenti* and theoreticians but of ordinary audiences, not of pundits but of punters. A splendid example is provided by Robert Darnton's account of popular reactions to Rousseau's *Émile*.[36] The modern reader of the work, armed with a powerful historical imagination, may be able to see why it evoked such responses. But he or she will surely be unable to respond in anything like the same way: the unaffected

---

[35] *Painting and Experience in Fifteenth-Century Italy*, Oxford, 1972.

[36] 'Readers respond to Rousseau: the fabrication of Romantic sensitivity', in *The Great Cat Massacre and Other Episodes in French Cultural History*, New York, 1984.

sentimentality invoked and evoked by Rousseau's masterpiece is no longer a serious option for us.

More directly relevant to our present concerns is the plentiful evidence of dissociation between past and present responses to natural phenomena. Looking at Turner's *The Great Falls of Reichenbach* or Kaspar David Friedrich's *The Wanderer above the Mists* we may achieve an insight into the Romantic sense of the sublimity of mountain scenery; but a comparable immediate experience is hardly likely to befall us as we wander in the Alps. Or, on a less exalted plane, consider the sententious, moralizing attitudes to the 'God-written Poetry of Nature' displayed in the flood of popular natural history books in mid-Victorian England.[37] Here even a vicarious insight is likely to be beyond our imaginative reach.

There are several ways in which we may seek to mitigate the force of this objection.

To start with, we should not be over-impressed by the historical diversity of aesthetic theories. Just as it is unwise to infer diversity in the practices of scientists from diversity in the general methodological pronouncements of philosophers of science, so it is unwise to infer diversity in aesthetic response from diversity in general aesthetic and critical theory.

Reflection on the nature of aesthetic competence may yield further mitigation. Aesthetic competence in appraisal of an art work of a given genre requires, at a bare minimum, a tacit grasp of whatever conventions and rhetorical strategies and repertoires are proper to the genre. In the case of classic works of our own culture our affiliation to a tradition of interpretation may create a measure of tacit familiarity with such matters. But the educative powers of traditions should not be exaggerated. Further, there are many instances in which aesthetic competence requires more than just a grasp of genre and convention. Specific and local knowledge may be needed as well: of provenance, of artist's intentions, of matters represented or alluded to in the work itself, etc. Clearly in the case of works from periods and cultures other than our own, aesthetic competence will often demand extensive historical knowledge and imagination. It is, therefore, reasonable to regard the evident

[37] See D. E. Allen, *The Naturalist in Britain: A Social History*, London, 1976, ch. 4.

diversity in aesthetic response to culturally and temporally remote works of art as in part the product of aesthetic incompetence.

Can diversity in aesthetic response to natural phenomena, the type of diversity that most directly threatens the reliability of the methods of assessment of theories with which we are concerned, be likewise attributed in part to aesthetic incompetence? A proper answer to this would require the development of a general account of competence in the aesthetic appreciation of natural phenomena, a task beyond the scope of this work. However, some tentative observations are in order. Our account of Type 2 and 3 appraisals of theories rests on the assumption that there are certain aesthetic qualities of natural phenomena whose perception is facilitated by, and may on occasion demand, competence in the form of understanding of the processes that underlie or explain those phenomena. This certainly does not imply the absurd view that all perception of aesthetic qualities of natural phenomena requires theoretical knowledge. However, it fits in most naturally with an account of aesthetic competence with respect to nature in terms of a capacity for informed and discriminating perception. Such an account has, I believe, great attractions. It would, presumably, entitle us to dismiss on grounds of incompetence aesthetic appraisals of nature that rest on gross pretensions about natural phenomena or on their facile and superficial observation. On this score we may well be entitled to dismiss many of the sententious Victorian appreciations of the beauties of nature, mentioned above.

Finally, it should be noted that diversity of competent aesthetic response is damaging to the claim that aesthetic properties are *in natura rerum* only if the diverse responses are genuinely inconsistent. Otherwise the proper conclusion to be drawn from diversity of response is simply that there are more aesthetic virtues than we might, from our temporally, culturally and socially limited standpoints, have supposed.[38] This last consideration is, I think, the crucial one. Much of the historical and cultural diversity of aesthetic response to natural phenomena is to be seen simply as testimony to the inexhaustible variety of their aesthetic virtues.

Aesthetic ambivalence

In my opinion by far the most serious challenge to the place of

---

[38] Cf. J. McDowell, 'Aesthetic value, objectivity and the fabric of the world', 3.

aesthetic qualities in the fabric of the world comes not from historical and cultural diversity of aesthetic response but from dissonance and ambivalence in the responses of aesthetically competent individuals. I may perceive in Schubert's *Unfinished Symphony* on occasion despair, on occasion triumph. I may perceive in Poussin's paintings both severity and sumptuousness, austerity and extravagance.[39] Darwin saw the entangled bank as grim, the locus of brutality and death, and as serene, the locus of co-operation and life. Nor is this to be accounted a local or exceptional feature of aesthetic experience. On the contrary, such multiplicity of aesthetic aspect is surely central to the phenomenology of all varieties of aesthetic experience.

This multiplicity of aspect forms a central part of the evidence for the involvement in aesthetic perception of a projection of imaginative expectations and constructs. As expounded by such influential aestheticians as Ernst Gombrich and Roger Scruton, the role of imaginative projection is such that there may be fully adequate aesthetic perceptions of one and the same object that are at odds in the sense that they could not possibly be combined in a single perceptual experience of that object.[40] Perception of aesthetic qualities is thus identified as a species of 'seeing as'. Just as in Wittgenstein's famous example one and the same disposition of lines on a paper may be seen as a duck or a rabbit, so one and the same aesthetic object may be seen as despairing or triumphant, as austere or extravagant, as pervaded by death or as infused with life. Such a theory of aesthetic perception makes it difficult, if not impossible, to sustain the view that aesthetic properties inhere in the objects themselves.

This challenge should, I think, be met by denying the analogy between perception of aesthetic qualities in objects and the seeing of 'aspects' of ambiguous figures of the duck/rabbit sort. As Wollheim has pointed out, the analogy breaks down even in the examples that are phenomenologically closest to perception of ambiguous figures.[41] In viewing one of Cézanne's paintings of Mont Sainte Victorie I may 'flip' from perception and appreciation

---

[39] I came across this example somewhere in Wollheim's writings.

[40] E. H. Gombrich, *Art and Illusion: A Study in the Psychology of Pictorial Representation*, Oxford, 1960; R. Scruton, *Art and Imagination: A Study in the Philosophy of Mind*, London, 1974.

[41] 'Seeing-as, seeing-in, and pictorial representation', in *Art and its Objects*, 2nd edn., with 6 suppl. essays, Cambridge, 1980.

of the painting merely as a painted surface to perception and appreciation of its content, a mountain in the distance, trees and houses in the foreground, etc. But these are not genuinely exclusive perceptions. In normal perception of the painting awareness of surface and awareness of content are combined—indeed, competent aesthetic response surely demands such a double awareness. Likewise, in other cases in which an object occasions apparently conflicting aesthetic experiences, reflection suggests that at least one of the dissonant experiences is of suspect authenticity unless there is the possibility of a perception in which they are combined or reconciled. It suggests, moreover, that the most significant aesthetic qualities are precisely those whose perception demands such reconciliation in perceptual experience. The living quality of Cézanne's painting lies in the marvellous integration of surface and content; Poussin's religious and mythological masterpieces are splendid in their sumptuous austerity; and the grandeur that Darwin saw in the entangled bank lay neither in its grim, death-pervaded aspect nor in its serene, life-infused aspect, but in a vision that reconciled the two. Thus we see that the freedom of the aesthetically competent imagination to project on to one and the same object a multiplicity of constructions does not entail the subjectivity of competent aesthetic response. However discordant the imaginative constructions may appear, their authenticity depends upon their reconcilability in experience.

My aim has been to pre-empt certain plausible across-the-board arguments for the unreliability and hence unamenability to calibration of uses of aesthetic criteria in the sciences. In the course of these refutations I have ventured a number of tentative theses, mostly negative ones, about the status of aesthetic qualities and the nature of aesthetic perception. It has become evident that some types of general aesthetic theory are much more friendly than are others to the possibility of successful calibration of certain types of appeal to aesthetic criteria in the sciences. Aesthetic theories that emphasize beautiful realization and embodiment of functions and processes obviously favour it; not so those that centre on the beauties of decoration, ornament and appearance. Aesthetic theories that impose strict conditions for aesthetic competence are much more hospitable to it than are those that licence free play and arbitrary appropriation. Aesthetic theories that foreground resolution of tension and conflict in aesthetic perception support it, where those that highlight irreconcilable aspects of aesthetic objects militate against it.

It might be thought that a proper case for the amenability to calibration of aesthetic appraisal in the sciences requires the construction of a systematic and general aesthetic theory. This is, I think, a thought to be resisted. The lack of significant convergence of belief in the history of aesthetic theory provides grounds for pessimism about the prospects for a credible general aesthetic theory. Moreover, it is likely that the aesthetic criteria legitimated by such a theory would be too general and too open to variant interpretation to place effective constraints on the practices of particular sciences. The only way to make a case for reliability of methods based on aesthetic criteria is, I believe, through calibration against precedents and standards. That is not a task for philosophers of science or aestheticians. It is a task for critical and reflective practitioners of the sciences themselves.

The amenability to calibration of methods based on aesthetic appraisal is, I am convinced, of crucial importance for our estimation of the claims of the sciences to have attained a modicum of reality in the questions they pose and of truth in the answers they deliver. Whether or not the factual and theoretical conflicts that have eventuated in current scientific consensuses are in principle underdetermined by empirical considerations, there can be little doubt that many of them are underdetermined by the empirical considerations that were actually invoked in the course of their resolution. Add to this the undoubted prevalence and frequent effectiveness in the sciences of uncritical appeal to authority and opportunist appeal to special interests, and the case for scepticism about the reality of current scientific questions and the truth of current scientific answers becomes strong. Now suppose that the various kinds of appeal to aesthetic criteria are, one and all, unamenable to calibration. Given the prevalence of such appeals in the sciences, the case for scepticism becomes overwhelming. But should calibration of the various methods based on aesthetic appraisal in use in the sciences speak in favour of many of them, then the cause of reality and truth in the sciences would be powerfully reinforced.

11
Conclusion: Beware of Science

In this work and its companion, *The Fortunes of Inquiry*, I have considered the status and credentials of the view that the natural sciences accumulate real questions and true answers. In the light of our deliberations how secure are the claims of the sciences to be accumulators of reality and truth? Before addressing that question, let us reflect briefly on the status and credentials of our own enterprise. Have we played the sciences fair in our accounts of truth and reality? Have we been sufficiently critical of our own theorizing? Does a philosopher have the right thus to pontificate on the credentials of the sciences? And if so, is there any concrete advice that we can offer to scientists?

There are two obvious ways of cheating when out to vindicate the accumulation of truth and reality in the sciences. One is to make the task of vindication too easy by a lowering of standards—by setting up or presupposing accounts of truth and reality that fail to do justice to their transcendence of error and partiality. The other is to overcome obstacles not by argument but by uncritical appeal to authority: by idolization of the real world, or of the objective standpoint, or of scientific rationality, or of science itself.

It is often maintained that only the construal of truth as correspondence to a mind-independent real world does justice to truth's transcendence of erroneous and partial perspectives. In *The Fortunes of Inquiry* I endorsed the Kantian charge of incomprehensibility against such theories of truth. I proposed instead a pragmatic account in terms of the eventual verdicts of inquiries that satisfy certain stringent conditions, and I argued that the account adequately dissociates truth from specific cognitive standpoints. In particular, I showed that the account comports happily with fallibilist claims that a substantial portion of our current beliefs may be false; and that it is consistent with strong claims about the elusiveness of truth, claims to the effect that there may be truths beyond the reach of all physically possible inquirers.

However, the account does place certain bounds on our insecurity of tenure of truth and on its elusiveness. It is inconsistent with the claim that every one of our beliefs may be false; and it is inconsistent with the claim that there may be truths beyond the reach of any conceivable form of inquiry. I do not think that the denial of these extremes constitutes a cutting of truth down to human size. Instead, I believe, these alleged possibilities are to be seen as metaphysical illusions generated by the metaphor of truth as mirroring, portraying, matching or fitting a mind-independent world.

There is another score, however, on which the charge of a lowering of standards is perhaps rather more pressing. Calibration, testing of the reliability of methods against precedents, has loomed large in this work. As noted in Chapter 8, calibration is not the only way in which the reliability of methods may be demonstrated. Suppose we are out to demonstrate the reliability of an instrument, a thermocouple, say. We may, of course, do so by calibration using objects and systems whose temperatures are reliably attested on independent grounds. But we may also do so by offering a causal account of the workings of the instrument, an account which explains why the readings of the instrument are, under certain circumstances and within a particular range, reliably indicative of the temperature of the measured object or system. Such a causal vindication tells us not only that the instrument is reliable under certain conditions and over a certain range, but also why it is reliable under those circumstances and over that range.

When we turn from the workings of instruments to the processes that eventuate in consensus on observations, experimental findings, hypotheses and theories, we are no longer in a position to spell out causal vindications. For we know very little about the causal mechanisms of processing of sensory input in individuals, and next to nothing about the causal mechanisms that may underlie the social processes that eventuate in consensuses. We can, however, envisage the possibility of such explanations, or so it seems. This general form would be as follows. They would specify causal chains emanating from the states of affairs in question, proceeding via phenomena (whether naturally occurring or instrumentally contrived) and the sense organs of inquirers and thence, via the cogitations, communications and negotiations of those inquirers, to the formation of consensuses about the initial states of affairs. Such explanations would, in effect, show that communities of inquirers who conformed to the method under consideration were, under appropriate circumstances, thereby constituted as reliable 'instruments' for detecting the relevant types of states of affairs. In Chapter 8 and in *The Fortunes of Inquiry* I drew attention to certain difficulties attendant on the programme of causal vindication of the methods of the sciences, difficulties having to do with avoidance of circularity, with specification of methods in forms amenable to causal vindication and with the coherence of the programme in the case of methods for the resolution of theoretical issues.

Suppose that the programme of causal vindication of the methods of the sciences should fail; and suppose too that the failure should be such as to suggest that many of the best calibrated methods of the sciences lack a causal underpinning of the requisite kind. Both scientific realists and holders of our pragmatic position would have cause for regret. For the programme is immensely attractive. It holds out the prospect of a fully naturalistic account of accumulation of truth in the sciences, an account which would show scientific knowledge to be, in Nietzsche's memorable phrase, woven by the 'great world-spider' herself. Moreover, it gives substance to the regulative ideal of a body of science capable of vindicating the methods by which it itself has come into being. Exponents of the account of truth as correspondence to a mind-independent real world would, however, have a very substantial additional cause for disquiet. From their standpoint it would be miraculous were a method reliable without that reliability being mediated by a causal story which anchored the deliverances of the method to states of affairs out there in the world. Faced with such failure, the metaphysical realist would therefore have grounds for global scepticism about the methods of the sciences, however well calibrated they might be. From our pragmatic standpoint such global scepticism would be quite unwarranted. Desirable though causal vindication of the methods of the sciences may be, there are no good grounds for insisting that behind every reliable method there must lurk a causally mediated reliable process. Calibration alone is for us enough to keep the sciences on the rails.

In denying the necessity of a causal underpinning of scientific methods have we cheated by lowering the standards of vindication for the methods of the sciences? I think not. Like the insistence that truth transcend the fruits of all conceivable inquiries this requirement is an illusion engendered by the idolization of the world.

We have charged metaphysical realists with idolatry. Are we too idolaters?

In a challenging recent paper Arthur Fine pleads for a 'natural ontological attitude', an attitude that will beware of adding 'metaphysical appendages' to science and that will forswear all attempts to specify the aim of science, to make sense of science as a whole or to vindicate science by appeal to 'outside authorities'.[1] Fine denounces three types of such appeal to outside authorities: appeal to The World, appeal to Method, and appeal to Semantics. Though we have echoed Fine in castigating invocations of The World and Method, has not our construction of theories of truth and reality placed us squarely in the camp of those who idolize Semantics?

By way of response to this charge we may start by insisting that what constitutes semantic idolatry is not the appraisal of science by semantic standards, but the uncritical invocation and application of such standards. In *The Fortunes of Inquiry* and the present work I have done my best to present cogent arguments for my accounts of truth and reality and to provide a balanced appraisal of the claims of the sciences to have accumulated true answers and real questions. However, there is a salient form of criticism to which I have not subjected my accounts of truth and reality, namely, reflexive criticism. What can be said in answer to the question: How do the accounts of truth and reality fare when applied not to the deliverances of the sciences but to themselves?

At the very least we may hope that such self-application does not vitiate our accounts, revealing inconsistency, vicious circularity, or regress. This is a non-trivial hope. We have already noted how self-applications of certain kinds of relativist accounts of truth and reality run into troubles on these scores. Self-application is equally problematic in the case of those metaphysical realist accounts of truth which attempt to spell out the notion of correspondence between semantic and worldly items in causal terms. The troubles here arise from the implausibility of consider-

[1] 'Unnatural attitudes: realist and instrumentalist attachments to science', *Mind*, 95 (1987), 149–79.

ing the alleged facts about the nature of truth as candidates for involvement in causal relations. (This is a special case of the general difficulty such correspondence accounts face in dealing with truth in fields whose subject matter manifestly does not consist of worldly states of affairs.)

More optimistically we may hope that reflexive appraisal of our accounts of truth and reality would strengthen them, confirming the relevance of the arguments we have used to support them and even indicating new kinds of evidence that might profitably be brought to bear on them. The following tentative reflections encourage this hope.

To start with let us consider the question: Are our accounts of truth and reality locally real, or, to be a little more precise, real for the community of intended readers of *The Fortunes of Inquiry* and the present work? To this modest question the answer is clearly in the affirmative. Some at least of the considerations that we have adduced for and against these accounts are patently of types taken by present-day philosophers to be relevant to questions about the nature of reality and truth. So, on our account of local reality of assertions, our accounts of reality and truth are locally real. It may be added that should our accounts of reality and truth cohere with the beliefs of a section of the intended readership, then those accounts are at least locally true, that is, true-from-a-standpoint in the sense set out in *The Fortunes of Inquiry*.

The aim of *The Fortunes of Inquiry* and the present work is, of course, to convince the intended readership of the absolute truth and reality of our accounts of truth and reality. In addressing this issue at the reflexive level we must consider the prospects for applying within the discipline of philosophy the arguments that have been used in support of the claim that the sciences have shown accumulations of true answers and real questions. Our principal arguments have depended crucially on historical considerations. Thus we have been much concerned with the historical roles of calibration against precedents and standards, seeking to substantiate the claim that, at least in certain traditions and disciplines in the sciences, calibration has been the predominant factor in bringing about changes in methods and that appeal to well-calibrated methods has been the predominant factor in securing doctrinal consensuses. And in *The Fortunes of Inquiry* the crux of the argument for the accumulation of truth in the sciences is a defence of the claim that in certain scientific traditions there have occurred historical series of theories or hypotheses showing the following 'progressive' features: cumulativeness, whereby from the standpoints of later theories earlier theories show an accumulation of truth; transcendence of error, whereby from the standpoints of later theories there is evident a successive over-coming of sources of error at the hands of earlier theories; resilience in the face of alternatives, whereby from the standpoints of later theories earlier divergent theories can be seen to have been either assimilated or 'explained away' as products of error or partiality.

Should it prove possible by appeal to the history of philosophy to affiliate our accounts of truth and reality to traditions that are calibrated and progressive in the senses indicated above, we would acquire, at the reflexive level, evidence of their truth. On the account of reality of questions and assertions that we have offered, the existence of such a domain of evidence guarantees the reality of our accounts of truth and reality.

To make out a reflexive case for the truth of our accounts of truth and reality we must first consider the general prospects for successful marshalling of evidence from the history of philosophy for claims about the predominance of calibration and the occurrence of 'progressive' series of theories or hypotheses. A proper treatment of these issues would be a massive undertaking, and the following remarks are tentative and inconclusive.

On the issue of the predominance of calibration as a factor in the establishment of doctrines and methods in philosophy there is one obvious ground for optimism. It has long been characteristic of philosophical writing to indulge in extensive critical reflection on the methods of the discipline itself; and criticism of methods by appeal to exemplary successes and cautionary failures has been, as in the sciences, a routine part of such reflection. On the other hand, there are major apparent grounds for pessimism. The challenge to the predominance of calibration posed by the prevalence of other types of legitimation—most notably appeal to literary and aesthetic sensibilities—seems in many areas of philosophy to be more blatant than is customary in the sciences.[2]

---

[2] For a brilliant and witty account of the constitutive roles of narrative conventions and strategies in the history of philosophy see J. Rée, *Philosophical Tales: An Essay on Philosophy and Literature*, London, 1987.

Further, in many fields there is an apparent lack of doctrines sufficiently generally agreed to serve as fair standards for calibration. Moreover, when the long-term history of the discipline is considered there is evident on a dramatic scale the dissociation of styles of inquiry that, as we have argued in Chapter 8, threatens the very possibility of fair calibration.

The following observations may somewhat mitigate our pessimism about the effectiveness of calibration in the history of philosophy. On the issue of strategies of appeal to literary and aesthetic sensibilities we should note that the threat is apt to appear yet more serious than it is if we allow ourselves to be prejudiced by canons of rationality which exclude literary and aesthetic strategies or by 'official' declarations by philosophers concerning the impropriety of rhetoric. In the previous chapter I argued that we should avoid such prejudices in the context of the issue of effectiveness of calibration in the sciences; and I believe that the same considerations apply in the various fields of philosophy. On the issue of shortage of standards for calibration of methods, it should be noted that such standards may not be in quite such short supply as at first sight it seems. For, as has often been remarked, the history of philosophy shows that when an effective consensus is reached on some range of issues the subject matter is often acquired by or formed into another discipline—logic, psychology, anthropology, linguistics, etc. Moreover, in many arts and sciences the boundary with philosophy is by no means clearly defined. The role of such disciplines derivative from or cognate with philosophy as sources of standards for calibration of methods should not be overlooked. On the issue of dissociation of styles of inquiry, it should be noted that in the history of philosophy as in the history of the sciences the extent of dissociation is exaggerated by concentration on the grand and universal methodologies articulated in canonical 'great' works. In philosophy as in the sciences we may hope to uncover methodological continuities by attending to the histories of the specific and often inexplicit practices and methods that have operated in particular fields and traditions of inquiry.

A similar attendance to particular traditions of philosophical inquiry is, I think, requisite if headway is to be made on the historical issue that is crucial for the reflexive assessment of the truth of our accounts of truth and reality, namely, the issue of their affiliation to traditions that are cumulative, transcendent of error and resilient in the face of alternatives. Exhibition of full genealogies of our accounts of truth and reality showing the required characteristics would be a major historical undertaking. But even short of such an undertaking there are, I believe, grounds for cautious optimism. To start with, it may be remarked that our accounts clearly satisfy a minimum condition for such a historical legitimation, that of affiliation to tolerably well-defined traditions. As suggested in *The Fortunes of Inquiry*, our account of truth is in the tradition of pragmatist theories of truth; and, as pointed out in Chapter 3 of the present work, there are precedents for our account of reality of questions and assertions in the tradition of hermeneutic philosophy.

Within these traditions it is, I am confident, possible to exhibit cumulative sequences of accounts convergent on our own, though it must be conceded that this would involve considerable interpretive and reconstructive licence. In the matter of transcendence of error too there are hopeful signs. Thus it is plausible to relate part of the divergence between our own account of truth and that of Peirce (a natural starting-point for the series of pragmatic accounts) to his, from our standpoint, excessive confidence in the existence and efficacy of a specific canon of scientific method. In the case of William James's various accounts of truth, which are in notable respects closer to ours, we can, from our standpoint, detect an overcoming of Peirce's methodological 'scientism': moreover, it is possible, from our standpoint again, to relate some of the substantial remaining differences to another form of scientism, James' confidence in certain highly contestable doctrines of empirical psychology. A similar transcendence of error could, I think, be made out in the successive approximations to our account of reality to be found in the hermeneutic tradition.

Resilience in the face of alternatives poses the most serious problems. But even here, there are some grounds for optimism. In *The Fortunes of Inquiry* and in the present work I have attempted to demonstrate the resilience of my pragmatist account of truth in the face of the divergent traditions of realist and relativist accounts. In particular I have argued that many of the central tenets of scientific realism can be conceded within the framework of the present account of truth as can many of the historical and sociological data which motivate relativist accounts of truth; and I have attributed the prevalence of the rival accounts to the specious plausibility of what are, from our standpoint, misleading meta-phors, unwarranted extrapolations, etc. (Similar attempts to 'capture' both realist and relativist premises whilst arguing for a denial of realist and relativist accounts of truth are to be found in Hilary Putnam's recent pragmatist writings.)[3] Resilience of the tradition of hermeneutic treatments of the reality of questions and assertions is harder to demonstrate for lack of currently salient alternatives. But even here some progress can be made. One can, for example, detect in positivist writings of the 1920s, 1930s and 1940s a strongly divergent tradition of verificationist accounts of the reality (in positivist jargon 'cognitive meaningfulness') of scientific questions and assertions. In Chapter 3 I argued that my account captures the acceptable elements of verificationism; and it would not, I think, be difficult to contrive an explanation of the divergences between positivist accounts and accounts of the type I have offered in terms of positivist commitment to what are, from our standpoint, erroneous views about the methods and cognitive status of the sciences.

I conclude that reflexive assessment of our accounts of truth and reality is indicative of a distinctive domain of historical evidence in which we may profitably seek evidence of their truth.

Both in the sciences and in philosophy it is, I have argued, history that constitutes the ultimate arbiter of questions about truth and reality. Are we then to be charged with idolization of History? I think not. History is no standard external to the arts and sciences: for all of them it is, as Schleiermacher called it, 'the realm of reflection'.

But there are grounds for a more aggressive reply to Fine's charges of idolatry against those who dare to criticize science. Historical and sociological studies show beyond a shadow of doubt that the working practices of scientific disciplines are both incompletely and inaccurately portrayed by the methodologies to which scientists officially subscribe. The challenges to the preten-sions of the sciences that are posed by such discrepancies are surely not to be dismissed as illegitimate interventions from 'outside' science. Rather, they arise from within the sciences, though from aspects of them of which most of their practitioners have only limited awareness. In the face of such discrepancies it is

---

[3] See especially his *Reason, Truth and History*, Cambridge, 1981, and *The Many Faces of Realism*, LaSalle, Ill., 1987.

surely indefensible to renounce interpretation and criticism of the sciences. To follow Fine in approaching science 'with trust and openly' is to submit to the most jealous of all the idols, Science Herself.[4]

What is science? Our deliberations have been unfriendly to the usual metaphysical criteria of demarcation: to positivist demarcations in terms of answerability to experience; to rationalist demarcations in terms of conformity to a canon of scientific method; to scientific realist demarcations in terms of possession of the real world as the object of inquiry and of a privileged causal ancestry for scientific knowledge. One might well suppose, as Fine evidently does, that recognition and admiration of the *de facto* category of science is harmless provided we reject the idea that there is 'an essence of science'. That this is not so will be the burden of my concluding remarks.

Just how much trust in science is in fact warranted by our assessment of the claims of the sciences to have accumulated real questions and true answers?

Against the standard general philosophical arguments for scepticism and relativism in the sciences—the arguments from underdetermination, meaning variance, dissociation, etc.—I hope that I have put up creditable and credible defences. However, I have not attempted to refute outright the specific doubts raised by sociologists' revelations of the prevalence and effectiveness in the sciences of uncritical appeal to authority, of opportunist appeal to vested interest and of the exploitation of literary and aesthetic sensibilities. Here I have offered only some grounds for supposing that despair would be premature. The positive task of vindicating the methods of the sciences is not, I have urged, for philosophers. Rather it is the business of practitioners of the sciences themselves to calibrate their methods against precedents and to replace or modify those that fail the tests.

This naturalistic view of scientific methods by no means implies, however, a subscription to a *laisser faire* attitude to science. Philosophers, or at least those of them who are prepared to inform themselves about the history and sociology of the sciences, have both the right and the duty to offer to scientists useful advice on methodological matters. Both in *The Fortunes of Inquiry* and in

---

[4] Fine, 'Unnatural attitudes', 177.

the present work there has been plenty of implicit advice to practitioners of the sciences. Let us conclude by making some of it explicit.

Our principal injunction to scientists is that they should take extremely seriously the findings of sociologists and social historians about the practices and negotiations whereby closure of debate on both methodological and doctrinal issues is in fact mediated in the sciences.

It is tempting for scientists and admirers of science when reading the more 'subversive' portions of such works as Collins's *Changing Order* or Shapin and Schaffer's *Leviathan and the Air-Pump* or Latour's *Science in Action* to react dismissively—to suppose that these sociologists are deliberately rubbishing science, that the disciplines, practitioners and institutions they have studied are atypical or deviant, that their accounts overlook some range of genuinely scientific practices. Underlying such dismissals is a series of comforting but highly questionable assumptions.

Crucially, there is the assumption that scientists are properly aware of the ways in which consensuses are achieved in the sciences. The assumption is evidently called in question by the division and delegation of labour characteristic of mature scientific disciplines and by the substantial roles of habitual competences resistant to articulation. And it is further called in question by the mass of recent sociological studies which show that accounts of the means by which discoveries have been achieved in the sciences, given by scientists involved in those discoveries and speaking in good faith, often have the character of *et post facto* rationalizations at odds with the practices and procedures that were in fact operative.

A further common basis for dismissal is the assumption that there is general conformity by scientists to a canon of rational or scientific methods. If sociologists and social historians fail to detect such conformity, that can only be because they have misinterpreted the practices they have studied or because those practices were not genuinely scientific. It has been a principal burden of *The Fortunes of Inquiry* and the present work that scientific rationality is a myth: that in fact the methods and practices of the sciences show an irreducible diversity; and that what matters in the sciences is not conformity to a canon of rational methodology, but the reliability and power of the methods employed as evinced by their calibration against precedents and standards.

Perhaps most insidious of all the bases for dismissal of sociologists' and historians' findings, however, is faith in the destiny of science, the belief that whatever the local aberrations of scientists the juggernaut of science is fated to go on revealing truths about nature.[5] This superstition is oddly tenacious. It seems that we have tacitly invested in the fate of science much that was once openly invested in sacred and spiritual histories of mankind with their promises of redemption and a millennium.

To repeat, scientists should take seriously the findings of historians and sociologists about their practices. This is not just a matter of preparedness to face up to criticism. To be sure, some of the practices uncovered are evidently unreliable, others suspect on the score of reliability and in obvious need of calibration. But on occasion what historians and sociologists uncover are not suspect practices but potentially powerful resources for the advancement of the sciences: promotion of hypotheses by appeal to aesthetic criteria; jocular and satirical critique of standard and entrenched practices; legitimation of methods in a discipline or tradition by appeal to its history.

Finally, we urge scientists not to be lured into complacency by the spectacle of fields of inquiry in which it seems that resolution of questions proceeds exponentially or that emergence of an ultimate theory is imminent. For the history of the sciences strongly hints at an inverse relation between the productivity of a science as measured by its capacity to solve questions within a fixed scene and creativity as measured by the deconstruction or enrichment of existing scenes and the generation of new scenes. Certainly bold claims about scientific progress and the imminence of grand, unified and final theories have often heralded great shifts in the scenes of the sciences.[6]

What makes such admonishments necessary? Why should scientists need to be advised of the dangers of the myth of a unique scientific method, given the manifest diversity of styles of inquiry in the sciences? Why should they need to be warned of the frequent discrepancies between their *ex post facto* accounts of the

---

[5] On the 'fatalization' of the history of science in the latter part of the 19th cent. see D. von Engelhardt, *Historisches Bewusstsein in der Naturwissenschaft von der Aufklärung bis zum Positivismus*, Munich, 1979, pt. 4.

[6] See e.g. R. Fox, 'The rise and fall of Laplacian physics', *Historical Studies in the Physical Sciences*, 4 (1974), 89–136; L. Badash, 'The completeness of nineteenth-century science', *Isis* 63 (1972), 48–58.

routes to consensus and the paths they actually followed? Why should they need to be told of the importance of disciplinary histories, given the obvious roles of retrospective chronicles and surveys in the prosecution of scientific controversies and in the teaching of the sciences? Why should it be worth informing scientists who look askance at literary and aesthetic appeal in scientific publications of the prevalence and effectiveness of such appeals in the sciences? Why, above all, should scientists need to be reminded of the need to articulate and calibrate the methods through which they attain their consensuses?

Part of the answer to these questions has already been given. The prevalence of tacit and habitual methods in the sciences together with the division and delegation of labour make it generally impossible for practitioners to have comprehensive knowledge of the practices of their own disciplines. But this is only a partial explanation for uncritical acceptance of existing practices; and it does little to explain cases in which there is apparent repression and forgetfulness of practices once explicit and articulate. Here much of the blame lies with the prevalent 'ideologies' of the natural sciences, complacent images which portray science as a disinterested and dispassionate enterprise, free of literary contrivance and rhetorical artifice, possessed of a special rationality, fated to reveal ever more of the inner workings of nature.

The alliance of disciplines that we call 'natural sciences' is of much more recent origin that is often supposed. Even in programmatic and utopian writings it is hard to detect such a category before the 1820s; and it is not until the 1870s and 1880s that this disciplinary complex becomes securely institutionalized and enshrined in the curricula, social structures and economic and political strategies of the industrialized nations.[7] Promotion of a unifying empiricist methodology played a major role in this consolidation of the natural sciences. Indeed, there is an element of truth in Habermas's dramatic claim that the end of the nineteenth century sees the replacement of traditional epistemology by the methodology of science.[8]

---

[7] On the 19th-cent. formation of 'science' see e.g. S. F. Cannon, *Science in Culture: The Early Victorian Period*, New York, 1978; E. Bellone, *A World on Paper: Studies on the Second Scientific Revolution*, trans. M. and R. Giacconi, Cambridge, Mass., 1980.

[8] *Erkenntnis und Interesse* [1968], trans. J. J. Shapiro, *Knowledge and Human Interests*, London, 1972, ch. 4.

In Chapter 6 we touched briefly on the great impoverishment of historical concern and awareness within the natural sciences that coincided with their separation from the human sciences towards the end of the nineteenth century, and we related this to the widespread reaction against a previously rampant historicism in the sciences. The repression of aesthetic awareness in the sciences that occurred in the same period can be similarly related to reaction against what were perceived as the excesses of Romanticism.[9] Sociological awareness too was, it seems, repressed with the growing social and political entrenchment of the natural sciences. Certainly we find in the nineteenth century explicit and detailed reflections by practitioners on the most effective institutions and forms of division, delegation and reward of labour in the sciences, reflections of kinds that scientists themselves rarely indulge in today.[10]

The time has come for scientists to break with science. What started life as a creative programme, liberating inquirers from limited scenes of inquiry, has become itself a limitation on scenes of inquiry. Freed of the mythology of science, scientists might become more perceptive of their varied practices and of the

---

[9] Notable attacks in the name of empiricism on aesthetic sensibility in the sciences include the assessments of Goethe's scientific work by Hermann von Helmholtz and Émil du Bois-Reymond: Helmholtz, 'Über Goethes naturwissenschaftliche Arbeiten' [1853], trans. H. W. Eve, in *Popular Lectures on Scientific Subjects*, London, 1873; du Bois-Reymond, 'Goethe und kein Ende' [1872], in *Reden*, iii, Leipzig, 1912. (Helmholtz, however, later took a very different line relating the beauty of works of art to the 'unconscious inferences' which enable the artist to express in his creations the unifying laws that underlie phenomena: 'Goethe's anticipation of subsequent scientific ideas' [1892], *Selected Writings of Hermann von Helmholtz*, ed. R. Kahl, Middletown, Conn., 1971.)

[10] See e.g. John F. W. Herschel, *A Preliminary Discourse on the Study of Natural Philosophy*, London, 1830, pt. 3, ch. 6; W. Swainson, *A Preliminary Discourse on the Study of Natural History*, London, 1834, pt. 4; Charles Babbage, *Economy of Machinery and Manufactures*, 4th edn., enlarged, London, 1835 (repr., Fairfield, NJ, 1986), §§217–46; J. C. Maxwell, 'Introductory lecture on experimental physics' (1871) and 'General considerations concerning scientific apparatus' (1876), in *Scientific Papers*, ed. W. D. Niven, i, Cambridge, 1890. In this connection outstanding interest attaches to two recent articles by Sophie Forgan which explore the ways in which the planning and architecture of scientific institutions expressed 19th-cent. conceptions and ideals of the organization, pursuit and teaching of the sciences: 'Context, image and function: a preliminary inquiry into the architecture of scientific societies', *British Journal for the History of Science*, 19 (1986), 89–113; 'The architecture of science and the idea of a university', *Studies in History and Philosophy of Science*, 20 (1989), 405–34.

workings of their own social and political institutions. They might
recover their lost literary and aesthetic consciousness. They might
re-engage in historical reflection. Then we should surely see a
wonderful proliferation and enrichment of the sciences and of the
lived experience of all who partake in them.

Index of Names

Abbe, Ernst 159
Achinstein, P. 110 n.
Adams, E. W. 82 n.
Adanson, Michel 19
Alembert, Jean le Rond d' 12, 85
Allen, D. E. 16 n., 105 n., 117 n.,
  220 n.
Altham, J. E. J. 157 n.
Ampère, A.-M. 85
Amrine, F. 37 n.
Anderson, W. C. 91 n., 93 n., 200,
  201, 202, 203, 204, 205, 207
Apollonius of Perga 134
Appel, T. A. 50 n., 108 n., 116 n.,
  141 n.
Appignanesi, L. 172 n., 184 n.
Archimedes 81, 132
Ariès, Philippe 92
Aristotle 81, 99, 100, 111, 112, 123,
  134, 136, 197, 198
Ash, M. G. 131 n.
Asquith, P. D. 82 n.
Atran, Scott 96, 97, 98, 99, 117
Averroës 111

Babbage, Charles 238 n.
Bachelard, Gaston 131
Bacon, F. 14, 76, 85, 86, 102, 104, 131
Badash, L. 236 n.
Baer, Nicolai Reymers, see Ursus
Balan, B. 21 n., 102 n.
Balss, H. 36 n.
Barckhausen, J. K. 137
Barnes, B. 178 n.
Barthez, Paul-Joseph 22, 85
Bastide, F. 195 n.
Bateson, W. 121
al-Battani 133
Baxandall, Michael 219
Bazerman, C. 89 n., 91 n., 206 n.
Beiser, F. 35 n.
Bellone, E. 237 n.
Ben Chaim, Michael 149 n.
Benjamin, A. E. 89 n., 91 n.
Berenson, Bernhard 219
Berman, M. 90 n.
Bernard, Claude 123 and n.
Bernard, J. H. 30 n.

Beutler, E. 37 n., 38 n.
Blackburn, P. 84 n.
Blumenbach, J. F. 11, 22, 23, 25–8, 32,
  33, 36, 37, 50, 52 n., 53, 54, 55, 81,
  85, 87, 101, 112, 142, 143, 162, 166
Bloch, Marc 92
Bocheński, I. M. 99 n.
Boer, S. 57 n.
Boerhaave, Hermann 103
Boissier de Sauvages, F. 18
Bowker, G. 207 n.
Boyle, Robert 104, 106, 175, 176, 178,
  189, 198, 199, 200, 203, 204
Bradbury, S. 166 n.
Bradley, F. 67 n.
Brahe, Tycho 132, 133, 134, 135, 136
Brannigan, A. 80 n.
Braun, L. 126 n.
Bräuning-Oktavio, H. 37 n., 49 n.,
  80 n., 86 n.
Brinkmann, R. 45 n.
Brown, O. 166 n.
Brown, T. M. 21 n., 85 n., 103 and n.
Browne, J. 20 n., 116 n.
Bruford, W. H. 70 n.
Buchdahl, G. 66 n., 165 n.
Buchenau, A. 28 n., 29 n.
Buffon 20, 21 n., 24, 28, 113 and n.,
  144, 193
Burke, U. P. 92 n., 93 n.
Busse, G. 45 n., 52 n.
Butler, S. 166 n.
Butts, R. E. 196 n.
Bylebyl, J. J. 111 n.
Bynum, W. F. 131 n.

Cagogni, A. 74 n.
Cahan, D. 114 n.
Callon, Michel 185, 186, 187, 195 n.
Camper, Petrus 42 n., 105
Cannon, S. F. 237 n.
Cantor, G. N. 89 n., 196, 198 n.
Carus, K. G. 50
Cassini, J. D. 122
Cassirer, E. 29 n.
Cézanne 222, 223
Charlton, D. G. 17 n.
Choulant, L. 117 n.

Christie, J. R. R. 89 n., 201 n.
Churchill, T. 34 n.
Churchland, Paul M. 209, 210 n., 211
Churchman, C. W. 82 n.
Cicero 100 n., 101
Clark, R. T. 35 n.
Coleman, W. 36 n., 114 n.
Coleridge 109
Collingwood, R. G. 1, 2, 69
Collins, H. 84 n., 89 n., 169, 170–7,
    208 n., 235
Conan Doyle, A. 97
Condillac 143
Copernicus 123, 133, 134, 135, 136,
    197, 209, 210, 211, 212, 215, 218
Corbin, A. 17 n.
Corsi, P. 102 n., 113 n., 141 n., 144 n.
Cortázar, Julio 84 n.
Crichton, A 23
Crombie, Alistair 196
Cross, S. J. 22, 104 and n.
Cummins, R. 81 n.
Cunningham, A. 50 n.
Cuvier, Georges 32, 52, 53 and n., 98,
    108, 113, 138, 139, 140, 141, 142, 143,
    144, 145, 150, 166, 208

d'Alembert, *see* Alembert, Jean le
    Rond d'
Dance, S. P. 16 n.
Darnton, R. 15 n., 93 n., 219
Darwin, Charles 52, 76, 125, 131, 212,
    216, 217, 218, 222, 223
Daubenton, L. J.-M. 17 n., 21 and n.
Daudin, H. 18 n., 102 n., 108, 108 n.
Day, R. A. 206 n.
Dear, P. 196, 198
Delambre, J.-B. J. 138, 140
Descartes 76
Desmond, A. 50 n.
De Solla Price, Derek 94
Dibon, P. 112 n.
Diderot, Denis 12, 17 n.
Dilthey, W. 130
Dineen, D. A. 59 n.
Diogenes Laertius 126
Dirac, P. A. M. 114
Drake, Stillman 196
Dreyer, J. L. E. 132 n.
Droysen, J. G. 130
Du Bois-Reymond, Émil 113, 238 n.
Duchesneau, F. 21 n., 22 n., 27 n.
Duhem, Pierre 174

Ecker, A. 45 n.

Eco, U. 74 n., 97 n.
Edgerton, Stanley 119, 204 n., 207 n.
Einstein 61
Eisenstein, E. 119
Engelhardt, D. von 105 n., 126 n.,
    129 n., 130, 236 n.
Englehardt, H. T., Jr. 67 n.
Eve, H.W. 238 n.

Febvre, Lucien 92
Feyerabend, Paul 196
Fine, Arthur 228, 233, 234
Fischer, K. 43 n.
Fish, Stanley 74
Fleck, Ludwik 67, 110, 111, 125
Forgan, S. 93 n., 115 n., 238 n.
Forster, Georg 30
Foucault, Michel 52 and n., 53 and n.,
    67, 204, 205
Fox, R. 236 n.
Frank, M. 117 n.
Franklin, Allan 158, 159
Freind, John 123, 136, 137, 138
Freud, S. 97, 98, 131
Friedrich, Kaspar David 220
Fyfe, G. 204 n.

Gadamer, Hans-Georg 5, 68–76
Galen 111, 113
Galileo 97, 98, 159, 196, 197, 204
Galison, P. 87, 89 n., 94, 95, 110 n.,
    184, 189, 190 and n., 198
Gallo, R. C. 125
Garcia-Bellido, Antonia 212, 213, 214
Garfinkel, H. 67 n., 74, 91 n., 178,
    207 n.
Gasking, E. 22 n.
Gauss, J. 39 n.
Gehring, W. J. 214 n.
Gelfand, T. 114 n.
Geoffroy Saint-Hilaire, Étienne 50,
    108, 142
Giacconi, M. 237 n.
Giacconi, R. 237 n.
Gieryn, T. 208 n.
Gilbert, G. N. 91 n., 103, 194, 207 n.,
    208 n.
Gilbert, M. 61 n.
Gillispie, C. C. 17 n., 36 n.
Ginzburg, C. 97, 98
Giseke, P. D. 19
Gismondi, M. A. 92 n.
Goethe 11, 33–43, 45, 49, 50, 54, 55,
    80, 86, 105, 113, 193, 238 n.

Goffman, Erving 61 n., 90, 115 n.
Goldman, Alvin 164
Golinsky, J. V. 201 n.
Gombrich, E. 222
Gooding, D. 158 n., 196 n.
Goodsir, John 50
Gould, S. J. 45 n., 48 n.
Graham, L. 125 n., 130 n., 131 n.
Gross, A. G. 80 n.

Habermas, Jürgen 68 n., 237
Hacking, Ian 155–67
Hafen, E. 214 n.
Hahn, M. 105 n.
Haller, Albrecht von 15, 16, 21, 23, 24, 25, 27 n., 131, 142
Halstead, H. B. 82 n.
Hannaway, O. 91 n., 93 n., 110 n., 115 n., 200, 201, 204, 205, 207
Harrison, T. R. 157 n.
Heath, P. 106 n.
Heidegger 67, 68 n.
Helden, A. van 122 n.
Heller, J. L. 107 n.
Helmholtz, Hermann von 113, 163, 238 n.
Herder, J. G. 33–43, 47 n., 50, 54
Hermann, Johann 19
Herschel, J. W. F. 85, 238 n.
Hirzel, R. 100 n.
Hoeniger, F. D. 111 n.
Hoffmann, Friedrich 142
Hollis, M. 155 n., 156 n., 163 n.
Holmes, F. L. 114 n.
Home, Henry (Lord Kames) 28
Howell, W. S. 112 n.
Hunter, John 22, 85, 104
Hunter, M. 90 n.
Husserl 67
Huxley, T. H. 87, 109, 113
Huygens 106, 122, 175, 176

Inge, C. 195 n.
Iser, W. 74 n., 195 n.
Ivins, William 118

Jacyna, L. S. 131 n.
James, William 232
Jardine, N. 42 n., 50 n., 133 n., 136 n., 197 n.
Jungnickel, C. 114 n.
Jussieu, Antoine-Laurent de 18, 19

Kahl, R. 238 n.
Kant 11, 28–33, 35, 37, 39, 40, 41, 42, 43, 44, 50, 52 n., 53, 54, 55, 66, 67, 81, 87, 101, 102, 106, 112, 143, 162, 204, 225
Karl Eugen, Duke of Württemberg 36
Kelley, D. R. 197 n.
Kepler, 123, 133, 134, 135, 136
Kermode, F. 71 n.
Keynes, J. M. 114
Kielmeyer, Karl-Friedrich 33–43, 50, 54
King, H. C. 166 n.
Knight, D. 50 n., 109, 117 n.
Knorr, K. D., *see* Knorr-Cetina
Knorr-Cetina, K. 149 n., 194 n., 207 n.
Knox, Robert 50
Koch, Robert 189
Koelreuter, J. G. 25
Koyré, Alexandre 196
Krausz, M. 161 n.
Krohn, R. 194 n.
Kuhn, D. 36 n.
Kuhn, Thomas 131
Kuroiwa, A. 214 n.
Kyburg, H. E. 82 n.

Laissus, Y. 16 n., 17 n.
Lamarck 142
Larson, J. L. 33 n.
Latour, Bruno 87, 90 n., 91 n., 97, 107, 118, 119, 149 n., 169, 170, 173, 184, 185, 187 n., 188, 189, 190 n., 193, 195 n., 207 n., 235
Laudan, L. 165 n.
Laudan, R. 20 n., 125 n.
Lavater, J. C. 42
Lavoisier 201, 202, 203, 205, 207
Law, John 119, 169 n., 185, 195 n., 204 n., 207 n.
Lawrence, F. 68 n.
Lawrence, C. J. 131 n.
Lawson, H. 172 n., 184 n.
LeClerc, Daniel 137
Le Goff, J. 92 n.
Lenoir, T. 21 n., 27 n., 32 n., 36 n., 37 n., 39 n., 50 n., 52 n.
Lepenies, W. 105 n., 113 n., 125 n., 204 n.
Lesch, J. E. 123 n.
Libavius, A. 199, 200, 201, 205
Liebig, J. 85
Limoges, Camille 17 n.
Linacre, Thomas 138
Linnaeus 15, 18, 19, 28, 83, 107, 108, 142

Livingston, E. 207 n.
Locke, John 143
Löw, R. 52 n.
Luckmann, T. 67
Ludwig, C. G. 18
Lukes, S. 155 n., 156 n., 163 n.
Lycan, W. G. 57 and n.
Lynch, M. 88 n., 91 n., 194, 204 n., 207 n.

McClellan, J. E. III 90 n.
McCormach, R. 114 n.
McDowell, J. 216 n., 221 n.
McLaughlin, P. 27 n.
Mach, E. 196
MacLeay, W. S. 109
Macquer, Pierre, Joseph 201
Madden, E. 165 n.
Maestlin, Michael 134
Mandelbaum, J. 113 n., 141 n.
Marks, R. 43 n.
Marsh, D. 100 n., 197 n.
Martin, Julian 104, 105 n., 136, 137, 138
Maxwell, J. C. 238 n.
May, J. A. 28 n.
Meckel, J. F. 50
Medawar, Peter 207
Meiland, J. W. 161 n.
Melanchthon, Philipp 201
Mendel 122
Montagnier, Luc 125
Montalenti, C. 102 n.
Moran, B. T. 116 n.
Morelli, G. 97, 98
Morrell, J. B. 90 n., 114 n.
Moss, J. D. 197 n.
Mueller, B. 37 n.
Müller, Johannes, *see* Regiomontanus
Mulkay, M. 91 n., 103, 194, 207 n., 208 n.

Napoleon 139, 144
Naylor, R. 196, 197
Needham, J. 125
Newton 26, 27 n., 76, 81, 85, 101, 103, 104, 114, 131, 137, 138, 184
Nicolson, M. 20 n., 116 n.
Nietzsche 227
Nisbet, H. B. 21 n., 34 n., 37 n.
Niven, W. D. 238 n.
Noblet, J. de 91 n., 119 n.
Nora, P. 92 n.
Nuttall, R. H. 166 n.

Oh, C.-K. 59 n.
O'Hear, Anthony 218 n.
Oken, Lorenz 1, 2, 5, 11, 43–50, 51, 55, 56, 64, 86, 102, 166
Oldroyd, D. R. 107 n.
Outram, D. 33 n., 138, 140, 142 n., 143
Owen, Richard 50

Pallas, Simon 19
Paracelsus 137, 156, 162, 200
Pasteur 107, 121, 188, 189
Pater, Walter 219
Pierce, C. S. 232
Peter of Spain 99
Pfannenstiel, M. 45 n.
Pickering, Andrew 169, 178
Pinch, T. 158 n., 169, 178, 196 n., 208 n.
Pitt, J. C. 196 n.
Pitcairne, Archibald 137
Podro, M. 106 n.
Poincaré, Henri 81, 82 n.
Pomian, K. 16 n., 93 n.
Popkin, R. H. 197 n.
Popper, K. 103
Porter, R. 131 n.
Pouchet, F. 121
Poussin 222, 223
Prelli, L. J. 208 n.
Priestley, J. 85, 203
Ptolemy 133, 134, 135, 210 n.
Putnam, Hilary 233
Pythagoras 133, 136

Querner, H. 45 n., 50 n.
Quine, W. V. O. 174
Quintilian 100, 101

Ramée, Pierre de la, *see* Ramus, Petrus
Ramus, Petrus 101, 112, 112 n., 201
Ranke, L. von 130
Ratoosh, P. 82 n.
Rée, Jonathan 113 and n., 230 n.
Regiomontanus 135
Rehbock, P. F. 50 n.
Reidel, M. 35 n.
Rescher, N. 81 n.
Riccioli, G. B. 127
Richards, E. 50 n.
Rip, A. 195 n.
Roe, S. A. 23 n., 27 n.
Roger, J. 17 n.
Rossi, P. 102 n.

Rousseau, J.-J. 16, 219, 220
Rudolph II 133
Rudwick, M.J. 87, 91 n., 93 n., 189, 190
Rupke, N. 105 n.
Ruskin, J. 218, 219
Russell, E. S. 50 n.
Russo, L. 197 n.

Salomon-Bayet, Claire 17 n., 89 n., 149 n.
Sandkühler, H. J. 105 n.
Sargent, Rosemary 104, 105 n.
Schaffer, S. 80 n., 84 n., 87 n., 92 n., 106 n., 110 n., 114 n., 158 n., 169, 175, 178, 179, 184, 189, 196 n., 235
Schaper, E. 216 n.
Schelling, F. W. J. 11, 43–50, 54, 55, 64, 86, 87, 98, 101 and n., 102, 106 and n., 113, 129
Schelling, K. F. A. 43 n.
Schleiermacher 233
Schubert, F. 222
Schuster, J. 45 n.
Schutz, A. 67 and n.
Scruton, Roger 222
Sebeok, T. A. 97 n.
Secord, J. A. 110 n.
Seemen, H. von 112 n.
Semmelweis, I. P. 121
Serres, Étienne 50
Shapin, S. 84 n., 87 n., 92 n., 106 n., 110 n., 169, 175, 178, 179, 181, 184, 189, 199, 200, 207, 235
Shapiro, J. J. 237 n.
Sheets-Pyenson, S. 115 n.
Sheridan, A. 107 n., 169 n.
Shirley, J. W. 111 n.
Simons, H. W. 80 n., 91 n., 208 n.
Sloan, P. R. 32 n.
Smith, James Edward 127
Sonntag, O. 15 n.
Southall, J. P. C. 163 n.
Stafleu, F. A. 15 n.
Stahl, G. E. 142
Stallo, J. B. 45 n.
Stearn, W. T. 107 n.
Stevens, S. S. 82 n.
Stevenson, L. 161 n.
Strawson, P. F. 66 n.
Stroup, A. 91 n.
Suleiman, S. R. 195 n.
Swainson, W. 238 n.
Swoyer, C 161 n.

Taton, R. 16 n., 17 n.
Thackray, A. 90 n.
Tort, P. 27 n.
Tournefort, J. P. de 18
Travis, G. D. L. 194 n., 208 n.
Trenn, T. J. 67 n.
Trevelyan, H. 41 n.
Trunz, E. 39 n., 40 n.
Tucker, J. 117 n.
Tuckfield, C. J. 126 n.
Tufte, E. R. 206 n., 215 n.
Tulk, A. 45 n.
Turner 220
Tycho Brahe, *see* Brahe, Tycho

Ursus (Nicolai Reymers Baer) 133, 134, 135, 136
Uschmann, G. 38 n.

Van Tieghem, P. 17 n.
Vasoli, C. 100 n.
Vater, M. G. 101 and n.
Vickers, B. 197 n., 204 n.
Vicq d'Azyr, Félix 21, 22
Vorländer, K. 39 n.
Vossius, Gerard Jan 127

Wallis, R. 178 n., 208 n.
Watson, P. 214 n.
Weber, Joseph 122, 172, 173, 174, 176
Weingart, P. 125 n.
Westman, Robert 116
Wheeler, H. 37 n.
Whewell, W. 85
Whitley, B. 194 n.
Wilkinson, C. M. 41 n.
Williams, R. J. 207 n.
Williamson, G. 100 n.
Willoughby, L. A. 41 n.
Wisan, W. 196
Wittgenstein 222
Wolff, Kaspar Friedrich 23, 24, 25, 26
Wollheim, R. 217 n., 222
Woolgar, S. 80 n., 90 n., 177, 193, 207 n.
Wren, Christopher 122
Wundt, W. 131

Yeo, R. 85 n.

Zaner, R. M. 67 n.
Zaunick, R. 49 n.
Zimmermann, R. C. 38 n.
Zucker, F. J. 37 n.